SLEEPWALKING INTO A NEW WORLD

THE LAWRENCE STONE LECTURES

Sponsored by
The Shelby Cullom Davis Center for Historical Studies
and Princeton University Press
2014

A list of titles in this series appears at the back of the book.

SLEEPWALKING INTO A

NEW WORLD

THE EMERGENCE OF
ITALIAN CITY COMMUNES
IN THE TWELFTH CENTURY

CHRIS WICKHAM

PRINCETON UNIVERSITY PRESS
PRINCETON & OXFORD

ISBN 978-0-691-14828-1

Library of Congress Control Number: 2014947305

British Library Cataloging-in-Publication Data is available

This book has been composed in Adobe Jenson Pro and Trade Gothic LT Std

Printed on acid-free paper ∞

Printed in the United States of America

1 3 5 7 9 10 8 6 4 2

CONTENTS

MAPS

ACKNOWLEDGEMENTS

I am very grateful to Princeton University and Princeton University Press for inviting me to give the Lawrence Stone Lectures in May 2013, which were the basis for this book: and in particular to my hosts, Philip Nord and Brigitta van Rheinberg; to Peter Brown, Pat Geary, John Haldon, Bill Jordan, Helmut Reimitz, and Jack Tannous, who made the stay of myself and my wife Leslie Brubaker so welcoming; and to all of these for questions and critical commentary which greatly improved the subsequent book. I am also very grateful indeed to Eddie Coleman, who critiqued the whole text, Leslie Brubaker, who critiqued chapters 1 to 3, Paolo Grillo, who critiqued chapter 2, Mauro Ronzani, who critiqued chapter 3, and Sandro Carocci and François Menant, who critiqued chapter 5. Alessandra Mercantini, of the Archivio Doria Pamphilj in Rome, kindly made my consultation of a crucial cartulary easy. And I had essential help, in the form of advice and unpublished work, from other old friends, Maria Luisa Ceccarelli Lemut, Maria Elena Cortese, Alessio Fiore, Pino Petralia, Gigi Provero, Gianluca Raccagni, and Enrica Salvatori. As usual, without friends, whatever merits my book has would have been very much fewer.

Birmingham, October 2013

A NOTE ON PERSONAL NAMES

As elsewhere in my books on Italy, almost all personal names are here rendered into Italian, except for the names of popes and emperors, which I have put into English. But I have here also put Archdeacon Hildebrand and Matilda of Tuscany into English, on the grounds that these two are widely known in the English-speaking world under these names, and much less so as Ildebrando and Matilde.

1

COMMUNES

In 1117, after a great earthquake which devastated northern
Italy, the archbishop of Milan and the consuls of the same
city—the city's leaders—called the people of other northern
cities and their bishops to a great meeting in Milan, in the
Broletto, an open space beside Milan's two cathedrals, now
part of the Piazza del Duomo. There, in the words of an eyewitness, the chronicler Landolfo of S. Paolo, writing two decades later:

> The archbishop and the consuls set up two *theatra*
> [stages]; on one the archbishop with the bishops, ab-
> bots and leading churchmen stood and sat; in the other
> the consuls with men skilled in laws and customs. And
> all around them were present an innumerable mul-
> titude of clerics and the laity, including women and
> virgins, expecting the burial of vices and the revival of
> virtues.

It seems that this meeting was called in response to the earthquake, and Landolfo mentions shortly after 'the whole people
congregated there out of fear of the ruin of the rubble, so that
they could hear mass and preaching'; it was also, however,
seen as a moment in which people could ask for justice, and
Landolfo himself was there to seek restitution, for he had recently been expelled from the church (S. Paolo) of which he
was the priest and part owner. He failed in that; his enemy

Archbishop Giordano was never going to let him have his church back, and nor (although with less venom) would his successors. Landolfo's remarks about the revival of virtues should be read as sarcasm, in that context. But his image of the set-piece meeting with its stages is a striking one; and so is the image of the separation of powers, the Church on one stage, the consuls and men of law on the other.[1]

This narrative can be set against a document from July of the same year, surviving in a contemporary copy, stating that 'in the public *arengo* [perhaps in the same open space] in which was lord Giordano, archbishop of Milan, and there with him his priests and clerics of the major and minor orders of the church of Milan, in the presence of the Milanese consuls and with them many of the *capitanei* and *vavassores* [the two orders of the Lombard military aristocracy] and *populus'*, the consuls of Milan decided a court case brought there by the bishop of the neighbouring and now-subject city of Lodi. This is only the second text which mentions consuls in Milan at all, and the first in which the consuls are actually named—nineteen of them—and shown acting in a judicial role. Landolfo's account and the consular document seem to refer, if not to the same assembly, at least to rapidly succeeding versions of the same occasion, and thus reinforce each other: the one showing a highly orchestrated event, the other showing its effective legal content. And they have also been seen—and heavily emphasised—as a pair ever since modern historiography began to concern itself with the origins of Italian city communes, which in the case of Milan goes back to Giorgio Giulini in the 1760s: in this dramatic moment, we can see the consuls of Milan begin to take on their new and future role as urban rulers, and Italian history took a decisive new path from then on.[2]

Map 1. Communal Italy

In what follows, I intend to nuance that moment, quite considerably. But let us begin by looking briefly at why the moment, and the new régime, has such historiographical importance. There are two contexts for this, seen very broadly, one Italian and one international (including, not least, American). For professional historians in Italy, the role of the middle ages in the grand narrative of the past was never that of the origins of the modern state, as in most of western Europe (or else its regrettable failure in Germany), but, rather, the victory of the autonomous city states over external domination, which made possible the civic culture of the Renaissance; indeed, external rule was only part of it, for Italians tended until recently to regard the genuine state-building of Norman and Angevin southern Italy as a wasted opportunity

3

and the origin of southern 'backwardness', in that it undermined urban autonomy there. The city was the *principio ideale*, the 'ideal principle' of Italian history, in Carlo Cattaneo's famous image of the 1850s, in the run-up to the Risorgimento. When the moment was which first produced urban autonomy was therefore of very great interest and importance for the historical community, and the *moto associativo*, the 'associative movement', which led to autonomous collectivities was a core focus of study, particularly in the decades around 1900, the period when scientific history developed in Italy. Indeed, its more-than-scientific emotional force meant that debates about the nature of medieval civic collectivity soon became metaphors for the main political and cultural battlegrounds of early twentieth-century Italian history; medieval historians were important in the socialist and fascist movements, in the Crocean idealist community, and also in the slower-burning clerical movement which would end up as Christian Democracy after World War II. One would think that this would mean that the subject was fully studied; that has unfortunately not been the result (I will come back to this), but its centrality remains taken for granted in Italy.[3]

As for the international interest in the subject, this was associated, from Burckhardt through to US Western Civ, with the Renaissance too, although here also with the addition of the supposed democratic, or at least republican, nature of the Italian communes, as a contribution to the origins of modernity. As the historian of Venice Frederic C. Lane said to the American Historical Association in 1965, 'My thesis here is that republicanism, not capitalism, is the most distinctive and significant aspect of these Italian city-states; that republicanism gave to the civilization of Italy from the thirteenth through the sixteenth century its distinctive quality. . . . The attempt to revive the culture of the ancient city-states strengthened in turn the republican ideal and contributed mightily to its triumph in modern nations and primarily in our own'. The US focus on the history of the Renaissance, which remains so strong, derives from both these strands.[4] The experience of the Italian communes has also been used surprisingly often as a point of reference by non-medievalists, as with the US sociologist Robert Putnam's influential co-authored book, *Making Democracy Work*, which attributes all contemporary civic solidarity in Italy to the influence of the Italian communes and their 'collaborative solutions to their Hobbesian dilemmas' in the eleventh century, or, in the UK, Quentin Skinner's well-known survey *The Foundations of Modern Political Thought*, which simply starts, without qualification, with the early Italian consulates, in a chapter titled 'The Ideal of Liberty'. These two important scholars have, I have to add, been content to get their information about communal Italy from fairly basic textbooks, but the Italian communes, and more widely the Italian city-states, have a notable place in their story-lines about what each sees as modernity.[5]

I could lengthen this list, but there is probably no need. The point is that the Italian communes have been widely used, often without much detailed thought, to denote one of the stepping-stones to the modern world, for their bottom-up collaboration, for their move away from monarchical institutions, for their institutional creativity, or for their secular (and therefore more 'modern') culture. This sort of interpretation to me is fundamentally mistaken, as are all teleological readings of history. But not all of these descriptions are incorrect; communes were indeed characterised by institutional creativity (if for no other reason than that their institutions tended to fail), and were also indeed founded on bottom-up collaboration (however fundamentally shot through they were with hierarchical and military-aristocratic values and rivalries as well). These were novelties, and their very contradictions make them interesting, as well as difficult to explain. The leitmotif of this book will therefore be such contradictions; and they are best summed up by a simple problem. North and central Italian cities in 1050 (say) were run by aristocratic and military—and also clerical—élites with much the same practices and values as those anywhere else in Latin Europe; and, even if they were sometimes hard to control, these élites were, just as elsewhere, fully part of hierarchies which extended upwards to bishops, counts, and kings/emperors, as part of a coherent Kingdom of Italy. By contrast, in 1150 (say) they were run by élites which may well have been from the same families, but which had developed autonomous and novel forms of collective government focused on annually changing consuls in fifty and more cities and towns, almost none of them looking more than nominally to any superior powers, which regularly fought each other; such governments seemed highly radical to outsiders,[6] and were organised enough and sure enough of themselves to be able thereafter to ally together and fight off the most serious attempt by an emperor to control Italy in depth for two hundred years, that of Frederick Barbarossa, in the years 1158–77. This was a new world. And yet they made this to-us dramatic change without, in all but a few cases, showing us any evidence of an awareness that they were doing anything new. What did they think they were doing? What did they *think* they were *doing*?

The short answer is that we do not know, and will never know, except very partially indeed. Our evidence is scarce, of course; this is the middle ages, and not the late middle ages of the documentary explosion, which in Italy was fully under way by 1250 but not at all a century earlier. But the question is important enough that it is worth trying to answer it. I have thus chosen to focus on three case studies, which are in each case characterised both by a relatively good set of documents (usually land transactions) and a varied set of narratives, the dialectic between which may get us somewhere towards the problem as I have posed it: Milan, Pisa, and Rome. They are in fact the best three cities in Italy for such a pairing. Genoa might have been a fourth, but its earliest evidence is too sketchy—as we shall see (pp. 162–66) in the fifth chapter here, which contains a briefer overview of other Italian cities, so as to locate the three in their wider typicalities and atypicalities. My three chosen cities are also well-studied, but these studies do not fully focus on the issues which most concern me here. Milan and Pisa are relatively often compared (largely because the University of Pisa hired several historians from Milan in the 1960s); Rome is seldom brought into the equation, however, and will be a useful contrast to and control on the other two. It is a mantra that every Italian city is different, and this is undoubtedly true, but the different experiences shown by each of these three have obvious parallelisms as well, and thus will go some way towards creating the sort of indirect, glancing picture of the way people made choices, which is the best the evidence can offer us. I am by training a social historian, so I am more experienced in analysing the results of such choices and the patterns they make than the mental processes involved, but those processes are crucial too, and I wish to set them out as clearly as I can.

Before we look at concrete examples in the next chapters, however, we need to look at the historiographical frame for how to analyse communes in more detail as it has emerged in the last generation; this is important to set out, in order to show where I am following others (including my own previous work) and where I am not.

The quantity of detailed and comparative Italian scholarship on early communes has not been as substantial as one would think. For a long time Italians concentrated on their immediate antecedents, and when consuls appeared they perhaps thought their job was done; for example, the leading Italian historians of the generation before this one, Giovanni Tabacco and Cinzio Violante, did most of their empirical work on the period before the late eleventh century.[7] In the last forty years, however, although the number of studies is still not huge (except for monographic analyses of individual cities, which are plentiful; but these do not often use their empirical data as a basis for wider rethinking), some important work has changed our view of what happened across the period 1050–1150 quite considerably.[8]

The first point that needs to be made (and it is one that is uncontroversial in the historiography) is that the leadership of medieval Italian cities was not ever exclusively commercial, whether mercantile or artisanal, unlike the picture often painted for northern Europe.[9] Most of Italy's major landowners lived in cities—that was the basic reason why Italian cities were so much larger, more powerful, and more socio-politically complex than those of the rest of Latin Europe, and had been for centuries—and they always had a central role to play in city politics. Indeed, economic development, although it was moving fast in Italy in the eleventh and twelfth centuries, was not in itself a necessary cause of the development of communes; the major ports of Pisa and Genoa were precocious communes, and so were the exchange foci of Cremona and Milan, but Venice was not, and plenty of relatively uncommercial centres, such as Bergamo or Parma, developed consular régimes at much the same speed as economic leaders; I will not have much to say about economics here as a result. Essentially, early city communes are by now generally recognised to have been, in the very loosest sense of the word, aristocratic: they were not usually the result of open conflict (Rome was the major exception here; see below, pp. 174, 184, for others), and they worked to perpetuate the power of landed élites of different types. It was the pre-communal period, above all the early and mid-eleventh century, that was the period of urban uprisings; the very earliest evidence for what could be called communes, by contrast, appears in the last decade of the eleventh century in the case of a handful of cities and the twelfth, often well into the twelfth, for the others. They appeared, historians often now say, in the context not of contestation but of compromise:[10] between the different factions or strata of urban élites, between bishops and secular urban leaders, and between those leaders and wider communities. This occurred above all as a result of the confusion caused by the Investiture Dispute in the decades after 1076, which pitted emperor against pope and led to a civil war in Italy (including, often, rival bishops in individual cities and thus a crisis of their traditional leaderships) in the 1080s–90s, and to the steady breakdown of the Kingdom itself from then on into the following decades; communes were thus a defensive reaction to crisis.

As we shall see, I will call some of the detail of that defensive reaction into question, to an extent; all the same, I would not disagree with most of the general picture. But the stress on aristocratic dominance has had its good and its bad side. It can be a reality check on older romantic notions of popular democracy winning out in the Italian city-republics, but it can also, even now, be based on a Paretoesque assumption that all historical protagonism is *really* aristocratic by definition. Some Italian historiography has been rather comfortable as a result, and has stressed how the real sources of political power did not change at all with the early communes. In favour of such continuitist readings are some unproblematic findings, such as (as Ottavio Banti showed) that the new city régimes were mostly not called 'communes' until the mid-twelfth century, but 'cities', *civitates*, as they had always been, thus hiding for us (and for them?) any changes in their governance—indeed, *commune* was not even a noun in sources for most cities before the 1120s, but an adjective or adverb, meaning 'collective' or 'in common'.[11] Furthermore, it is now often argued, not just that consuls had or could have a public role from very early— which is not hard to show[12]—but also that consular régimes simply inherited the public role that counts and bishops had in cities before them. A further element of continuity was the undoubted importance of *iudices*, men with legal training and experience, for they had run cities under bishops in the eleventh century, under some mixed régimes in the early twelfth, and then under more clearly consular-dominated régimes in the mid-twelfth: it has been argued that as long as they controlled public acts, the legal basis of such acts was unlikely to be very different.[13]

These latter arguments, however, risk flattening out the period so completely that the real novelties of the consular period, whether consciously perceived at the time or not, become invisible. For example: the main way in which the traditional *regnum Italiae*, which united Italy north of Rome from the seventh century to the eleventh, showed its public identity and legitimacy was through assemblies called *placita*, where justice was done on a regular basis in the sight of large numbers of people; these judicial assemblies vanished in almost the whole of north-central Italy in the late eleventh century, and communes did not seek to re-create them.[14] Either the *placitum* tradition, with its strong 'public' element, did not work any more; or consular régimes felt that they did not have access to it; or else public power had become differently located. Whichever way, a basic underpinning of political power was lost or greatly changed; and legal experts visibly adapted to that, indeed took it for granted. We will come back to this.

Where historians have disagreed more in the last generation is over the nature of the élites which ruled early communes. For a start, if major landowners were important in communally ruled cities, how different were such cities from the countryside at all? Hagen Keller, already author of some of the best general articles on the formation of the communes, in 1979 published a major book which (among other things) argued strongly, based largely on evidence from Milan, that the élites of northern Italian cities in our period were divided into defined strata, *ordines*, and were headed by military aristocrats (he called them *Adel*) defined by feudo-vassalic relationships and also different social origins: *capitanei*, who held fiefs from the local bishop and had private (signorial) lordships in the countryside, and *valvassores*, who were the vassals of the *capitanei*; there were also 'citizens', *cives*, among these élites, leading figures outside the narrower aristocratic hierarchy, but they were a minority in early communal leaderships, and anyway even men devoted to commercial activity could have vassal ties to the military *ordines* or to bishops.

This might not seem so controversial (I myself happily accepted it at the time, and still accept its main lines), but it coincided with an important and polemical article by Philip Jones on the 'legend of the bourgeoisie', generalised later in another large book, which argued—again among many other things—that Italian cities were not fully 'civic' in the ways in which medieval historians were accustomed to seeing them, and that the importance of landowners in cities meant that the latter were long dominated by aristocratic values (the communes were 'born seigneurial'); and Pierre Racine's *thèse* on Piacenza, which proposed (and this did go too far) that early communes were so much under the control of landed aristocrats that they could be seen as a 'seigneurie collective', and were not really typologically distinct from signorial lordships in the countryside.[15] None of these historians were Italians, and their views did not by any means seem as useful to Italians in the 1980s as Keller's conclusions did to me; Italians broadly, and not always helpfully, responded by stressing how 'civic' Italian cities were in all periods after all, and how different they were from the countryside, notwithstanding the attempts by foreigners to make them like northern Europe.[16] They also made some better-aimed points about Keller's 'society of orders': that its two-fold nature did not characterise more than a minority of north Italian cities (and none in central Italy); that it was more rigid than it needed to be, as exactly who *capitanei* were and how they behaved was different from place to place; that aristocratic strata and episcopal vassals did not dominate early communes everywhere either; and that Keller had understressed the important fact, demonstrable for example in Milan as Paolo Grillo has shown, that there was quite a sharp difference between *capitanei* who were involved in city politics and members of the same *ordo* who were not—and that the former, although still episcopal vassals, were less interested in signorial rights and other elements of rural power, and much more interested in more 'civic' activities.[17] One can accept most of these points without thinking any less of Keller's book, but the debate leaves open some crucial issues as well, such as what exactly the 'civic' values of twelfth-century cities did consist of, if they were indeed so different from those of the countryside and of northern Europe. (This was explored by one of Keller's critics, Renato Bordone, but far from completely.[18])

A more fully accepted work, but actually more critical of others, and arguably more radical, was Jean-Claude Maire Vigueur's 2003 book *Cavaliers et citoyens*, on urban militias, in the twelfth and (especially) thirteenth centuries. Maire Vigueur argued that the political core of the commune across both centuries was not the military *ordines* as characterised by Keller (and plenty of other people), but, rather, the collectivity of mounted knights of every city, which extended far beyond a narrow set of feudo-vassalic aristocrats, to 10–15 percent of the urban population, and certainly included richer members of the commercial and artisanal strata, as well as judicial experts and notaries. He argued for the twelfth century that the hegemony of this very wide militarised élite stratum produced a 'very great stability and a very strong homogeneity of the class which governed the commune' for the entire consular period, and that studying the (few) prosopographical analyses of consuls produces 'a feeling of boredom, an impression of déjà-vu' because of the total homogeneity of the stratum, based as it always is on an 'honest' landed patrimony, tenurial links to local churches, and a tight set of kinship and business links to other consular families.[19] There is no doubt that this book, by extending the scale of urban élites very greatly, has given a new framing to research in the field, and has the ability to get scholars to sidestep older debates. I will have it in my mind often in what follows; in particular I am sure, with Maire Vigueur, that the importance of feudal ties to bishops has been overplayed in communal analyses, and that communal activity belonged to a relatively wide stratum. I have my doubts about the total homogeneity of that stratum, however. As we shall see, it included, in each city, more diversity than that; and I shall stress in what follows a stratification inside it based on wealth, which in my view helps us to get closer to real social and political differences in the experiences of the early city communes—which are important, as we shall see when we reach the empirical evidence for my three case studies.

Let us pause on definitions for a moment. I have been referring to 'aristocrats' and to 'élites'; I shall stick to 'élites' for the most part when talking about urban leaders, as it is suitably vague—it can certainly extend to all of Maire Vigueur's urban militia—and will restrict references to the military 'aristocracy' to people who are definitely *capitanei*[20] and their equivalents (though how rich they were, and how different they really were from leading *cives*, is another matter, as we shall see). But what about the word 'commune' itself? Scholars have traditionally regarded it as meaning the urban government of people called *consules* (the near-universal word for city rulers in north-central Italy by 1150, except in Rome, where *senatores* was preferred, and in Venice, where dukes remained central), and have tended to regard communes as starting with the first references to consuls—there is a well-known list of such first references, beginning with Pisa in 1080–85, then Asti in 1095, Milan in 1097, Arezzo and Genoa in 1098, and so on. But these references are all entirely chance citations, and consuls or their equivalents could have existed a long time earlier in most cases. As Keller has said, we do not know the date of the passage to a consular régime in a single Italian city (although Rome, as we shall see later, is a partial exception).[21] In addition, is the simple appearance of the word *consul* enough to mark a new form of government? Many early references to the word are to very generically defined figures, who may well have had no official status, as has been convincingly argued for Pisa and Arezzo out of the canonical list, and also Lucca, where the word is first used in the 1090s, in a poetic text referring to 1081.[22] So our evidence for consuls may have either preceded or succeeded the crystallisation of the 'real' commune, which also, as we have seen, was not called a *commune* in most cities until well into the twelfth century. Given that, how can a 'real' commune be characterised?

Put like this, it should be fairly clear that it is up to any historian to use the characterisation which s/he finds most useful. I would prefer to use, not a definition, but an ideal type, a collection of related elements which may not all be present in every city, but which, as a whole or in part, can be used to characterise and compare the city communal phenomenon from place to place. These would include in particular, for the Italian commune in its twelfth-century version: a conscious urban collectivity, which included either all (male) city-dwellers or a substantial part of them, usually held together by oaths;[23] a regularly rotating set of magistracies, chosen or at least validated by that collectivity (not often in any 'democratic' way, but at any rate not chosen by superior powers such as kings or bishops); and a de facto autonomy of action for the city and its magistrates, including in warfare and justice, and eventually taxation and legislation—the basic elements of early and central medieval government. Not all communes were in practice autonomous (e.g., from bishops), particularly at the start; and not all communes had magistrates regularly chosen or assented to from below (Frederick Barbarossa chose many urban rulers for a decade, and the dukes of Venice, who were life-long rulers even if themselves elected by complex processes, doubtless had a strong voice in the choice of their *sapientes* and *consiliatores*), but the point about an ideal type is that it allows a focus on why certain elements are absent, rather than provoking often unhelpful arguments about whether a city without one element or another is 'really' a commune at all. Nonetheless, it also allows one to see that a city with only a single one of these elements might not so usefully be compared with cities with most of them: a city with a community of the oath, for example, and no other autonomy (Milan in the 1040s is a clear instance) could well be difficult to control, and in Milan's case was, but found it hard indeed to maintain the continuous protagonism that annual magistrates and a city-based judicial remit would later bring; similarly, a wholly autonomous city which nevertheless firmly looked to a single ruler for life (as were both Rome and Venice before 1143) had a markedly different political practice from one where the rotation of powerful offices was already the norm.

Consuls were very widely accepted as city rulers in northern and central Italy by the 1150s. They are taken for granted as rulers in narratives of that decade, whether written by men holding communal office themselves, such as Caffaro in Genoa, Ottone Morena in Lodi, and Bernardo Maragone in Pisa, or by an outsider as unsympathetic as the highly aristocratic German historian Otto bishop of Freising, uncle to Barbarossa himself; by now we begin to get our first clear references to early communal fiscal exactions; and the 1150s was also the decade in which Pisa took the important step of preparing the first version of a comprehensive local law-code, an undoubted claim for full practical autonomy.[24] These are the main reasons why I will regard 1150 as an endpoint for my discussions, for communes were fully established in most major cities in north-central Italy, in one form or another, by then. Earlier, it would depend on the city; but for me a crucially important marker is the appearance of regular consular judicial records, which are the first documents which show consuls or their representatives autonomously in action in any systematic way, sometimes describing themselves as *electi a populo* and similar phrases, significant ones for our recognition that this was a very different form of government from the traditional hierarchies of the Kingdom of Italy. Such records also soon show a claim to legal supremacy over parties even if they did not consent to it (an important sign of legal authority), which is shown by the preparedness of consuls to reach judgements even when one of the parties did not appear in court.[25] If so, the consolidation of a communal régime can be regarded as first attested in the 1130s in most of the precocious cities: Milan again, plus Piacenza, Lucca, Padua, Cremona, and Verona, with Pisa and Genoa, as we shall see, clearly the first of all, with a similar consolidation partially visible already around 1110—but this time the group definitely does not include Asti and Arezzo, where consular courts are not recorded until as late as the 1180s and 1190s respectively.[26] Keller has argued for the 1120s–30s as the moment of the institutional crystallisation of communes, which fits these dates well enough, at least, again, for the earliest-established communes.[27] I would also prefer this to his other main argument, set out in the context of Milan, in which a collective oath of peace between the *civitas* (or *populus*) and the *nobiles* of the city, at the end of an urban uprising in 1044–45 against the aristocratic *ordines* and the archbishop, and then the punctuation of religious disputes among the Milanese *populus* by collective oaths (called *iuramentum commune*) in the 1060s and 1070s, are 'primitive forms of communal organisation and self-government'; these oaths were too inchoate and ad hoc to be straightforward harbingers of a new political régime, and there is for me a clear danger of a teleological reading here.[28] But it must also be recognised from the outset that, if the full set of elements of my ideal-type commune only appear in most cities in the 1130s to 1150s, then this is rather later and slower than some other historians have argued, which has implications for our understandings of causation—and for the self-awareness of the people who moved these developments along.

A final element in this historiographical survey is a closely related point which I have argued myself, and which I wish to continue to develop here: that communes at their inception were very informal bodies. They had, in the end, to become more formal, to replace the old formal hierarchies, public and private, of the Carolingian and post-Carolingian world, which lost force, sometimes finally, with the civil wars of the late eleventh century; but that process was by no means immediate. Consuls were creating a new structure, based on elements (such as collective oaths and rotating offices) which had never been used on their own for government before; their leaders were often from traditional élite families, who in the past had been in the entourages of kings/emperors, counts/dukes, bishops, and will often have found the *habitus* of royal or episcopal courts and formalised *placitum* assemblies much more familiar and congenial than that of the city gatherings which marked the early communal period in most places. Why would we assume that they had a clear and consistent idea of what they were doing? Why would we assume that they would automatically feel that ruling their peers, and those less powerful than they, would be more honorific than remaining in the traditional hierarchies accepted by their ancestors, which they were, indeed, sometimes still members of, again royal and episcopal ones above all? And why would we assume that, once consular systems were established, their leaders would recognise that this was The Future, and simply set about consolidating them? They were most likely making it up as they went along; they may well have thought of themselves as simply modifying earlier forms of political practice, and they may well have preferred to think this, too. Indeed, some consular régimes do not seem to have been permanent, or very high-profile, at the start; they were 'latent' in Giuliano Milani's nice phrase, as in the cases of Vercelli, Ravenna, and Florence, discussed later.[29] Some elements of the future communal ideal type did become formalised relatively early, notably the city assembly, as we shall see. But even the solidest régimes otherwise developed very informally for a long time, adding on elements as they became necessary and possible, certainly borrowing them from neighbours in one of the classic examples of 'peer polity interaction' (by 1200 most communes had very similar institutional structures, in fact), but proceeding along very ad hoc paths at the start.

It can be added that those who led cities at the end of the eleventh century did not necessarily all want to become consuls at all. Links to kings and bishops, even if by now less power-enhancing on their own, could remain more attractive. The Avvocati family in Lucca, for example, major city figures throughout the eleventh century, and the lay leaders of the city in the thirty years after 1080, do not appear among the city's consuls in the first generation after their first real appearance in Lucca in 1119–20, but instead are attested as imperial representatives (*missi*), as 'counts of the sacred palace', an even higher-flown imperial title, and also as episcopal advocates (hence their later surname): these titles and roles seem to have been more prestigious than 'mere' consular office. Once the Lucchese consulate had fully stabilised, they did join it, but that was not until the 1150s.[30] Perhaps they were the family who saw this period most clearly, whereas the actual consuls had less idea of what they were doing. It is hard to tell in Lucca, as there are too few discursive texts which might give us a clue as to people's motives—the major reason why I do not include Lucca, which I know well, among my case studies. But the Avvocati have plenty of parallels in the earliest communes elsewhere, as we shall see. And it is this initial, uncertain, informal period which I shall be concentrating on here, when city leaders of different types—and we shall look at a whole set of different types in our three case studies—were sleepwalking into a new and often radically different régime: all the while, for the most part, pretending that they were doing nothing of the kind.

2

MILAN

Milan is our starting-point in this sequence of case studies. Not because it was the first commune fully to develop (Pisa and Genoa have the best claims to that); not, as we shall amply see, because it was typical; but it was powerful and influential in central northern Italy (in the region now called Lombardy, and indeed farther afield), and held the attention of contemporary observers, as also of the historians of the last century and more. Recent historians have, indeed, often seen it as typical; we therefore have to understand how its development did work if we want to call that into question. The city is also a good place to start from in terms of its evidence. It has a relatively rich documentation, and also has several local histories in the century we are looking at: two from the 1070s, by Arnolfo and the anonymous author known as Landolfo Seniore, which recount the uprisings against Archbishop Ariberto da Intimiano (1018–45) and the activities of the purist popular religious movement of the period 1057–75 known as the Pataria—they are very hostile to the Pataria, but we also have pro-Patarene texts which show local knowledge—and then one from the 1130s, that of Landolfo of S. Paolo already cited. The younger Landolfo relates the travails of his uncle Liprando, a survivor of the Patarene movement of the previous generation, and then of himself, deprived unjustly (he says) of his church, inside a framing of archbishops and their own, often insurmountable, problems.[1] These histories allow a narrative characterisation of the development of the various strands of what would become the commune which, in its main lines, is not controversial. Let us first look at the overall development of Milan and its government, first archiepiscopal, then communal, in the century 1050–1150, and then, in the second part of the chapter, focus on who its consuls were and how their social composition changed. For, in a world of considerable informality of governmental structures, exactly who directed them and for what purpose become particularly important. In Milan, as in most other cities, it was the practices of that informal period which would frame how any given commune actually did develop when it finally institutionalised itself.

Milan had always been the largest and one of the dominant cities of the Kingdom of Italy. It had been a major political centre since the Roman empire, and was, although not on a significant river, a road-centre for transalpine traffic, and a major entrepôt for exchange between the Alpine foothills (a large-scale producer of iron and wool) and the great route of the river Po, thirty miles to its south. These were the bases of an industrial development in cloth and metal in and around the city which was moving fast by the twelfth century.[2] Milan far outmatched the old capital of the Kingdom, Pavia, its southern neighbour and enemy, and it was also the seat of the archbishopric for most of the Po plain; the archbishops of Milan—almost all from capitaneal families—were very powerful and rich, and had steadily displaced the counts of Milan (last documented in 1045) as the de facto rulers of the city.[3] Its large size and growing wealth also meant that it was the focus for a particularly active and complex urban aristocracy, of the *capitanei* and *valvassores* mentioned in chapter 1, and it was hard to rule peacefully—between 1050 and 1150, indeed, in the context of the internal troubles referred to above (and there were plenty of others), five archbishops were deposed. In that context, it was necessary to do one's best to seek a wide base of support if one was to rule the city successfully.

Archbishop Ariberto in the 1030s rode the tide of trouble between the different strata of his military vassals and the intervention of the emperor Conrad II. In the early 1040s, however, he faced an uprising of the 'citizens', *cives*, who in this context have been interpreted by a succession of scholars since Cinzio Violante, I am sure rightly, as not the urban populace as a whole, but rather a militarised élite stratum of rentier, commercial, and judicial figures.[4] After the civic revolt, the agreement of 1045 gave to the *cives* a greater transactional power, with mutual oaths sworn, and a recognition that they had a role in the election of archbishops. Ariberto, according to the chronicler Arnolfo, had been elected in 1018 in consultation with the *maiores* of the city; but his successor, Guido da Velate, was elected in 1045, Landolfo Seniore says, with the involvement of an 'assembly [*collectio*] of all the citizens', and that wider tradition of election continued into Landolfo of S. Paolo's time—the *nobilis multitudo* and the *populus* in 1097 (two groups of citizens on different sides); or the *nobiles* and *viri*, in front of the *populus*, in 1102.[5] It is hard to know how wide this participation was, or how important it was—in 1097, at least, the fixers of the election apparently took the trouble to win over the *populus*, which indicates that, however socially restricted, it had some real role—but we can take an élite dominance on each of these occasions pretty much for granted as well. All the same, the Milanese laity, even if only its aristocratic strata, had long been a player in archiepiscopal elections, and, with that élite more widely based, it continued to be one.

This was the backdrop to the unrest of the period of the Pataria in 1057–75. This was a genuine bottom-up religious movement, focussed on the two moral panics most characteristic of the eleventh century, worries about buying clerical office (simony) and worries about the effect of married clergy on the efficacy of the sacraments. These concerns had an impact on plenty of cities—and, of course, on the papacy as well—but it is in Milan that they most clearly seem have been borne along by a wider lay popular movement, one which, as Bob Moore among others has stressed, was well-acquainted with the commercial role of money, and was less willing than were previous generations to regard giving money in return for office as a morally neutral exchange of gifts. (Patarene hostility to clerical marriage was however much more controversial in Milan, where the tradition of married clergy had a long history, as Landolfo Seniore, in particular, protested.) The Pataria came to focus on the election of Archbishop Guido, which they held to be simoniac—apparently because he had been chosen by the emperor Henry III from outside the list of candidates agreed inside the city—and tensions rose sharply. In Rome, after some hesitation, support for the Pataria became clear once Alexander II became pope in 1061, for he, as Anselmo da Baggio, was from a Milanese capitaneal family and had been a keen supporter of 'reform' before he left the city in 1056; Hildebrand, his right-hand man, was even keener, both as archdeacon in Rome and, from 1073, as Pope Gregory VII. After 1066, the Pataria were led by a lay *capitaneus*, Erlembaldo, who was regarded as an imposing figure even by his opponent Landolfo Seniore; he had a great deal of support in Milan, at every level of society, élites and non-élites alike. In 1073–75, when neither of two rival archbishops after Guido's death managed to establish himself in

Milan, Erlembaldo ruled the city more or less on his own, until a fire damaged the city in 1075 and a revolt led by aristocrats resulted in Erlembaldo's death in battle inside the city, apparently at the hand of the *capitaneus* Arnaldo da Rhò, and the rapid eclipse of Patarene power.[6]

It seems to me, as to most historians, that the Pataria was an essentially religious operation. Exactly how its development fitted into the history of political legitimisation in the mid-eleventh century remains to be determined in full; I will not focus on it here, however. It is certainly (as noted in the last chapter) important that Erlembaldo and his party swore together a *iuramentum commune*, which was often an oath sworn for the moment, but at one point, in 1071, seems to be a wider constitutive oath; that tells us about the considerable solidity of sworn collective action by then. All the same, although the survivors of the Pataria continued to have some purchase in Milan until the 1100s, it did not have much to do with the history of the commune as it developed in the twelfth century.[7] The Milanesi seem to have felt burnt by the whole affair, and in the next quarter century were internally quiet, under less contested archbishops, as well as being for the most part on the side of the emperor. Although the Pataria had support from all social levels, as probably did its opponents as well, its actual suppression seems to have been in effect a victory for the *capitanei*, whose members again filled the office of archbishop, and other senior clerical posts: Archbishop Anselmo III da Rhò (1086–93) was indeed from the family of Erlembaldo's killer.

Documents in the period after 1080 which list the composition of the main figures in the last Milanese *placita* (the last known is from 1093) and the archbishop's court show us a mixed élite in the city and around the archbishop. It was both aristocratic and judicial in composition: the *vicecomites* or Visconti, the da Landriano, the da Rhò, the da Melegnano, the da Baggio, all families who are elsewhere described as capitaneal; and a smaller set of *iudices et missi*, whose legal expertise was recognised by an official imperial title and whose local political position was central—above all, three frequently recurring figures, Alberto, the patriotically named Mediolano Ottone, and Ambrogio Pagano. Of the aristocrats, Arialdo da Melegnano is particularly visible in these documents as a political coordinator, and he must have had a central role.[8] Then, in 1097, a Cremona document shows us a formal agreement after a land dispute (we cannot tell whether it went to a *placitum* or not) which was made in Milan *in consulatu civium*, 'in the consulate of the citizens', for the first time. This was witnessed by an array of members of prominent families, including Arialdo da Melegnano again, Wifredo da Pusterla, and Anselmo Fanti, all of whom are known to have been *capitanei*, by Pagano Stampa, who was from a family of vassals of the monastery of S. Ambrogio, so was certainly aristocratic too, as well as by the three *iudices*, but now the group also included Pagano and Nazario Gambari, from a family which was not aristocratic but would be active in the city later in the twelfth century.[9] We cannot tell whether these names were or included people called consuls in 1097, but the same sort of people seem to be associated with the *consulatus* as we find in archiepiscopal documents, with, now, the addition of some prominent *cives*.

We need to pause here, however, and consider what the word *consulatus* could have meant. It clearly indicates that Milan now used the term *consul*, although it does not appear again in any other text for twenty years, until 1117. The word was previously used in Rome and then, in the 1080s, in Pisa (see below, pp. 77–78, 83, 129), but early uses of *consul* there simply referred to members of urban élites, and certainly not yet regularly rotating city rulers as developed in the twelfth century; it is entirely likely that Milan borrowed the word (most plausibly via Genoa, which had close links with both Pisa and Milan) to mean, initially, something just as generic. That Milan had done this by 1097 is indeed not surprising; already two important rural centres (or small towns) in the wider hinterland of Milan, Biandrate and Chiavenna, had prominent men called *consules* in this period, in 1093 and 1097 respectively.[10] But a *consulatus* is something else as well, and arguably more important: it is a collectivity of people, an assembly (and also the place where such a collectivity met). As such, it looks back to the assemblies (then sometimes called *collectio*) of the 1040s, and to the oath-based groupings of the Pataria, but the phrase in 1097 indicates that such an assembly was by now a more formalised and more regular occasion. It is also striking that in the immediately following years, 1098–1100, we have two texts—one surviving in an inscription, the other in a later copy—in each of which Archbishop Anselmo IV da Bovisio, who had been elected in 1097, founds a market and gives it toll exemptions with *comuni conscilio tocius civitatis*, 'the common counsel of the whole city', such *consilium* in the second text being given in a *conventus*, another word for assembly.[11] Such an assembly appears in Landolfo of S. Paolo's narrative too: in his text for 1103 it is called a *concio*, and in 1117 an *arengo*, as we shall see in a moment. This multiplicity of names implies that we should not put too much weight on the implications of the single term *consulatus*, but it certainly shows that the city's assembly was by now an organised body: happy to act closely with the archbishop, and with a demonstrably aristocratic element in 1097, but probably meeting autonomously, and also fairly often.

Urban assemblies can be tracked back to the ninth century; cities, or their élites, wished to express their will in public in every period, and this was a good way of doing it. Such assemblies had some parallels to the judicial assemblies of the *placita*, for obvious reasons, but they did not have the formalised public role that *placita* did; in particular, even if dominated by urban élites in practice, they were as yet ad hoc, not part of the public political hierarchy of the Kingdom of Italy, and were not headed or called by counts or *missi* or other royal/ imperial representatives.[12] They appear only occasionally, and particularly at times of crisis, as the 1040s surely were. But from the late 1090s in Milan they appear much more often; and their practical powers in the next decade or two became ever clearer, as we shall see in a moment. To repeat, the role of the assembly to ratify a settlement in 1097 implies that its role was by now in some way formalised. Why then? It was a decade of apparent calm in the city for the most part; whether or not the assembly (let alone its shadowy consular leaders) was the result of 'compromise', in Milan it seems to have appeared in a period of renewed and uncontested hierarchy inside the city, around traditional authorities—archbishops and their senior clergy and vassals, in particular. Milan itself was stable then, that is to say. Anselmo IV indeed took the youth of Milan on crusade in 1100, in a notably unsuccessful expedition which he did not return from, but which included members of all earlier factions, even Patarene families. But the wider context of 1097 in Italy was still one of continued civil war and political uncertainty; and it is not chance that the *placitum* tradition had by now ended in the city. In the absence of public judicial assemblies, the city's own gatherings gained more of a formal status in their place, and, increasingly, definable powers as well, as a defensive measure we can indeed say, even if in an environment when archiepiscopal authority was not any more—and not yet—in dispute. This is important. Not as a step towards 'the commune', for only a few elements of the ideal type I characterised in the last chapter are as yet visible here, and indeed the institutionalisation of the powers of ruling consuls was a much later process, as we shall see; but as a sign of a new local structuring of urban political action, in a period in which the wider institutions of the Kingdom were in increasing disarray.[13]

Once we get into the twelfth century, Landolfo of S. Paolo begins to give us some detailed accounts of major moments in the city's history, in most of which he was either an eyewitness or else informed soon after by eyewitnesses, notably the fall of Archbishop Grosolano in 1111 and that of Anselmo V da Pusterla in 1135. These deserve some discussion, because they give important—even if, as we shall see, problematic—information about how Milan's lay community, and the consuls as part of it, actually operated in the city by now.

Grosolano, who was, atypically, not from Milan (he had been bishop of Savona in Liguria), was not a much-loved figure in the city, and soon after his election in 1102 he was attacked by Landolfo's uncle Liprando for simony: a rhetorical charge which Landolfo does not even try to substantiate, but which resulted in an ordeal by fire in 1103 to justify it, which Liprando performed successfully. Landolfo writes this up in great detail and it has some prominence in the historiography as a result, but Grosolano had solid support from the clerical hierarchy and the pope, and this attempt to depose him went nowhere.[14] Landolfo claims several times that Liprando had massive popular backing; we can doubt that. But it is certainly significant that the ordeal was in the end organised by the *concio populi*, the 'assembly of the people'. That assembly was here acting separately from the archbishop, and not obviously to his advantage; and its regularity and potential independence slowly increased from here on. In 1117, Archbishop Giordano used the *arengo* to considerable effect, as we saw at the start of this book; in 1118, the *contio militum et civium* was the body which began the great war with Como (Giordano is here said by Landolfo to have 'inflamed it to do revenge' after the death of a Milanese *capitaneus* at Como's hands, but the archbishop apparently could not start a war on his own); in 1128 the *contio cleri et populi* decided that Anselmo V should crown Conrad, rival to the German king Lothar III, as king of Italy; in 1135 the *popularis contio* was the venue for the beginning of the overthrow of Anselmo, in part precisely because of that coronation, in which senior clerics spoke against him, turning the meeting, and the consuls agreed to take further action.[15] It is clear that this assembly by now, in the first third of the twelfth century, had a membership which could include both aristocrats and clergy; it is however, here as elsewhere, far from clear whether it included more than a minority of the inhabitants of the city, except in 1117, when it explicitly included women. But it is also important that these citations are all from a single work written in the 1130s (the word *concio/contio* does not, for example, appear in Milanese documents in this period), and that Landolfo, far from a neutral observer, wrote a carefully structured text; all we can really say is that in the 1130s he saw an apparently fairly loose and wide form of assembly politics as being a normal way for the inhabitants of Milan to express themselves politically, including in the presence of prominent clerics and lay leaders. I will come back to that.

Grosolano hung on in 1103, then; but he fell quite easily eight years later, when floods hit the city and he, although absent in Jerusalem, was blamed for them. A carefully constituted group of eighteen clerics and laity (all of the latter and many of the former apparently aristocrats; some are attested later as consuls), evenly divided between supporters and opponents of the archbishop, agreed to meet on the last day of IIII to determine whether Grosolano was rightly archbishop; they in the end all decided that he was not, apparently on the grounds that he was still bishop of Savona, and elected Giordano instead. This can easily be seen as the political community getting rid of an embarrassment, with some despatch; it turned out more muddily, though, for Grosolano attempted a comeback on his return to Italy in 1113 and there was a battle between his supporters and his opponents in which numerous people were killed—clearly the former archbishop was not friendless, and (Landolfo says) only Giordano's victory in a parallel war of bribery got Grosolano out of the city (he later appealed to the pope, without success). Here, though, the body which voted against Grosolano was by no means a *contio*; it was an ad hoc and self-selected group of city leaders. The word only appears in Landolfo's account here to describe Grosolano's faction, not any form of general assembly, unlike during Anselmo V's fall in 1135.[16] I would resist the idea that this marks a change between IIII and 1135, with the *concio* becoming more central; again, it is important to stress that we are dealing with a single text; but we can say at least that, for all Landolfo's interest in assemblies, he did not need to invoke them every time something important happened in the city.

And the same is true for consuls, in fact even more so. Landolfo says at one point, proudly, that he was an *epistolarum dictactor*, a letter-drafter, for the consuls, but they are far from prominent in his narrative. As Keller has remarked, they above all appear when Landolfo is going to a series of tribunals to try to get his church back, as in 1117. Twice he refers to them as the *archbishop's* consuls (*suis consulibus*), even if, conversely, they are among the political figures who bring Anselmo V down. Although plenty of lay figures appear as political players in Landolfo's account, he only mentions two consuls by name, both from the capitaneal da Rhò family. At the end of his history, in 1136, he actually got a hearing about his church from Lothar III, now emperor, but all Lothar did was refer the case to the consuls of the city, and the one who took it on was Arnaldo da Rhò, grandson of Erlembaldo's killer, whose family had got Landolfo out of the church in the first place: so no joy there.[17] That is the closest to any kind of consular protagonism that we get. Landolfo was a consular officer, and beyond that a member of an oppositional family with no connection to the city's traditional leadership (his relatives cannot be tracked in documents, even if they fought for the city quite often according to Landolfo, so may genuinely not have been prominent[18]), who had little sympathy with aristocrats; he might have been expected to talk up an autonomous city government, but he did not. For all the public separation of powers in 1117 (above, p. 1), it would be easy to conclude, on the basis of our main narrative source, that the consuls were indeed nothing more than ordinary members of the aristocracy, with strong ties to the archbishop, and only occasionally active as independent political protagonists: apart from the assembly, not much of the communal ideal type is visible here. But we should not simply accept Landolfo's imagery. We are all now much more distrustful of sources than that, and it is also pretty clear that Landolfo of S. Paolo, notwithstanding the title of his 'History of the city of Milan' recorded in the earliest, early fifteenth-century, manuscript, was writing above all a history of the Milanese church and its archbishops (including of his uncle and himself, both clerics as they were), and not of Milan's lay politics—even of its wars, which are the basic meat of urban histories and annals, but which, significantly, only appear as asides in his text. A letter casually surviving in a letter-collection of the 1130s indeed shows the *consules Mediolanensium et universus populus* writing to a lay lord to request military help against Cremona in, probably, 1132; consuls were clearly fronting the political actions of the city by now, which, joined to their rotation in office and their link to the *concio*, brings all the elements of the ideal type into view.[19] It is thus better to regard Landolfo as only a single and partial witness, to be set against other data as needs be. Conversely, it is at least important to remember that it was possible for a writer who, however unsuccessfully, appears as a player in urban and ecclesiastical politics in his own right (all the archbishops knew him personally), and who was also directly involved in the consulate, not to see the emerging commune as more than minimally centre stage.

Let us therefore turn to the documents of the commune itself. The first text which mentions and names consuls dates to 1117; the second to 1130. Both are atypical, and I will come back to them. There then follows a continuous series of consular judgements in legal disputes, starting in 1138 and reaching twenty in number already by 1150 (over two hundred by 1200), and covering nearly every year from then on—with the exception of the period 1163–66, after Barbarossa had the city destroyed in 1162 and its inhabitants temporarily exiled (the Milanesi reversed both, rapidly, after 1167, and Barbarossa lost the war only nine years later). These consular judgements from 1138 onwards are highly standardised; 1138 is thus unlikely to be the first one, and indeed Landolfo's case in 1136 implies that it was not. They consist of a set of consuls who hear a dispute, usually in a specified public place, which stabilises soon enough in the Broletto, near the cathedrals (see map 2), in front of what is already called in 1138 the *domus consulatus*; with then one of them—usually a *iudex*—pronouncing sentence with the agreement, *concordia*, of the others.[20] They also have audiences who are listed as witnesses, often made up of past and future consuls, who are numerous until the 1170s. These disputes generally concerned rural land, and often feudal and signorial rights as well; the jurisdiction of the consuls may not have spread everywhere in the diocese, but it certainly, given the origins of the parties to these disputes, could reach a long way out already by the 1140s.[21] They represent a regular and solid set of cases. They survive in a wide variety of Milanese archives, and sometimes in those of other cities too. The formulae for these texts do not say that Milanese consuls, unlike those for some cities, are 'elected' by the *populus*, but they are clearly autonomous figures. The texts have been edited since 1919 as a group, almost the only set of consular texts for any city to have their own publication, and have thus influenced everyone very considerably—as has the editor Cesare Manaresi's authoritative but highly institutional introduction.[22] When Hagen Keller says that communes became organised bodies in the 1120s–30s, he is largely thinking of this set of texts, and one can see why.

Where there is more room for doubt is in the earlier two cases, in 1117–30, and some associated documents. The 1117 text, discussed at the start of this book, is not at all like later consular sentences; it is in fact in the format of a temporarily revived eleventh-century *placitum* assembly, with the archbishop as the president, the legal authority, and the consuls doing the judging in the *arengo*—in effect, in the role taken in the eleventh century by imperial *iudices*. *Placita* had otherwise ended in most of Lombardy (they only by now survived

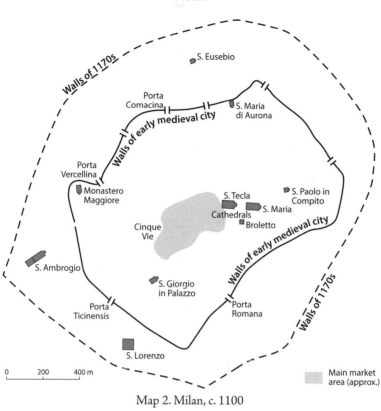

Map 2. Milan, c. 1100

intermittently, particularly in the Veneto[23]), so this procedure was a copy of a former judicial assembly, not its continuation. But, in that context, the significant novelty of this case is not only the consuls and the *arengo*, even though both clearly have a visible identity by now (the 1117 judgement was to be 'recorded [*inbreviare*] in their *consularia*', so the consuls had record-keeping too), but also, and much more, the absence of any imperial figure: it is as if Milan was by now presented as the archbishop's to rule, with the consuls as 'his' officials.[24] In the 1130 text, there is no archbishop, but, as Paolo Grillo remarks, Anselmo V was running into trouble then; here, one consul pronounces sentence (actually, he confirms a sentence already given by the bishop of Bergamo in a case inside that city's territory, so bishops are not absent here either), and a large number of other consuls (twenty-two in all) confirm. This, apart from the length of the list of consuls, fits later judgements; but we can easily see this text as in some sense midway between archiepiscopal and consular power. The 1130 text is, however, central to historians, because it is absolutely the only consular document ever to say that some consuls were *capitanei*, some were *valvassores*, and some were *cives*. Keller sees this as the tip of an iceberg, and argues that it is a guide to the fact that consuls were regularly chosen from all three strata, as Otto of Freising explicitly claimed in the 1150s; Grillo, among others, doubts that and stresses its one-off nature. We cannot, it must be recognised, easily tell, as it is unique—although this three-fold political representation turns up quite casually in Landolfo of S. Paolo too.[25] There are, conversely, no signs at all that by the 1140s there was any tripartite division in our consular lists, and, as we shall see, it is not very likely. But it is certainly demonstrably the case that some later consuls were aristocratic and some not. I will come back to this, for it seems to me more important than arguing about typicality here, and the balance between different social origins for consuls was also variable in practice, in significant ways.

What to me is equally important, however, is that these are not the only recorded disputes in the period. Four others are canon-law cases, which were ended by the archbishop, in each case in the presence not just of clergy but also of laymen who must in some way have been part of his court, his *fideles* or vassals. The lists of these men have many overlaps with the consular lists of 1117 and 1130. Two other disputes are what could be called 'quasi-consular', in that they are agreements confirmed by large bodies of important men who do not call themselves consuls, and the overlaps are here great as well. The second of these, from 1129, set in the *publico arengo* of Milan, still fronts the archbishop (although he was already in trouble in that year), who receives lands and rights previously held illegally by rural lords, but also cites an earlier legal decision by the consuls; one might regard the (highly aristocratic) witness-list as consisting of the consuls of that year, but the text definitely does not say so, and they could equally well be the archbishop's men—if, indeed, there was any concrete difference.[26] After 1130 there are fewer of these archiepiscopal judgements (although they continue, throughout the century, again in canon-law cases[27]), but earlier, in the 1110s and 1120s, the image of a consular world virtually folded into the archbishop's personal entourage, which can be extracted from Landolfo of S. Paolo, does seem to make some sense in the documentation at our disposal. The consuls before the 1130s did have some formal role, if Landolfo wrote letters for them; and already in 1117 they also kept records, as we have just seen.[28] All the same, the rather more institutionalised commune of the years after 1138 marks a break from that, and potentially quite an important one.

If we are to get further in our understanding of how the commune of Milan developed, we will have to look, as I stressed earlier, not at governmental structures, but at people, at exactly who it was that was politically active in the city in each period; that is to say, with respect to what I have just been discussing, who the public figures in our documents, whether archiepiscopal, quasi-consular, or consular, actually were. A detailed prosopography of all of them cannot be set out here; I will take a few typical examples and track them through, framed by some very basic statistics. I will draw a simple distinction of before and after the first 'regular' consular case in 1138, for the figures are different for each, and will also stop in 1150, my endpoint for these analyses—although I will follow some important individual figures until the end of their documentation.

The first thing that is clear is that the public world before 1138 was indeed very largely aristocratic. In the 1117 text, out of eighteen or nineteen consuls, a maximum of four were not visibly aristocrats; in 1130, out of twenty-three, only five were non-aristocratic *cives*. Most of the non-aristocrats turn up in the archbishop's documents too, and it is in fact interesting that the big archiepiscopal occasions often include, at the end of lists, rather more people who cannot be identified elsewhere than do the early consular documents—the archbishop was the focus of a wide civic aggregation; but the top names in these lists are again overwhelmingly aristocratic.[29] From 1138 onwards, however, the pattern changes substantially. There are no obvious aristocrats at all in the 1138 consular lists; in 1140 and 1141 they return, but the percentage has dropped to 50 percent. All told, of the consuls documented between 1138 and 1150, under 40 percent were aristocratic, as far as we can tell, a percentage which falls further if we count each office-holding stint, as many consuls held office several times.[30] Of non-aristocrats, by contrast, a high percentage were *iudices et missi*, legal experts with an imperial title, and these legal experts were by far the commonest examples of consuls who served several times: in some years, indeed, a majority of the consuls were *iudices*. So what happened

between 1130 and 1138 is both that the percentage of aristocrats who held consular office dropped substantially and that
legal experts came abruptly into the foreground. We saw *iudices* as active in the *placita* of the eleventh century, and also
in the 1097 text which mentions the *consulatus*, so there was
a continuity there, which in at least one case is probably a genealogical continuity as well, as we shall see. But legal experts
are almost absent from the consular texts of 1117–30, and also
from the archiepiscopal documents of the same period: they
were not part of the aristocratic early years of the commune,
even though they were so important in the 1140s—and in
every succeeding decade. All this seems to me to confirm a
break from previous practice, and indeed potentially quite a
sharp break; but it occurred in the 1130s, not earlier—the decade in which the commune became more of an institution,
and apparently also less of a spin-off of the archbishop's own
entourage, for the archbishop is, equally, much less prominent
from this moment on in city government.

The other thing that is worth noting after the 1130s is what
happened to the aristocracy. Up to 1130, we see a wide range
of urban aristocratic—especially capitaneal—families, both
around the archbishop and in the early consular documents.
Only the most rural aristocratic families (such as the da Carcano and the da Besate) do not figure in these texts, or indeed in most other Milanese documents from the early and
mid-twelfth century. Some of the urban aristocratic families
continued to be consuls afterwards too: the da Rhò, the da
Porta Romana, the da Settala, the da Soresina, the Visconti,
the Burri, the Crivelli.[31] But there are also several, equally
urban, aristocratic families whom we can track attached to
the archbishop, but *not* to the commune, at least after 1130:
the da Landriano (no consuls until 1155), the da Pusterla (no

consuls between 1117 and 1179), the da Melegnano (no consuls till 1181), the Stampa (no consuls till 1193), the Pozzobonelli (no consuls till 1198), the da Tenebiago, the Avvocati, and the Fanti (after 1130, never consuls again).[32] The Avvocati, who provided a consul in 1130 but not afterwards, kept their role as the archbishops' advocates, which was presumably enough for them to be important in the city without needing other offices, and also their tithe fiefs and signorial rights around Rosate in the south-west of the diocese, although they were less powerful there in the second half of the twelfth century than in the first.[33] The da Landriano are very prominent in all our early twelfth-century materials for Milan, and indeed earlier, although they were not actually consuls in 1117–30; later, by the 1170s, they are very visible in city politics again as well (indeed, two members of the family were rectors of the Lombard League, the urban alliance against Barbarossa, in that decade). But they for the most part dropped out in the formative years of the commune, and presumably (among other things) concentrated on the development of their rural signoria in Villamaggiore in the southern Milanese, where they can be seen as lords in several twelfth-century texts.[34] The Stampa were less powerful (they were vassals of S. Ambrogio, as we have seen, but we cannot find them with signorial rights), but we can see them active in land transactions, in particular in Quinto *de Stampis* south of the city (it is Quinto de' Stampi still today), where they must really have been dominant.[35] These three can stand as type-examples of families who did not need the commune, particularly after it crystallised as a body in the 1130s; the da Landriano came back into the communal orbit once there was a political structure which was solid enough to be interesting in its own right, but the others did not even do that.

I have already suggested that aristocrats might not necessarily have wanted to be part of an élite which simply ruled its inferiors rather than of the traditional hierarchies which looked to emperors and bishops; here are clear Milanese examples of it. It would be nice to be able to propose that richer or more signorial families kept out of the commune, whereas less rich ones did not, but our documentation is not good enough to do that (it privileges land, not commercial activity, as all early document collections do, which does not help assessments of urban wealth, and also tells us less about land held in fief, which was common in the Milanese, than we would like). Such a division by wealth is not inconceivable, and we shall see some examples of it in Pisa in the next chapter; but in Milan, actually, none even of these non-consular families stand out as being seriously rich by the standards of Italy's leading aristocrats, and indeed no urban capitaneal family can be shown to have had more than one or two castles; large sets of castles were restricted to rural families such as the da Besate.[36] All we can say is that a non-communal choice was certainly possible for political players in Milan— and, given Milan's prominence and the relatively early crystallisation of its communal structures, plus the considerable military aggression associated with it, which we shall come on to, we could say: *even* in Milan. So the Milanese commune of the 1120s might well have been an extension of the archbishop's entourage, but the commune of the 1140s was fuller of legal experts than it was of aristocrats, and many aristocrats by now avoided it. This shows that there was indeed something new and different going on by the 1140s; and it was that commune, not its predecessor, which determined how the city's government would develop in the future.

Let us look at some of the families which actually did provide consuls, so that we can see the sort of people the city had to deal with in the years after 1138. I will single out seven, two aristocratic, one possibly more commercial in orientation, and four judicial, for a brief analysis; they will give us an idea of the range. This sort of family reconstruction, however summary, is also essential if we want to gain any sense of what they actually thought they were doing.

The da Rhò were a clearly capitaneal family who committed fully to the consulate. As we have seen, they played an active part in the movement against the Pataria, and provided an archbishop, in the eleventh century; they were associated with later archbishops in the 1120s, and they were (among other, more important, things) enemies of Landolfo of S. Paolo. They remained active archiepiscopal vassals after 1130 as well, and close to the cathedral church; in 1149–50 Anselmo da Rhò was a deacon of the cathedral and Arderico da Rhò was its advocate. They held tithes in fief in Arnate, Varano, and Ternate in the north-west of the diocese, well past their political centre at Rhò, quite far out in fact, although the (scarce) attestations to their landholding show them in the city too (see map 3). But Arnaldo da Rhò was consul in 1130, 1136, and 1140, Giovanni in c. 1134 and 1150, and Ottone in 1143, 1145, and 1154; and, in general, the family was very active as witnesses to urban transactions of all kinds across the same period. This family, similar in many ways to the da Landriano, was by no means as cautious about a consular and urban public commitment.[37]

The Burri family was even more visible. Malastreva, son of Eriprando Burro, was the only person to be as active in the earliest commune (consul in 1117 and 1130—when he was a *valvassor*—and in the archbishop's entourage in between)

Map 3. The territory of Milan, c. 1100

Legend:
- • City
- † Rural monastery
- – – Approximate diocesan boundary
- R Land of da Rhò family
- B Land of Burri family
- C Land of Cagapisto family

as he was in the commune of the 1140s, for he was consul three times in the latter decade, while remaining close to the archbishop, as a document for 1148 attests. In that text, he is named alongside Gigo Burro, who was himself a consul five times between 1140 and 1151; a third family member, Anselmo Burro, was consul in 1144, and the family remained active in the consulate in the 1170s and onwards—in the next century, indeed, they were also frequently podestà for other cities. So there is no doubt about the Burri family's commitment to the commune, however close they were to the archbishop too. The range of landholding which this very extensive family had is also visible: they had some in Villamaggiore in the far south of the diocese (as did many influential Milanesi, possibly all in fief from the da Landriano), in Melegnano not far away, in Gudo to the south-west of the city, in Magnago to the north-west, and in the city itself, as well as some tithes (but no documented signorial rights) at Vimercate to the east (see again map 3). This spread is wide, covering nearly half the diocese, which would certainly help to explain their involvement with the city, at the centre of the web. The data are too fragmentary for us to get a sense of a scale here, but Ottone di Amedeo Burro could afford a dowry of £40 in 1121, a figure which is well above average. Prosperous landowners with an urban base and considerable public ambition: we might imagine that they used their wealth for commercial purposes, although it has to be said that this is not very visible later, in the richer commercial documentation of the thirteenth century. Either way, however, they stand as the archetype of aristocratic consuls, and if they and the da Rhò had been typical of consuls in the 1140s, they would have shown a notable continuity with the previous generation. But they were not.[38]

Non-aristocratic and non-judicial families who provided consuls are much harder to trace, and this fact is significant; they may well have sometimes held less land, and they certainly rather less often witnessed the sort of charters which ended up in ecclesiastical archives. They may have sometimes gained prominence through commercial activity, although we cannot simply assume that; it may well be that we are dealing with smaller-scale rentiers here as often as with a stratum of merchants and workshop-owners. If we do find evidence for any of them, this might simply show atypicality, too. But we can at least, thanks to research by Livia Fasola, say something about the Scaccabarozzi family, a family which produced two consuls, Guilielmo in 1150 and 1155, and Giordano in 1157. This was a family which went over to Frederick Barbarossa after he destroyed Milan in 1162—and indeed even before; Giordano is called *proditor*, 'traitor', by the Milan *Annals*—and never became consuls again. It was a family of prosperous landowners, particularly active in the city, but also owning land both in the far south of the Milanese and the far north-east. They had no tithes or signorial rights, important signs of aristocratic identity, but did later acquire fiefs, and they may well have matched some of the lesser aristocratic families in the scale of their landholding. Very unusually, the Scaccabarozzi are directly attested in commercial activity, for in 1143 they leased from the cathedral church a *pristinum*, a bread-oven, in Cinque Vie, a city quarter. An at least occasional commercial investment might be what marked out people defined as *cives*, as opposed to aristocrats, but, again, we would be unwise to assume that automatically; more important in my view is that, when we can see the landed resources of leading *cives*, they could be substantial and wide-ranging.[39] What we are in fact looking at here is a second stratum of the urban élite, one less rich and certainly less signorial than the leading *capitanei*, even if for a time as involved in consular politics as the da Rhò and the Burri were. In this second stratum we could probably also put some of the families of *valvassores* who have relatively little impact on our documents, and so were probably less rich than the Burri; this was a stratum defined by wealth, not military-aristocratic status.

Very different, however, were the judicial consuls. Let us here start with Gualterio *iudex* and *missus*, consul three times between 1138 and 1142. He may have died soon after, for he was a professional *iudex* already in 1109, when he guaranteed the land sales of two under-age owners, as Milanese custom required; he was then said to be son of Ariprando *iudex*. Ariprando *iudex* and *missus* is equally attested in a public role, consistently, between 1095 and 1115; he was in his turn son of Pagano *iudex*, who must be the Ambrogio Pagano we have already met, a notarial and then a major judicial figure between 1069 and 1114 (by when he must have been very old). These genealogical links are not certain, for Ariprando is a common name, but they are very likely; they also allow one to speculate that the later Ariprando *iudex* who was consul four times between 1147 and 1162 might have been the next generation along (he went over to Barbarossa after 1162 as well).[40] Here we have the continuity of judicial involvement in the public world of the city which is invoked by those who think that nothing changed much with the commune, even if it is far from clear that lawmen thought the same in each generation, and members of this family are also notably absent from public documents in the formative years of the consulate. But the other striking thing is that, for all the frequency of citation of the first three generations in texts, they are not once referred to as landowners in any shape or form. They were, apparently, a purely judicial family. *Iudices* were often from families of high status in the eleventh century, and could have substantial lands in many cases. There were counter-examples even then, and by the early decades of the twelfth legal experts in many cities tended not to be in the ranks of major landowners. This family was clearly one of the counter-examples: even their eleventh-century forebear Ambrogio Pagano, who ran *placita* in the 1080s and was present in the first consular document of 1097, cannot be seen as active in land transactions in any documentary collection.[41] Whether or not judicial roles were remunerative enough to make a career out of on their own, it is at least clear that this family's prominence was not linked to landed wealth.

Stefanardo *iudex* and *missus* appears as a consul in 1138 too, and then four more times up to 1149, but was younger than Gualterio. His hinterland is clear; he was from the rising small town of Vimercate, where he is attested with land from 1133; between 1150 and 1153 he left Milan and retired back to Vimercate, where he was a land dealer (as *iudex de Vicomercato de civitate Mediolani*) and also active in judicial roles, until his death after 1183, by when he must have been around eighty; his family remained there after that, and never supplied consuls again—even if they did not abandon an attachment to Milan, for the Stefanardi family still referred to themselves as being from the city in 1211, and their descendants had a city base too.[42] Why Stefanardo himself gave up on a Milanese career is unknown, but he was certainly prominent in Vimercate afterwards, thanks in large part, one assumes, to the prestige of his past history. We can at least in this case (thanks to the survival of Vimercate's church archive) say roughly what his economic resources were based on: the small scale of his transactions (a few fields at a time) makes it hard to see him more than as a medium owner, for all his success as a city figure.

Oberto dall'Orto was similar as well. He was consul seven times between 1140 and 1158, and then, after a break, twice in 1169–71; his son Anselmo was consul three times in 1155–62. Anselmo, too, joined Barbarossa after that, and was not consul again, but it is significant that this family did not face eclipse, for Oberto was important enough to be recalled to serve after the city was rebuilt. Again, we cannot trace Oberto's family in our land documents, except as witnesses (an earlier Anselmo was a land-measurer for the monastery of Chiaravalle in 1139, but this is our only clear reference to a wider activity).[43] But both Oberto—called *vir sapiens* by the German chronicler Vincent of Prague and also in his death entry in the cathedral necrology in 1175—and Anselmo appear, uniquely, as authors of short legal text-books which still survive, showing that both were trained in Roman law; indeed, Oberto's texts, about the law of fiefs, are in the form of letters to Anselmo while he was away studying, probably in the 1140s. This latter study was almost certainly in Bologna, for one of Anselmo's own law tracts says that he had been there; but Oberto, whose title of *iudex et missus* is initially attached to King Lothar III (so he got the title between Lothar's accession in 1125 and Oberto's own first appearance in 1131), must have himself trained in the early 1120s or indeed earlier, when Bologna was much less prominent. Peter Classen thinks he was trained in Milan itself; Pavia is a possible alternative, for its legal teaching was well-established in the eleventh century.[44] But Oberto's work shows us that the legal training available to him, and thus presumably his contemporaries also, must have already been complex in the 1120s at the latest, wherever it was based. We shall come back to this later, as these texts are important for us, but they are relevant here as a marker of the depth of legal knowledge in the city, one which might well have meant that being a *iudex et missus* was also remunerative: it is reasonable, then, to see Oberto as on Stefanardo's level in terms of resources. It was knowledge which was valued outside the city too. Oberto had so much prestige that he was called on to arbitrate a boundary dispute between the communes of Verona and Ferrara in 1151 on his own—a remarkable prominence for a single lawyer; furthermore, a Verona text of 1147 shows six Milanese legal experts, including Oberto and Stefanardo (flanked by four non-judicial Milanesi, including Malastreva Burro and a member of the da Rhò family), called in to give a highly Romanist *consilium*, legal opinion, during a dispute about feudal law.[45]

Girardo Cagapisto was in Verona in 1147 too, and he was the most active consul of the entire period we are dealing with here, with as many as fourteen stints as consul between 1141 and 1180—almost as many as he could have had, given that consuls seem not to have served for two successive years, and given the break in consuls in 1163–66—and was a representative of the city at the great peacemaking meeting in Venice in 1177 after the Lombard cities' victory over Barbarossa the year before. He too was an expert in Roman and feudal law, for he calls himself *causidicus*, jurist, and his name is cited together with Oberto's as constant points of reference in the basic text of feudal law (partially drawing on Oberto's letters), the *Libri* or *Consuetudines feudorum*. He was evidently a close colleague of Oberto, even if they often served in alternate years, and they were together as consuls in 1154, active protagonists in the first stand-off between Milan and Barbarossa. (This did not go well; they guided the German army out of the richer areas of the Milanese, the army ran short of supplies, and Barbarossa destroyed the Milanese castle of Rosate in reprisal—the Milanesi, alarmed, responded by destroying Girardo's own house, and he did not serve again as consul until 1160, by when relations with the emperor had broken down, the biggest gap in his career.) We can say rather more about the Cagapisto family than about that of other *iudices*. Girardo was certainly its most successful family member, and was visible elsewhere in the city, as some of the other Milanese *iudices* were not; his heirs, who can be tracked into the next century, carried on his legal expertise, and were notaries as well. In 1188, after his death, the city consuls divided some of his land among his three sons, and the text lists the places where they were located, four in number, west and east of the city (a respectable range, even if we cannot be sure of the scale here); other citations of the family before that add references to urban land and rural land in a couple more places, including some tithes in Bruzzano, slightly farther south, which they bought in 1135 and ceded back to the Milanese church of S. Eusebio in 1151 (see map 3). The tithes were not enough to make the family aristocratic, but are certainly signs of prosperity; so is a land acquisition by Girardo north-west of the city in 1170 from the da Baggio for £110, although that turned into a legal battle subsequently, won by Girardo. We could see the Cagapisto as a reasonably well-off medium rentier family. Girardo may possibly have been better off than Stefanardo, whose landholding was more restricted; but the range between the two may be a guide to the economic level of these other judicial families as well.[46] These families did not make it in economic terms even into the second stratum of the élite, which included families like the Scaccabarozzi; it is best to see them as a third level, one which I will call the 'medium élite'. We shall meet this stratum again when we look at Pisa, and especially Rome.

Girardo Cagapisto is significant for another reason, too: his name. It has not been stressed by most historians that so many of the Milanese political leadership had surnames beginning Caga- or Caca-, that is to say 'shit'. The niceties of earlier generations of scholarship led them to neglect this, and older historians at most refer to it glancingly and uneasily, although an excellent recent article by François Menant finally lists the names and discusses their etymologies; but it was certainly important for Milanese identity and self-representation. (Similar names exist in other Italian cities too—Menant stresses Cremona in particular—but they are not usually so prominent.) Cagapisto probably means 'shit-pesto'—as, for example, in the pasta sauce. In the case of the two brothers Gregorio and Guilielmo Cacainarca, again both *iudices* and active consuls between 1143 and 1187, their surname means 'shit-in-a-box'. That of Arderico Cagainosa, consul in 1140 and 1144, means 'shit-in-your-pants'. Other prominent families included the Cagalenti, 'shit-slowly', the Cacainbasilica, 'shit-in-the-church', the Cacarana, 'shit-a-frog', the Cagatosici, 'toxic-shit', and there were many more.[47] The twelfth century was a period when nicknames became surnames or even first names in Italy; there was a vogue for Mala- names, boasting of evil, among the aristocracy, for example (as with the Milanese aristocratic consul Malastreva, 'evil-stirrup'), whereas in more clerical Rome, alongside some Caca- names, many names were formed from Deus-.[48] But what would, say, the German court have thought, full of snobbish aristocrats from old families as it was, to find an authoritative representative from northern Italy's biggest city called Shit-pesto? In fact, we can tell; for one of them, Otto of Freising, when he narrates with some schadenfreude the travails of Girardo in 1154, calls him Girardo Niger, 'the black', a name never attested in Milan, which Otto must have invented as a politer alternative. This may have also been in the historian's mind when, just before, he wrote his famous trope about how awful it was that Italians allowed 'youths of inferior condition' and even 'workers in the contemptible mechanical arts' to assume the *miliciae cingulum*, that is to say public office.[49] Not that it is likely that any of the people we have just looked at were also artisans, as Otto implies, but there is no reason to take that statement too seriously—anyway, for Otto, a medium landowner called Shit-pesto with a leading civic role would have been quite as bad as a rude mechanical. It is important to recognise that shit-words were not taboo in Europe in this period; medieval Europe did not ever match the squeamishness of polite society in the years 1750–1950 in this respect. The Investiture Dispute, for example, has clear examples of Hildebrand being called Merdiprand and similar by ecclesiastical polemicists on the opposing side.[50] But this in itself shows that shit-names were at least insulting, in many contexts, in our period. Not always in Milan, though, evidently. The earthy sensibility shown by local naming, I would go so far to say, is one of the major Milanese contributions to the 'civic' culture of the twelfth century; and it was both new and, as they must have soon realised, aggressive to outsiders.[51]

To sum up here: the Milanese commune after 1138 had aristocrats involved in it, to be sure, but they were in a minority; and its most recurrently active members, some with goliardic names, were all judicial experts, with relatively few resources. This certainly fits the fact that far and away the best-documented activity its consuls engaged in was judging court cases. Justice and internal peace were explicitly important virtues in this period. Mosè del Brolo, a noted city intellectual in nearby Bergamo, wrote a poem called the

Liber Pergaminus in praise of his city around 1120 in which his only reference to what must have been consuls (twelve *viri sancti*, changing annually) focussed on their day-and-night engagement with law and justice, which created so great a peace in the city that there did not need to be tower-houses there. All the same, it has to be added that this cannot by any means have been all that consuls did: for cities also fought wars (Mosè said the consuls trained Bergamo's youth in fighting, too), in particular, in Milan's case, against Como between 1118 and 1127, Pavia and Cremona in 1129 and 1136, Cremona again in 1137–38, Pavia again in 1154–55, and of course against Barbarossa after 1158. The Como poem on its losing war with Milan makes it clear that *iudices* were among the combatants.[52] Legal experts did not seem inappropriate for war, it is clear; they had swords as well as robes. And it is even clearer that they did not seem inappropriate ambassadors, including in difficult negotiations, as with Oberto dall'Orto and Girardo Cagapisto in front of Barbarossa in 1154—Oberto was indeed praised not only for his wisdom but for his eloquence in a second meeting with Barbarossa at Roncaglia in 1158 (in both Latin and Italian; evidently this was no longer to be taken for granted among the laity) by Vincent of Prague.[53]

Judicial expertise was thus essential for consular government, and not inconsistent with fighting; and the latter brought *iudices* closer to the aristocracy again. I have been dividing the city's leadership into three economic strata, with the top level holding lands in a wide variety of localities, including tithes held in fief and up to a couple of castles, roughly corresponding to the military aristocracy; some *valvassores* nonetheless operated at a second level, together with leading *cives*, with no castles and less land; judicial experts tended, for their part, to come from the next level down again, the 'medium élite', with rather fewer (even if not trivial) landed resources. These distinctions mattered, and had parallels elsewhere, as we shall see in later chapters. On the other hand, this was not an enormously wide economic spectrum, for, even if aristocrats certainly had much more land than legal experts, such landholding was never visibly very extensive in the case of city-dwellers: in Milan and its territory, only rural families had the large collections of castles which were the normal prerequisite for aristocratic status elsewhere in Europe. Inside the city, aristocrats (especially *capitanei*) were the only holders of castles, but these rarely appear in our sources for the families; they were most of the holders of signorial rights,[54] although seldom in more than a couple of villages; they were most of the holders of fiefs of tithes, but here some clearly non-aristocratic families like the second-level Scaccabarozzi and the third-level Cagapisto could buy them too. Furthermore, we find both aristocrats and non-aristocrats with the same sort of landholding structure: whether larger or smaller, it was fragmented, scattered across much of the Milanese, and also almost never, in our documents, consisted of whole estates. This parallelism is important for our understanding of the lack of obvious tension between the strata of the Milanese landowning élites. (It also gives a further context to Otto of Freising's distaste: indeed, none of Milan's aristocrats may have seemed like 'real' aristocrats to him; all of them were too urban, and, overall, not rich enough, to be fully taken into consideration.) On the basis of Milanese material, indeed, Maire Vigueur is quite right to refer to the 'honest' landed patrimony of consuls; and he is almost certain to be right that what we are seeing here is in some sense a single group, members of what he calls the mounted militia, and, indeed, that this commonality of social standing was—at least after the 1130s—more important than the traditional division between *milites* and *cives*, let alone between *capitanei* and *valvassores*, which has made Milan's commune seem unusually aristocratic to many scholars.

I would indeed push this point further: Milan is well-known for being the type-example of an aristocratic commune, but actually, it was almost the opposite. In its opening decade or two, it certainly was aristocrat-dominated, but after the 1130s the consuls who take centre stage for the rest of the century were not aristocrats, but members of the third level of the urban élite (or of Maire Vigueur's militia), by no means particularly important in landed terms, and also outside the archiepiscopal entourage which had dominated the city hitherto. It is not possible to refigure Milan's crystallising commune as a radical undermining of aristocratic power, however; that would go too far the other way. There were, even in the years of hegemony of Oberto, Girardo, and their successors, more aristocrats among Milan's consuls than there were in most cities, as we shall see in chapter 5. It is clear, indeed, that—even if plenty of urban aristocrats did keep out of the early commune, showing that political homogeneity in the city was not total—the city's aristocracy, taken as a whole, was not opposed in principle to the local influence of the judicial families; that something linked them together. Put another way, the economic and status differences that did exist between aristocrats and jurists did not stop them from all being accepted as political players in Milan. But this creates a further problem of explanation. We cannot simply take for granted that city aristocrats and jurists formed a single political or military community; for they demonstrably did not in other cities, including in my other two case studies, Pisa and Rome. Why at least some aristocratic families such as the da Rhò, with a long tradition of political activism in favour of the status quo and a continuing closeness to the cathedral, were happy to participate in such a single community in Milan needs more discussion; and here we need to come back to the issue of culture.

We do not have any contemporary narrative sources for Milan between the end of Landolfo's chronicle in 1136 and the start of the Milanese *Annals* in 1154, which depicts a consular régime going it heroically alone against Barbarossa, until the disaster of 1162 and the revival thereafter.[55] It will be clear that I see the intervening period as the crucial moment of change, when the Milanesi developed a communal structure which was indeed new, and was by now partially dominated by men who had far fewer links to the traditional hierarchies which still persisted in Milan, the archbishop's entourage, the cathedral chapter, the vassalic network of the *ordines*. Whether this means they were also more 'civic' in their self-image, as Italian historiography often stresses, seems to me a misleading problem; the best example of a novel civic sensibility which I have so far been able to offer is Caca- names, and what I take away from all recent scholarship on the Milanesi and other Italians at war is that military values, far from being 'aristocratic' and thus opposed to the *vita civile* of later fame, were not just necessary, given all the local wars just mentioned, but one of the major markers of civic identity itself. A clear demonstration of this indeed comes from exactly this period, even if not precisely from Milan: it is the *Liber Cumanus*, an anonymous 2030-line poem about the heroic defence of Como against Milan in the war of 1118–27. This text has not been studied much, partly because its length and poetic diction have put off military historians, and partly because its relentless focus on the joys, horrors, and stratagems of what must have been the closest the early twelfth century came to total war has put off literary scholars. Here, the Comaschi are, precisely, the *cives*, all of them, fighting both on horseback and on foot; the Milanesi are mostly *hostes*, the enemy. The poem does, once, mention consuls as the leaders of the war from Como's side, but they are called *proceres*, aristocrats, rather more often, and the collectivity is seen as consisting of the whole city rather than any hierarchy, whether feudo-vassalic or consular.[56] This is not a text which will tell us much about the move to a consular régime, then, whether consciously or unconsciously, unlike some of the parallel Pisan poems which will be discussed in the next chapter. But it certainly tells us that civic and military values were in this context absolutely unitary: including in the fact that someone who was transparently a direct participant in the war—and perhaps a layman, for Christian imagery is virtually absent from the text—had a full control over the rules of poetry. I shall not be claiming any different 'civic' sensibility from this for anywhere in Italy, indeed. But what it was that the Milanese consular élite did think they were doing as they led the city away from the archbishop's court and towards a largely judicially led set of mid-century political structures is not something we can sidestep. So here let us look more closely at what Oberto dall'Orto and his son wrote; for these are the only known texts from the pen of any of our consuls, and they deserve some attention in their own right—and as works by consuls, not just as contributions to the development of law, which is the context in which they have mostly been studied.

We have to recognise from the start that Oberto and Anselmo wrote law tracts, not musings about politics; what they
thought about the consular office or communal identity was
not part of their chosen remit in the least. Anselmo is the easier to deal with, for he essentially wrote Roman law—a tract
on initial actions in cases, and a (very short and less Romanist) tract on forms of leasing. The latter at least has some link
to contemporary leasing activities; the former, however, had
particularly little resonance in Milan, where Lombard law and
legal procedure remained dominant, and Roman law, even
if—evidently—it was studied by legal experts, and also was a
recognised resource for judges (as we shall see for Oberto in a
moment), was not explicitly cited in consular judgements. This
contradiction has long been known; Antonio Padoa Schioppa
and Peter Classen developed the point thirty years ago, when
they showed (thanks in part to the evidence of the Verona
judgement) that there was much more Romanist knowledge
in Milan than the consular sentences would allow one to
think; Anselmo is simply the best example of that.[57] Whether
he regarded his Bolognese training as simply a legal qualification, or whether it underpinned his wider conceptualisation of
how law worked, cannot be said from these texts, although we
should not discount the latter: in the next generation, Rolando
di Guamignano of Lucca, a highly trained jurist who had a
long career as a public official in a city which, like Milan, did
not follow Roman law, wrote a detailed commentary on part
of the Digest, the very size of which (over five hundred pages in
the new edition) implies that he saw the principles of Roman
law as potentially relevant in a non-Roman city.[58] The density
of legal culture is anyway very clear here.

Oberto's two letters are more unusual in that they deal
with feudal law; they in fact became core sections of the later

Libri feudorum, and are almost the only sections ascribed to a named author. They are intelligent and practical guides from an experienced magistrate, who refers to himself at the start as frequently judging disputes in Milan—i.e. as a consul— and, in the second letter, as being too busy to write because he is 'often busy with the care of our *respublica*, and held [up] by many disputes of private persons, and other impediments of innumerable things'.[59] They set out rules for feudal investiture, for the alienation and inheritance of fiefs, for disputing between lords and vassals, and for the situations in which fiefs might be confiscated. They do so in a constant mental framework taken from Roman law, with verbal echoes of Justinian's *Corpus iuris*, occasional direct citations of it, and references to Titius and Sempronius, the John Doe and Richard Roe of Roman law, although not to any of the cuter distinctions of subsequent Romanist law tracts. They also refer to the long-established tradition of Lombard law, and to slightly earlier tracts on feudal law. Oberto at the start remarks that, although cases are (by implication in Milan) sometimes decided by Lombard, sometimes by Roman, and sometimes by customary law, and customary law is different from place to place, he at least wishes to set out how it works in Milan, with respect to feudal law, in which Roman law does not 'extend its force enough to defeat *usus* or *mores*', local customs. This phrase has often been used to show Oberto's exaltation of Milanese customary law over Roman law, but that is not what he means; he is explicitly talking about the law of fiefs here, which Roman law indeed does not cover, given that fiefs had not been invented yet in the sixth century.[60] Rather, Oberto is trying to elevate feudal law to the level of Roman law, a task in which he (and the authors of the rest of the text) succeeded, for the *Libri feudorum* became a standard addition to the *Corpus iuris* thereafter, and also the basis for all later medieval understanding of how feudal law worked—as well as, on a more local level, a core element in Milan's own customary laws, when they were written down in 1216.[61]

One can thus see these letters as Oberto trying to create more system in his normative arsenal: Lombard and Roman law are both stable written corpora, but feudal law is not, and it should be. This seems to reflect his practical experience as a judge of disputes—and as a judge of feudal disputes too, which did indeed come to the consular court with a certain regularity.[62] But there is another way of looking at these texts: when an experienced and educated consul and judge in Milan, from an urban and non-aristocratic background, wanted to fill gaps in the legal systems at his disposal, what he focussed on was the law of fiefs, which was rarely of relevance to more than the few families who were part of the military *ordines*. Indeed, he tells us much more about feudal relationships in the Milanese than does any other source at all, even if we exclude from his text (and I am not sure that we should) the famous section in which he explains what the difference is between *capitanei* and *valvassores*—which is, whether accurate or not, the only such explanation surviving anywhere.[63] So, what is a 'civic', Roman-law-trained consul doing in the 1140s? He is thinking about the feudal world.

We come full circle here. Oberto was not part of the archbishop's entourage, nor, as far as we know, did he hold any fiefs; and I do not think it would be too much to suppose that he was very happy about an environment in which it was legally trained men like him who ran the commune and not (or not only) those from the feudal/signorial world; but all the same, when he sought to put his mark on law, it was that world which was his main concern. Bureaucrats in the Third Reich had the concept of 'working towards the *Führer*', trying to get inside his supposed mind-set;[64] Oberto could be seen, with no more than a little exaggeration, as 'working towards the aristocracy'. Oberto's lifetime political practice took Milan away from traditional hierarchies; furthermore, he (unlike his son) was sufficiently opposed to Frederick Barbarossa to be recalled as a consul when Milan was rebuilt after 1167, and we need not doubt that had he still been alive he would have been with Girardo Cagapisto in Venice in 1177. But in his thought-world, those traditional hierarchies took centre stage. When, earlier, Barbarossa used Roman law to justify his claims to sovereignty at Roncaglia in 1158, and the consuls of the Italian cities conceded his right to do so,[65] Oberto (who was a consul in that year, and present at Roncaglia), given both his Romanist training and his thought-world, must have been particularly easy to convince—at least before the war between the emperor and Milan showed him what that sovereignty meant in practice. This sharp opposition between practice and thought sums up what I mean by sleepwalking (above, p. 20). Oberto was (along with his peers) taking his city in a profoundly new direction, but his mind was elsewhere. And that contradiction—or, perhaps better, the fact that it was not perceived as one, as far as we can tell—also allows us to see that the fact that Milan's commune developed into a structure which was no longer aristocratic-dominated matters less than one might expect: it was run by people who were very often not from that world, and who in many ways worked against it, but they identified with it all the same. The aristocrats who kept out of the commune after 1138 were presumably only too aware of that new direction, but the acceptance of it by the da

Rhò and the Burri, and, over all, the absence of conflict about it in a city which had had its full share of internal turbulence, may well be because the aristocratic strata were also aware of Oberto's thought-world.

———

Milan's government in 1150 was quite different from that of the eleventh century in many ways. I have stressed the 1130s as the turning-point, and it is not only the prosopography of later consuls that makes it so; Milan's new governing structures became fully established in that period as well. Up to the 1090s, as we have seen, justice in the city was still run through *placita*, assemblies which, although given their legitimacy by large turnouts, and certainly choreographed by judicial experts (including the consul Gualterio's probable grandfather), were called by superior powers and shot through with aristocratic representation. *Placita* then ended, even if their top-down patterning was still attached to the archbishop's entourage. But by now, from the 1090s, there were also civic assemblies, the meetings of the *concio*, whose public participation was very wide, as it seems, and whose aggregation was almost certainly based on collective oaths of a type which had appeared in the city in the troubles of the middle decades of the eleventh century. Such assemblies were an old tradition too, but they were more regular and increasingly formalised now, in reaction to the weakening of public power, and they seem to have been both bottom-up deliberative groupings (not dependent on or looking to a superior power, that is to say; the archbishop did not call them, but went to them) and groupings with relatively little social exclusion (we cannot tell if they included the urban poor, and they may not have done so very often, but women, normally excluded from the very male politics of Italian cities, were at least part of the collective grouping of 1117, according to Landolfo of S. Paolo).[66] It was a *concio*, again according to Landolfo, which decided on the Como war in 1118, the most momentous decision of that decade, and another *concio* which brought down Anselmo V in 1135.

It was thus Milan's assembly which first developed a new formal structure, as a defensive reaction against the political and institutional crisis of the Kingdom of Italy; but this was only one element of the ideal-type commune as I have characterised it. Autonomous consular power developed later, and not necessarily as a defence against political breakdown, for it did so with respect to an archbishop who was clearly still powerful: although we cannot track direct conflict between the archbishop (and his entourage) and the consuls of the late 1130s and onwards, there was a structural opposition between them, which I have tried to characterise. All the same, it was the *concio* which acted as the alternative legitimisation for that newly developing consular practice, which, however élitist that practice in reality was, was for the first time separate from the power of the archbishop. Consular judgements did not adopt the older *placitum* tradition; even though they for long had many witnesses, which marks a form of continued collective basis for consular authority, that basis was the *concio* by now, and did not have roots in the hierarchies of the past. The consuls were, furthermore, no longer overwhelmingly aristocratic and more often from the 'medium élite', and the latter looked to that wider city community more than they did to the archiepiscopal hierarchy. Nor did they look to the archbishop's hierarchy ever again, and when the rest of the Milanese aristocracy came back to communal politics later in the century, they did it on consular terms, not their own. But it does also have to be said that the consulate took a long time to develop the same formalised power that *placita* had provided. To abandon the *placitum* tradition was to a large extent a retreat, at least in the initial decades when the legitimacy of the powers of the commune remained inchoate; and when consular power, and communal identity, gained a public standing and a formality in its own right, in the 1140s and onwards, the older tradition of the *placitum* was no longer relevant, and the institutions which embodied power had to be new. This novelty was not lessened by the fact that the whole of the rest of consular history was devoted to making any popular power less real: the consular élite was wider than the aristocracy, but the militia of horsemen was still only 10–15 percent of the population (indeed, perhaps less than that in Milan) and it wished to remain that way. In the end, after our period, the *concio* would be replaced by narrower collective bodies, or else turn back into a top-down ceremonial assembly.[67]

Milan, then, was, if not radical, at least a mixture of radical and conservative. Its commune first started to develop in a world in which archbishops had a very great transactional power, and its first leaders were part of the archiepiscopal entourage, as well as being, for the most part, from aristocratic families which had ruled the city constantly for a hundred years and more, including when the Pataria were powerful. It is indeed quite possible that it shifted in a judicial direction simply because the archbishop recognised that 'his' consuls were going to need to run court cases, and perhaps he thought that they could be left to do that, while the traditional hierarchy ran the rest of the city. I would guess that what may have begun to undermine that comfortable continuity, already in the 1120s, was the Como war, for that war, unlike its predecessors, was a long-lasting and bloody affair which exhausted both sides, and required a much more total organisation of the military resources of Milan to win—and indeed of its financial resources, for it is the context for the first documented attempt at a land-tax in the Comasco, of a type which would not be generalised in peacetime for another generation, which is likely to have been matched in Milan too.[68] That war could only be won by the militia in Maire Vigueur's sense, which certainly included the judicial stratum, and will further have legitimised their role as city rulers; and it was that war which was the template for those of the future, in the 1130s and later. But, however it happened, the increasingly formalised body of the 1140s had a quite different complexion from that of the 1120s, and one which pointed in a different political direction. The archbishop lost centrality, and half the urban aristocracy dropped out as well; the most frequent consuls—who became the city's ambassadors to Barbarossa—were not only judicially trained, but also had relatively restricted landed patrimonies. Conversely, notwithstanding this, if Oberto dall'Orto is any guide, it is far from clear that the consuls were fully aware of these major changes as a break; for the direction of their thoughts was bound up with the aristocratic world as well. I say 'thoughts', not 'values'. In fact, all the signs are that the range of prickly honour-based values which marked the aristocratic world marked all types of city leader as well; a popular distaste for rural oppression and élite bad-boy city rampaging, which is occasionally seen at the end of the twelfth century and was at the core of anti-magnate legislation later in the thirteenth, is not documented in any visible way in our period.[69] This will have made the mixture of radical and conservative still easier to manage. But thoughts are arguably more important here. That they worked in a different way from the practical politics of the early to mid-twelfth century in Milan is clear, at least to me; and it is that difference that I want to stress. But I also want to stress that thought-worlds and practices are *both* important: not least when people act without really knowing what they are doing, with Minerva's owl flying out at dusk, as it usually does.

The question now is how typical Milan was; so next we will test what I have proposed on Pisa. Pisa was a very different city, very focussed on the sea, and with a long-standing tradition of maritime aggression already by 1100; but its sources are rich in the same kind of way as those of Milan, and in some senses still richer, as we shall now see.

3

PISA

The 1110s were a difficult and uncertain time throughout the fragmenting Kingdom of Italy, and indeed beyond, as we saw for Milan and shall see again for Rome; but not in Pisa. Indeed, as it seems, the Pisans were having fun. On the sixth of August 1113, Pisa's lucky day, three hundred ships sailed out of the port of Pisa, on a raiding expedition to the Balearic Islands, which were then under Muslim rule. This was not itself unusual for Pisa; across the whole of the previous century the city had run such raids once every fifteen years or so. This was a large expedition, however—although definitely Pisan-led, other cities of Tuscany took part in it, and it soon had support from Catalonia and Languedoc as well—and also a long one, for it took two years, not a few weeks; and, not least, it was also enthusiastically written up soon after the event, not just in Pisan annals and short poetic texts as were the other raids, but also in a very long poem in heavily Virgilian hexameters, the *Liber Maiorichinus*, the *Book of Mallorca*, a third of the length of the *Aeneid* itself. This text shows very clearly how heroic the Pisans thought they were, how strong in resolve, how martial, how well-led, by their twelve consuls, their archbishop, and their viscount. The stress on the consuls is indeed much greater than on the archbishop and viscount, a point we shall come back to; but what is equally striking is the stress on very many other Pisans too: dozens of them are named in the battle scenes, with their father's name as well, so that even we can often identify them, and contemporaries must usually have been able to do so. It almost seems as if the author (anonymous, but possibly a cleric named Enrico) might have invited people to make a contribution so as to be included, as with the yellow pages of a phone-book. But, however they were chosen, they convey very strongly the sense of a victorious collective enterprise: not aristocrats together with commoners, or not explicitly so, but all male Pisans together, the Pisan *cives* or *populus*, devoted to destroying their enemies (or, if you prefer, victims) and taking their treasure.[1]

Milan in the 1110s, as we saw in the last chapter, was also run by the archbishop and consuls, and we have analogous poetic texts from Lombardy as well, at least from Como and Bergamo. Whatever divided Italian cities in this period, they were going through many similar social and political processes, and reacting to them in some similar ways. But all the same, the experience Pisa had of the slow development of the city commune was very different from that of Milan. Milan's commune, for a start, although it developed early by Italian standards, did not begin to institutionalise itself until the 1130s; but Pisa had one of the earliest established communes of all, together with Genoa, with the years around 1110 being the most likely period for its crystallisation—as the Balearic campaign itself shows, but not only that—and the first references to men called 'consuls' in the city going back to the 1080s. This cannot be a mere chance of the documentation; too many different sorts of source give us the same sorts of evidence here, as we shall see later. Pisan historians have, for the last century and more, been transfixed by this, and have engaged in a good deal of research on the wide period of the origin of the commune, the century 1050–1150; the eleventh to thirteenth centuries were, after all, the high point in Pisan history, and Pisa University is a large and active one. There is good-quality work on our period as a result, some very recent, and it is much more comprehensive than that on Milan—nearly every élite family has a detailed study, for example; I will use them heavily here.[2] Oddly, however, the early twelfth century lacks a full study, and certainly deserves another look.

Pisa was a rather smaller city than Milan, but it was both on the Mediterranean coast and on the river Arno, and the port of Pisa was the main funnel for goods into Tuscany from the outside by the end of the tenth century; commerce was sufficiently important in the city by the twelfth century that evidence for it sometimes intrudes even into the land transactions which are, here as elsewhere, our most substantial source for the period.[3] The Pisan diocese was also relatively small, and much of it was the marshland of the Arno delta; local agriculture was rich, but its acreage was not enormous. The Pisans could have moved against their urban neighbours, as the Milanesi did at the expense of the cities around them, and they certainly engaged in border wars with Lucca, their nearest rival, throughout much of the twelfth century; but the two were fairly evenly matched, and the Pisans could not easily have copied the Milanese delight in destroying their neighbours. They did expand their territory, quite substantially, but above all into less populated inland and coastal regions which were outside the control of other cities. By contrast, however, Pisans had an interest in the sea which soon developed well beyond simply having a port.

The early eleventh-century western Mediterranean had an active commercial network, based on the sea-routes between southern Spain, Sicily, and Tunisia and extending from there east to Egypt, always the Mediterranean commercial powerhouse.[4] It was therefore focussed on the Muslim-ruled

Mediterranean, and Pisa was for long rather marginal to it. So the Arno city began, every so often, simply to raid the rich cities of the Muslim world; the size and ferocity of the Pisan fleet was sufficient to overmaster urban centres which were not expecting such systematic assaults. In 1005, the Pisans attacked Reggio Calabria, in 1015–16 Arab bridgeheads in Sardinia, in 1034 Bona (modern Annaba in Algeria), in 1064 Palermo, in 1087 Mahdīya and Zawīla in Tunisia, in 1092 Tortosa in Spain (a rare defeat), in 1098 east to Palestine as part of the First Crusade, then the Balearic Islands in 1113–15.[5] Like the Vikings, or the Portuguese in the Indian Ocean, the Pisans were here focussed on booty; but merchants and pirates were always hard to distinguish in the medieval world. The historian Goffredo Malaterra, writing in late eleventh-century southern Italy, indeed saw the 1064 Palermo campaign as simply a violent mercantile operation, by Pisans who were 'normally dedicated more to commercial gain than warlike exercises'—an illuminating phrase, not least because it is by no means intended as a compliment. In effect, in fact, what the Pisans did with their intermittent eleventh-century raiding was to establish a sufficient respect and fear of them as military players that they could become more fully a part of the pre-existing network of commercial relations in the western Mediterranean, a network which then extended eastwards with the First Crusade, and was institutionalised in the twelfth century in Pisan trading agreements from Morocco via the Byzantine empire to Syria.[6] Parallel to this was also their establishment of what slowly turned unto a small maritime empire, on the islands of Corsica and (later on) Sardinia; the bishop of Pisa indeed became an archbishop after 1092 because Pope Urban II put Corsica under his jurisdiction.[7] They were matched in all of this step by step, for almost identical reasons, by the Genoese, some-times their allies but also, structurally, their rivals and enemies. But the Genoese did not document their early activities with the detail and brio that the Pisans did.[8]

In the 1060s, the Pisans began to build their stupendous new cathedral, that white marble extravaganza, innovative in a dozen ways, which is still there today, along with its oddly angled bell-tower. The left side of the façade of the cathedral is studded with inscriptions, dating from the broad period 1070–1150. These inscriptions include some epitaphs—three for the main cathedral architect, Buscheto (documented 1104–10), one of which compares him favourably to Ulysses and Daedalus—but also two poems about Pisan victories: the just-listed sequence of heroic (to Pisans) sackings of islands and cities, the booty from which indeed in large part explic-itly paid for the building of the church. This commemoration in stone of bold military operations, and its close association with such an innovative and ambitious architectural project, has no parallels anywhere in this period. It clearly conveys civic pride in a very general sense; and the *cives* are regularly fea-tured in the texts: *maiores*, *medii*, and *minores*, rich and poor alike, as the epigraphic poem on the sack of Palermo says.[9]

The Pisans were indeed not short of civic pride in any way. The classical comparisons already mentioned for Bus-cheto had plenty of parallels in other things the Pisans did and said. They compared themselves to ancient Rome on nu-merous occasions—Pisa was *Roma altera*, the second Rome, as one mid-twelfth-century poem says, copied into the *Liber Maiorichinus* manuscript; an inscription formerly on the Porta Aurea, the city's river-gate, referred to Pisa as the 'gen-eral ornament of empire', i.e. that of Rome.[10] There are other such comparisons in the *Liber Maiorichinus* itself.[11] A slightly earlier text, the *Carmen in victoria Pisanorum*, a bloodthirsty poem about the Mahdīya campaign of 1087, starts 'I renew the memory of the ancient Romans', and refers to the fall of Carthage (and also Troy), as well as paralleling the Pisans to Old Testament heroes such as Gideon and the Maccabees.[12] That poem itself survives in a fascinating miscellany dated to 1119 called the *Liber Guidonis*, compiled by a certain Guido of Pisa who may have risen to become a cardinal in the next decade, which attests to a true obsession with ancient Rome, in that much of the rest of the texts of the miscellany is about it: classical histories of Troy (seen as a proto-Rome), Paul the Deacon's *Historia Romana*, and one of the earliest descriptions of the surviving classical buildings of the eternal city. Rome here is a metaphor for the confident and 'belligerent' Pisa of the 1110s.[13] This would reach its culmination in 1155 when the Pisans decided to create their own Romanist law-code, the double *Constitutum legis* and *usus*, which was entrusted to *constitutores* or *sapientes*, local legal experts, in a carefully planned five-year process which ended with the first of the two codes coming into force on 1 January 1161, and the other shortly after. The *Constitutum usus* proudly states that the Pisans had mostly lived by Roman law 'for a long time', *a multis retro temporibus*, a statement which, as earlier documentary sources show, was totally false, but one which was a preparation for the fullest reception of classical Roman law into any part of twelfth-century Latin Europe. The Pisans' absorption of Roman law was rapid and complex, and also not always obviously useful for the conduct of their daily business; it must have been part, and the most committed part, of this constant reiteration of Roman-ness by Pisan texts—one which certainly has parallels in the classicising trends of other cities, but one which the Pisans were self-satisfied enough to carry through to the end.[14]

But 'civic pride' is also a fairly vague term. What it meant in concrete—perhaps institutional, and certainly political—terms is another matter; and what Pisans meant by it in the twelfth century was not by any means necessarily the same as they had meant in the eleventh. The marquis of Tuscany was dominant in Pisa until the mid-1070s at the earliest, for example, and the city's autonomy cannot yet be assumed. The Pisans raided abroad for their own benefit, but usually with the encouragement, and perhaps sometimes at the request, of other powers: the pope and the powerful marquise of Tuscany Matilda for the Mahdīya campaign, and maybe already pope and marquis for the Palermo campaign; certainly pope and archbishop for the First Crusade (Pisa's first archbishop Daiberto, who led the joint Pisan-Genoese expedition in 1098, also became the first Latin patriarch of Jerusalem); fifteen years later, the archbishop accompanied the Pisans on the Balearic campaign and the pope sent his legate and a flag, which was assigned its own consular standard-bearer, although that campaign was certainly a city initiative.[15] The constant reiteration in our sources of the use made of the booty thus gained to build the cathedral also attests to a religious edge to this raiding, even if crusading imagery is not as pervasive in these texts as historians often say.[16] The cathedral's building campaign was itself by the 1090s incorporated institutionally into its own body, the *Opera* of the cathedral, whose lay administrators or *operarii*, under archiepiscopal control, were as prominent as consuls in some of our early twelfth-century documents;[17] indeed, the bishop/archbishop of Pisa was equally prominent in many of our sources, as we shall see.

Given all this, Pisan armies abroad are not an inevitable sign of a move towards lay and civic independence. Indeed, our eleventh-century texts simply praise the Arno city as a *civitas*, as all urban praise texts had done in the early middle ages, which does not in itself show that Pisa was acting as an autonomous body. The most one can say is that, to be able to organise such large expeditions abroad, the Pisans must have been able to operate as an effective and coherent collectivity already in the third quarter of the eleventh century, no matter on whose behalf they acted. The same is true for the expensive building of the cathedral, entrusted, as we have just seen, in large part to lay *operarii*. That was of great importance when the Pisans did develop their own urban autonomy, which they did in as unplanned a way as did the Milanesi. We cannot say that the Pisan raids prefigured the city commune, nor that the commune was the natural result of the 'private organisation of ship-owners and sea merchants', in Gioacchino Volpe's famous phrase at the opening of his history of the city;[18] all the same, when the Pisan leadership sleepwalked into the commune, they found that quite a lot of the work had already been done.

To get a sense of how the commune developed, we need to look at the political history of the city across the century we are focussing on—here shortened to the period between around 1060 and 1130, for after that there is no doubt of the stability of the Pisan commune—a history which is, fortunately, illuminated by some unusual documents, as unusual in their own way as Pisa's war poetry; then, as with Milan, we will look at exactly who the consuls of Pisa were, for here too we can understand much more about what the city's leaders thought they were doing if we see what sorts of

background they had. We have no writings from Pisan consuls themselves, unfortunately, at least until the city's *Annals*
were written by Bernardo Maragone, a second-rank official
and magistrate, from the 1150s onwards;[19] but the hunting
of family affiliations here is illuminating in itself, as I hope
to show.

Pisa in the 1060s and 1070s was firmly under the rule of
the marquis of Tuscany Gottefredo (d. 1069) and then
his widow and ruling marquise, the *ducatrix* (or *comitissa*, or
marchionissa) Beatrice, and then her daughter Matilda. Tuscany was the part of the Kingdom of Italy whose eleventh-
century political structure was the most solid, and the most
traditional in format (far more so than it was in Milan), with
political life dominated by the marchesal entourage, and the
public assembly of the *placitum* law-court very visible in our
evidence, into the 1070s in most places. Half a dozen surviving *placita* show this system in operation in Pisa, where the
marquises were often based in this period; they were standard
events, and widely attended by members of Pisa's urban élite.[20]
This is our starting-point, then; and it is one which was never
at any point visibly contested by the Pisans. The city had no
traditions similar to the urban uprisings which studded the
history of Milan, and, actually, even the civil war period of
the 1080s–90s only brought a brief period of tension in Pisa,
perhaps restricted to the later 1080s as we shall see, and then
no major internal trouble again for at least sixty and perhaps a
hundred years:[21] and that tension was not visibly one between
social strata either, unlike often in Milan. Matilda, when she
succeeded to the March of Tuscany at the age of thirty at her
mother Beatrice's death in 1076, had less traction in her early

years; she never visibly came inside the walls of the city of Pisa, for example, and she shared her judicial role with her viscount of Pisa Ugo II in the only Pisan *placitum* for her, in 1077.[22] But she also showed herself to be a willing patron of the Pisan church, and gave the cathedral a large set of estates in the same year, on condition that the cathedral chapter maintained a regular canonical life—a standard element of the package of ecclesiastical 'reform' in the period, of which Matilda was a committed supporter.[23]

Once the wars broke out after 1080 between the emperor Henry IV and Pope Gregory VII, Henry deposed Matilda from her March in 1081. When he entered Lucca and Pisa in that year, giving each of them major privileges, the Pisans switched to a pro-imperial position. But after he left central Italy in 1084 they returned to Matilda, and were certainly allied again with her and her popes by 1087.[24] Marchesal authority was thus not ended by Henry's acts, but it certainly took a considerable hit—Henry did not appoint a new marquis at all, and Matilda, although she remained very powerful and active in northern Italy, did not reappear in Tuscany for fifteen years. All the same, the wars had less direct effect on Pisa than on many cities; Lucca had two bishops for some time, but Pisa's pro-Gregorian bishop Gerardo does not seem to have been under threat in the 1080s. Pisa did have more than one family of viscounts, and the imperial-supported family is more prominent in the 1080s, but Matilda's vicecomital family was back by 1087 (Ugo II was romantically killed on the Mahdīya campaign), without rivalries between the two families being obvious in our sources for later decades.[25] The Pisans made sure to have some of Henry's specific gifts of property confirmed by Matilda later, as with the castle of Pappiana, a major marchesal centre, which Henry had given to the cathedral in 1089, in his last Pisan act, and Matilda gave again in 1103; and otherwise they sat out the war.[26]

Henry IV's 1081 diploma to the Pisans has always been seen as a founding charter by historians of the communal movement, and it is certainly the case that the Pisans benefited greatly from its terms, especially in trading privileges. The sentence in it which says that the Pisans could veto any future marquis, as represented by twelve men elected in an assembly, *colloquium*, called by ringing bells, is now accepted to be a later interpolation into the text (it survives only as a copy of the 1130s), which rids it of its status as a potentially communal charter. Conversely, the document still refers to the *communis consensus* of the *cives*, which was needed for anyone wishing to pull down houses in the city, to the Pisan *consuetudines de mari*, 'sea customs', which the emperor recognised, and to a newly legitimised local control over common lands, which were economically very important around Pisa, set in the Arno marshes as it was (not least for timber for shipbuilding, as we shall see). The city existed as a collectivity, then: it consisted of the 'faithful citizens', undifferentiated by social group, to whom Henry addressed his diploma.[27]

This, to modern Pisan historians, goes rather well with the first-ever reference to Italian city consuls. This is a document of 1080–85 (probably 1080–81) in which one of the Sardinian rulers, Mariano I *iudice* or king of Torres, frees his Pisan 'friends', *ammicos* (this is a nominative; the document is in the Sard language) from all trading tolls and gives them judicial privileges, 'for the honour of Bishop Gelardu [Gerardo], viscount Ocu [Ugo], and all the consuls, *consolos*, of Pisa'. The *ammicos* are then listed; they are from the leading families visible in the marchesal *placita*, and their heirs will often become consuls of the city commune. This document has successfully withstood attempts to declare it a forgery, but, notwithstanding that, it too is less clearly part of the 'move to the commune' than people often claim. It does not by any means show that consuls were at that point the city's formal rulers, or indeed that the word *consolos* denoted any official position; it seems simply to mean members of the city's élite, and is in this context a synonym of the *ammicos*.[28] This is no less the case with the poem on the Mahdīya campaign, which features two Pisans called *principales consules* and two called *cives nobiles*, acting together as military leaders: these men are all or mostly again from the same group of leading families, and we cannot distinguish here between the *consules* and the *nobiles*. We cannot, indeed, track any formal lay leadership in the city in the 1080s; even the viscounts are not so prominent in our texts that we could be sure of their directive role (Ugo II gets killed in 1087, but he does not obviously lead the Pisan forces).[29] We have a sense of a body of prominent citizens acting collectively, but that is all.

Bishop Gerardo died in 1085 and was not replaced for four years (for the Pisans, an episcopal vacancy was doubtless less bad than rival bishops), and maybe Viscount Ugo's death created a vacuum too, for his son Ugo III was a child. It was probably in this period, with hot civil war in Italy between two popes, Clement III and (from 1088) Urban II, that political relationships inside the city reached their most difficult point. The Pisan triumphal narratives do not allow themselves the rhetorical space to say so (they are snide about the Genoese and the Lucchesi, but not about fellow-Pisans), so we could not catch tensions from them, but two documents from 1090–92, both surviving as originals, tell us more. In 1089, Daiberto was chosen as bishop: a clever choice, for he had been consecrated priest by a pro-imperial bishop in

Germany but then had switched to the Gregorian side and was now enthusiastically backed by Pope Urban.[30] In around 1090 (certainly before 1092, for Daiberto is not yet archbishop), he appears in one of these texts as an arbiter over a major civic issue: the height of tower-houses in the city.

Tower-houses for urban élite families were a new development in Italian cities in the later eleventh century, and were regarded as a symbol of potential civic discord and unrest everywhere, for they were certainly defensible (some still survive in Pisa from this period, so we can see it for ourselves), and their tops were excellent locations for ballistas and the like; the bishop says in the text that the 'ancient plague of pride' has led to homicide, perjury, incest, and the destruction of houses, which is too generic to tell us much about what was going on, but is at least a marker of trouble—as indeed does the fact that he has been called upon to do such an arbitration in the first place. Daiberto enacts that no future tower should be more than thirty-six *brachia* (sixty-nine feet) in height—a figure taken straight from Henry IV's diploma of 1081—and he names the towers which should not be surpassed in height in the future, two north of the Arno, one to the south (two of the towers were those of the future Baldovinaschi and Sismondi families). Only two lay towers (those of Viscount Ugo III from the marquisal vicecomital family, whose family had earned the city's formal protection after his father's death, and Pietro di Albizo of the future Casapieri family) and one church campanile, which were already higher, could remain, and in each case no-one could in future go up to the top.[31]

The naming of important citizens is interesting, and once again they match those of city leaders in other sources. But what is most interesting about this text is the city decision-making which it invokes, and also does not invoke. On one level it is not so surprising that Daiberto was the arbiter, and not any lay figure, for if there was tension it was between lay élites; but, anyway, he says he has been advised by *sociis viris strenuis et sapientibus*, 'vigorous and wise associates', who are listed and are indeed from those lay élites, including some of the owners of the towers he names, and also Viscount Pietro, from the family of imperial viscounts—this being a hint that the tension was in part, as already proposed, between pro- and anti-imperial alignments. He does not say they are consuls, however, and consuls do not appear in the document. What does, on the other hand, several times, is the *commune colloquium civitatis*, 'the common assembly of the city', to which anyone can complain about illegal tower activity; this assembly can make exceptions by its *commune consilium*, 'common discussion', if they are for the 'common utility of the city', although, if they are not, the *populus* will take action against infractions. There also appears a formal oath to keep this arbitration, which everyone (we assume every male) over the age of fifteen in the city and its suburbs must swear to, and so must all future fifteen-year-olds. This arbitration was sufficiently important that it was itself sworn to by later consuls, as part of the basic set of laws and customs of the city, as we find from the texts of such oaths in the 1160s; but it is nonetheless not a consular text.[32] Rather, it is the establishment of an oath-backed agreement, by a bishop and his *sapientes*, which—this is the document's clear implication— has been called for by the 'common assembly' and its leaders, and which looks to that assembly for its execution in the future. The assembly has taken on more of a formal role than the one which it had in 1081, a decade earlier, indeed a locally central one, even if it has had to call in the bishop to sort tension out.

The second document is rural, and dates to the end of 1091 or the start of 1092. It relates the bad behaviour in the Valdiserchio, in the delta some five miles north of the city, of a group of lords called the *longubardi Pisani*—*longubardus* or *lambardus* being a Tuscan term for small military aristocrat (it has some parallel to *capitaneus* in the north, although it is a rarer word)—who have introduced 'evil customs', *malae consuetudines*, which evidently include forced guard duty in castles, money for wood rights and pasturing on common land, and the taking of grain and linen: in other words typical signorial rights, exactions which were markers of private lordship (and also called 'evil customs') everywhere in Europe. But this is to the disadvantage not only to the locals but also to 'some Pisan citizens', so they meet together to resolve it. They elect five or six *consules de Pisanis*, and several *boni homines* from the Valdiserchio, to resolve the issue, and the signorial rights are for the most part abolished forthwith. This is then ratified by the *longubardi Pisani* themselves, all named, and then the Pisan *populus* confirms it 'by common agreement', and Bishop Daiberto backs it up with an anathema.

These signorial rights were doubtless very new indeed. They are hardly attested in Tuscany earlier, and a similar document of complaint to the city a decade later—to the cathedral, the consuls, and 'the whole Pisan *populus*'—by the inhabitants of the small village of Casciavola, against the lords of San Casciano (one of the *longubardi Pisani* families), gives a date for them. That text says explicitly that Marquise Beatrice had previously prevented the lords from acting in this way by a legal judgement, but then 'all power lost its strength and justice was dead and perished in our land', and the da San Casciano behaved worse than ever—that is to say, in the 1080s–90s, which are thus presented here as a period of confusion and injustice. Here, as in the Valdiserchio, it is important to add, the Pisans did indeed put a stop to such lordly aggression, for the area around Pisa was almost devoid of signorial rights thereafter: the city had no intention of allowing rivals to its own jurisdiction, and acted far more determinedly here than (for example) Milan did. But its task in the Valdiserchio was made easier by the fact that the *longubardi* were, in fact, all themselves from city families, and indeed from many of the same élite families whose names we see in other texts, including (to name only one) Viscount Pietro; and also that the *consules de Pisanis* named here, who decided against them, were in some instances—again including Pietro—explicitly the same people too: they ruled against themselves, that is to say. As *consules*, and as city-dwellers, it was evidently in their interests to judge against their own accumulation of rural power; it was better to rule the countryside as a stable part of an urban élite than as a local lord. This must have been all the more true in that the individual *longubardi* families evidently could not gain such rights in the Valdiserchio on their own. In an area where very many influential people owned land, they had to operate as a sort of collective, which was not a strong basis for signorial coercion. The city was a much better venue for that.[33]

Now: we have more consuls here. In the Casciavola case, which dates to around 1100, the un-named consuls do seem to be the lay leaders of the city in some way, as they will, much more clearly, in a group of texts from 1109 onwards, as we shall see in a moment. This is less clear in the Valdiserchio case. In part, it hangs on an ambiguity in the text: when the people at the meeting 'elect consuls of the Pisans', are they choosing ad hoc representatives called consuls to arbitrate this particular dispute, or are they choosing from *among* consuls, who already exist as city rulers? One might think at this point that, in the end, whether there are 'real' consuls in Pisa only in 1100/1109 or else already in 1092 (and thus demonstrably earlier than all other cities—let alone in 1080–81, with the Sardinian document) is not one of the crucial historical questions. I would agree in part, but the important point is a different one; in fact it is three related points. One is what the word *consul* meant in this period; one is how Pisa as a city was actually organised; and one is who ran it and what they thought they were doing. All three are more interesting than arguing about single documents, even if we have needed a relatively detailed exposition of several single documents to get an idea of what the issues are. Let us look at them in turn.

In the 1080s, or 1090s, what does using the word *consul* mean? We certainly cannot assume that it meant a fully autonomous city ruler when the Pisans used it for the first time in 1080 or so (and there is no doubt that they did so first in the Kingdom of Italy); it meant that by 1150 everywhere, but it cannot have done so when there was as yet nothing autonomous for them to rule—and if the Sardinian citation of *consolos* predates 1081, the word dates from a time when Matilda's power was still untroubled by war. In that period, the word *consul* was certainly known to have once meant an annually changing city leader in ancient Rome, but it was most often used figuratively in narratives across Europe to mean any form of non-royal ruler—dukes or counts (such as William of Normandy before 1066) were called *consules* often enough;[34] and, in Italy, the city where it was most consistently used at that time was Rome, where it had meant any member of the traditional aristocracy of Rome in the tenth century (usually in the form *consul et dux*), and in the eleventh it meant in particular a member of the Tuscolani family, the city's rulers until the 1040s, and major dealers thereafter as well.[35]

Pisa had quite close links with the city of Rome in the century after 1050. This is shown, for example, by the habit of many of Pisa's judicial establishment to call themselves *iudices sacri Lateranensis palatii*, judges of the Lateran palace in Rome, throughout our period; I would indeed argue that the Arno city's later Roman-law commitment involved substantial borrowing from Rome's own twelfth-century judicial practice too.[36] I would make the same argument about the borrowing of the word *consul*: it was used to mean city leader in the most prestigious, and still probably the largest, Italian city, and that was good enough for Pisans whose desire to be Roman (at least, ancient Roman) we have amply seen. So the Pisans first used this contemporary Roman term to mean leader in quite a general sense, as in the Sardinian document and the Mahdīya poem (if it is as early as this), and by 1092 they happily used it to mean any prominent and publicly active person—for that is the minimum meaning of the term in the Valdiserchio document. Other cities picked up that usage from them quite quickly, as we have seen in the case of Milan's *consulatus*, documented from 1097 (above, p. 26). The word 'consul' was then available in people's vocabulary, ready to shift meaning and to become the technical term for city-chosen rulers: once such rulers came to exist. That is explicit for the first time in a Genoese document of 1098, which lists Amico Brusco *qui tunc erat civitatis consul*, 'who was then consul of the city', as giving *consilium* in an informal dispute; to use 'consul' as a title in this way strongly implies some form of rotating city leadership.[37] This may well therefore be a *terminus ante quem* for Pisa too, if my argument about the genealogy of the term, from Rome through Pisa, is accepted; the Arno city's consuls might perhaps have become in some sense urban rulers by the mid-1090s, that is to say, which also fits the reference to them in the Casciavola case. But we cannot get any earlier than that; and, in general, we absolutely cannot assume that, every time we see the term *consul* in the eleventh century (or indeed, in other cities, in the early twelfth), we have any of the institutions of the commune set up before our eyes. I am here fully in agreement with Mauro Ronzani, who out of current authors argues this point most forcefully for Pisa; indeed, as we have seen (p. 15), Lucca and Arezzo, also Tuscan cities, have other early references to *consules* which substantially predate the city commune in any of its other manifestations. So what we have to do is to try to track when the term actually does change meaning, and clearly comes to denote—to repeat my formulation of an ideal-type commune in the first chapter—a regularly rotating set of magistracies, chosen or at least validated by a conscious urban collectivity, with a de facto autonomy of action for the city and its magistrates, including in warfare and justice, and eventually taxation and legislation. It is not only hard, but impossible, to track the moment of the shift exactly,[38] but at least we can say that few of these elements (only the collectivity and the warfare) are visible in Pisa before 1100.

How Pisa as a city was organised in 1090 seems clear enough from Daiberto's arbitration on the towers, as we have seen: it was run by a collective assembly—here called a *colloquium*, but identical to the *concio* or *arengo* of northern Italy, and indeed the word *concio* occurs occasionally in Pisa.[39] It was like the *consulatus* or *conventus* or *concio* which appears at the end of the same decade in Milan, then, but it is more visible than is Milan's assembly in its early years. It was the assembly of the *populus* or *cives*, and there is never a hint in Pisa that this citizen collectivity was divided into aristocrats and others, unlike in Milan; nor indeed did it yet have any formalised leaders. There can be no doubt that it was in practice dominated by the same set of ten to fifteen families which appear in all our sources for our entire century (including in Daiberto's arbitration) as Pisa's leaders, as well as, at a military level, by the wider militia of horsemen which, as we have seen, Jean-Claude Maire Vigueur has described for all of north-central Italy—for Pisans of all social levels participated in its maritime wars, cavalry and footsoldiers alike, but horsemen are mentioned as being of particular prominence in our poetic narratives, as when the consul Lamberto di Uberto in the Balearic war of 1113–15 is made *dux equitum*, leader of the cavalry.[40] But these dominating groups had no established presence yet. Even if the 1092 consuls were 'real' city leaders, they certainly did not control the dispute-settlement procedures outlined in the Valdiserchio text, which are depicted as very informal indeed; even if rotating leaders had developed before the Genoese example from 1098, what they actually did remains obscure for another decade and more. And it is also hard to be sure that the assembly was a necessary sign of real autonomy for the city around 1090, as opposed to being simply the growing formalisation of an ad hoc body which had always existed for local affairs (and the organisation of campaigns)—as the references to collective agreement in Henry IV's diploma would indicate. One could best see it as simply gaining coherence to fill a particular power-vacuum, one which affected even Pisa during the civil wars, for Matilda, as I have already indicated, made no appearance in Tuscany between 1081 and 1096, and Pisa had no bishop either for four years in the 1080s—as also between when Daiberto left for the East in 1098 and his death in 1105 (his successor Pietro first appears in 1106[41]). The *colloquium* was thus prominent around 1090 because it had had to formalise itself to deal with the absence of both; as in Milan (p. 28), it was a defensive reaction to the absence of traditional hierarchies.

This picture of the formalisation of a city assembly in a period of a vacuum of power is part of the established argument that city communes themselves were defensive reactions to the civil war period in Italy. From now on, indeed, one can find such assemblies over most of north-central Italy.[42] But an assembly is not the same as a commune. One could, in particular, develop an active civic assembly and still be loyal in principle to a traditional ruler, as we have already seen for the relationship between Milan's early assembly and the archbishop. In the case of Pisa, the archbishop, as he now was, was much less dominant than in Milan (I will come back to that), but Matilda was still potentially powerful in Tuscany; and she eventually came back to the Pisa area in 1100, issuing several charters to the cathedral and other churches (and to one layman, of the future Orlandi, one of the *longubardi Pisani* families) before her death in 1115.[43] Would that have had an effect on Pisa? Matilda's twelfth-century presence in Tuscany might be said to have prevented Lucca from developing in a communal direction before her death—Lucca's first consuls are documented only in 1119, and are first seen representing the city in 1120.[44] In Pisa we cannot say that, however; for the last years of Matilda are indeed those in which we can see the commune appear in a much more organised form. Let us look at its signs.

Pisa's consuls first appear as real city representatives in 1109, in a set of documents in which a signorial family, the descendants of the tenth-century counts of Pisa, sold off two of their castles to the city of Pisa, here in the form of Archbishop Pietro and four *consules Pisani*, who are clearly here acting together for the city. This is followed by several parallel documents from 1110 in which the lords of Ripafratta ceded control of their castle to the city, a particularly important act because, although the family was by now associated with Pisa, their castle was a strategic centre inside the diocese of Lucca, with which city the Pisans had recently fought and won a war; here the castle is formally granted to the archbishop, but the political assurances which are attached are to the archbishop, the *operarii* of the cathedral, and the Pisan consuls, and the latter represent, for the first time (indeed, for probably only the second time in Italy), the *commune Pisane civitatis*, a noun not an adjective, 'the commune of the city of Pisa'.[45] These consuls were associated with the city's assembly and in some sense responsible to it, as is clear in our sources already in 1111;[46] all the same, they operate by now autonomously, as city leaders, and, increasingly, rulers.

This mix of protagonists appears quite often in the next years. One instance is when in 1114 the count of Barcelona made a formal alliance with the Pisan *populus* (or *exercitus*, army) for the Balearic war, who were represented by the twelve consuls of the city, and the document for it was prepared by the 'chancellor (*cancellarius*) of the Pisan consuls'—here the archbishop was less central, even though the text says that Pope Paschal II had put him at the head of the army, but he counter-signed as well; another is when in 1116 the new (and much weaker) marquis of Tuscany Rabodo pledged the castle of Bientina to Archbishop Pietro and to the *iudex* and *operarius* Ildebrando, with four consuls witnessing the document; another is when in 1120 the same Ildebrando, in that year not only *operarius* but also consul, sold the castle of Livorno, which Matilda had given to the *Opera* in 1103, to the archbishop, again with other consuls witnessing. But, inside that political mix, with archbishop, *operarii*, and consuls all active in the city's name, the core structure was coming more and more to be consular—once the latter appear in 1109, they are suddenly everywhere. Already in 1111, the Byzantine emperor Alexios Komnenos made a trade agreement with the Pisan people, the first we have that survives, and here they are represented by the consuls (*hypatoi*) of Pisa, and not the archbishop at all. The fact that the consuls have a chancellor in 1114 is another sign (by 1126 there is also a scribe of the Pisan *respublica*); so is the presence of consuls in acts of cession of castles to the cathedral, in effect to ratify the cessions, which are notably frequent in these years.[47] So, above all, is another document, from 1 January 1112, in which the consuls ran a court case about land of the cathedral which was held illegally, and got the holder to concede it to the archbishop, for not only is this almost the first Italian document in which the consuls of a city are seen running justice on their own (it is preceded only by a handful of Genoese texts: below, p. 164), but the text is also the only one from any city at all in which consuls use a *placitum* format, clearly in this case showing a claim to the public traditions of the past: here the consuls and *populus* meet and discuss the case in the '*forum* of the city of Pisa, which is called the court of the marquis', and make their 'decree' by common agreement. The solidity of consular authority by now, and its association with the city's assembly, is further emphasised by a document of the previous day, in which one of the consuls, in a document witnessed by many of the others, cedes in a different dispute with the archbishop, in the same court of the marquis, in the Pisan *colloquium*, 'in the time of the *consolatus* of the consuls of the Pisan association [*societas*]'.[48]

This pattern, established by 1112, continued. The growing centrality of the communal polity is clearly shown in a later text, of 1126, in which Archbishop Ruggero sold the estate of Pappiana (another Matildine cession to the church, as we

have seen) to the cathedral canons, again an entirely ecclesiastical financial transaction, and one done for the benefit
(*causa*) of the cathedral, but also one which Ruggero says he
is doing 'for the peace and quiet of the common Pisan *populus*', and one which is done with the 'advice of the consuls
and *sapientes*, both *iudices* and jurists, of the city of Pisa, and
the whole Pisan *populus*'.[49] By 1138, communal judges were
'given by the consuls and the whole *populus* to end disputes
and controversies both public and private'. Not all Pisan land
disputes went to the consuls yet; in our documents, private
arbitrations outnumber consular decisions until the 1150s.
The institutionalisation process in the Arno city was not fully
complete until the creation of the two *Constituta* at the end
of that decade, in fact. All the same, the structures were set
up for situations like the great assembly of 1153, in which the
consuls, 'in the public *contio*' (also called a *parlamentum*), acting for 'the commune of the city [which] we must love with
intimate charity and carefully preserve the ruling of its honour', abolished residual vicecomital rights, expelled Viscount
Alberto (son of Ugo III) and his family from the city, and
deprived his supporters of 'public office' for a decade.[50] The
system had by now been in place for forty years.

I argued for Milan that the earliest city consuls were
essentially part of the archbishop's entourage and power-
structure, and that the commune did not gain institutional
autonomy until the consuls became less often aristocrats and
more often judicial experts, and moved away from that archiepiscopal politics, in the 1130s. In Pisa, the archbishop was
a central figure in these early decades of consular activity as
well; but the situation was different, and the consuls appear
as separate from him from the start. We see the archbishop
accumulating castles in a whole set of documents in the 1110s

and later, enough for him to end up as by far the largest land-owner in the diocese of Pisa, and also the only lord with significant sets of signorial rights in the countryside. Volpe saw him as fronting for the commune here, in a period when the consuls and the commune had no legal identity, which he saw as a situation continuing right up to 1162, when Frederick Barbarossa recognised the city's government; but that is both less and more than what he was doing. These castles stably remained in archiepiscopal hands, and they were not cessions to the commune; but, conversely, Volpe was also wrong to suppose that the commune had, or claimed, no legal identity or public role, for the 1112 consular *placitum* already clearly shows otherwise.[51] By contrast, the archbishop of Pisa, public figure or no, is not seen judging a civil dispute after the arbitration over the towers; he was also happy to seek an arbitration in a rural dispute from an ex-consul by the early 1120s.[52]

When consuls appear in archiepiscopal transactions, one could, it is true, see them as being as much in the archbishop's entourage, as ratifiers of the acts, as we did in Milan. After all, many members of consular families are documented as archiepiscopal *fideles* and/or feudal dependants; Ildebrando *iudex* and *operarius*, and in 1118–21 'now by the grace of God consul of the city of Pisa', is also very likely to have been introduced into the consulate by his patron Archbishop Pietro, evidently an influential figure. When the commune developed its own standardised judicial system, from 1135 onwards, the first surviving document for it refers to the magistrates as '*iudices* elected by Archbishop Uberto of the Pisans and by the consuls and the whole *populus*', which is a clear indication of archiepiscopal protagonism—even if we have just seen that the second such case in 1138, and later ones too, just mention the consuls and *populus*.[53] The archbishops remained active players in the city thereafter, too. But they were not patrons of consuls in any systematic way; the consular families did not owe most of their prosperity to archiepiscopal leases;[54] and, indeed, the great landed wealth of the archbishops by 1150 was to a substantial extent gained after the commune was established, not before. The fact is that episcopal power in most of Tuscany had never been great, if one compares it with that of many north Italian cities. Up to around 1080, the marquis in Tuscany had had too firm a control over its political structures, in both city and country, much firmer than almost any lay office-holder did in the north. The bishop of Lucca, for example, in 850 a far larger landowner than his Pisan counterpart, leased away most of his properties and rights over tithe to major Lucchese city families in the next century, as bishops did, but then found that he could not get most of them back, and that these had turned into effective alienations; he did not have the political clout to make good his property rights.[55] After 'all power lost its strength' in Tuscany, as the men of Casciavola said about the 1080s, bishops had the opportunity to gain a new centrality; and we see the archbishops of Pisa doing their best to take it up (as also, later, did some bishops of Lucca). But bishops had to begin from the same standing start as did the lay citizens, and were not in a position to dominate urban political structures, as they crystallised, without considerable lay support and consent. Pisan archbishops were also not usually from the major city families, unlike in Milan, so could not lay claim to pre-existing networks of élite support.[56] They were allies of the commune, not its patrons, and certainly not, as in part in Milan, its progenitors.

This situation is actually already clear in the *Liber Maiorichinus*. Even though we might expect its clerical author to write up the role of the archbishop on the Balearic expedition, he in fact appears relatively seldom. That the pope had put him in command is hardly visible in the text; all we find him doing is preaching or exhorting the army, on a few occasions, and he is far from the only person who does that. It is the consuls who are throughout in the foreground, Dodone di Teperto 'famous, born for war', and so on—as well as Viscount Ugo III, and Pietro di Albizo, the main private citizen who is flagged in the text (more often indeed than Ugo), who is 'adorning the Pisan *cives* with the image of probity'.[57] As was noted at the start of this chapter, the *Liber* is aiming to create the image of a Pisan collectivity which is essentially lay and led by the twelve consuls, most of them named on several occasions, who ran the whole campaign— and who, it is almost unnecessary to say, came from the same set of families as did all other Pisan leaders.

Pisa's commune was thus fully in charge of the city by the 1110s, with its consuls running the political cessions of castles by 1110, a treaty with Byzantium by 1111, justice by 1112, and warfare by 1113. The wide range of this authority might make us conclude that the consular régime had already come to be established rather earlier, which gives some support to my cautious proposal of the mid-1090s for the appearance of ruling consuls, but, conversely, we need to remember that a similar range of documentation does not show any signs whatsoever of an active régime of this kind in the years before 1109, and the powers of the consuls must only have become established bit by bit. It has again to be recognised that we will never know exactly when they appeared in this new guise; I will come back to this in a moment. It is however not necessary to push, improbably, the establishment of all the elements of a fully autonomous and organised commune of Pisa back to the 1090s to have it be the front-runner here; Milan's commune did not show similar levels of organisation until the 1130s, and nor did any other, with the exception of Genoa, the pacing of whose early commune is almost identical to that of the Arno city.[58] It is necessary to say that the appearance in 1135 in Pisa of more regular communal judicial magistrates is much less precocious; many cities had developed consular justice by the 1130s, as we have seen (p. 17), and Genoa, the first in this respect, had walked this path already by 1110 at the latest. The 1130s were the key moment of institutionalisation of most of the early communes, that is to say. But this simply means that other cities soon caught up; Pisa was still the precursor. I have not chosen to discuss it first, for Milan's development has been more central to Italian historiography, so it was useful to start there, and Milan, dominant as it was in its region, is also unlikely to have been influenced more than terminologically by the experience of a city which was some way away and very different. But Pisa was not influenced in any way at all by anyone else; whatever it was doing—that is to say, whatever its leaders thought they were doing—they thought it up themselves.

We can see fairly clearly *what* happened in Pisa, at least around 1090 and then after 1109, and I am not the only person to set this process out, as my notes clearly show. But *why* is a rather different matter, and I want to spend the rest of this chapter considering just that. To many analysts of the early commune of Pisa, including some who are writing today, there is no problem here; the city commune was a development waiting to happen, implicitly indeed a wholly positive one, and it is a waste of time to spend too much effort unpicking its uncertain path when the end result is so obvious. But when we are dealing with something as potentially momentous as the abandonment of traditional hierarchies of government, and the development (among other things) of concepts of popular election or choice (the word *electio* means both) of city rulers, then—again, as we have seen for Milan—we are dealing with a change which was not automatic, at all; and it is fair to propose that absolutely no-one in Pisa in 1075, say, would have had any idea of what direction city government would have moved in by 1115, forty years later—in a world in which the stability and relative peace of the March of Tuscany had also virtually disappeared, at Matilda's death at the very latest, so that these rapidly changing city governments thus also had to deal with long periods of local (i.e. not just maritime) war. What people thought was going on in Pisa at each intervening step, in 1080, 1090, 1100, 1110, and whether they realised anything had changed, would have to be looked at entirely without hindsight as a result. We cannot, with the evidence which survives (most of which I have already set out), answer the question at that level of detail; but we can get a little further if we look at who the families of city leaders actually were and what sorts of resources they had, for that will help us gain a sense of their political choices.

We can clear away some general themes at the outset. The first essential point is one that has already been mentioned: Pisa's military experiences cannot have hurt. It was used to planning war already by the mid- to late eleventh century, and on a much larger scale than most other cities had to deal with until the wars between individual cities developed considerably in seriousness from the 1120s onwards. It must also be added, as a second point, that the economic importance of the large amount of non-agricultural land in the Arno delta was very great and, even though much of this was owned by lay families or churches (who doubtless largely got it from the marquis), there were also wide areas of common land, which was run by the city, as we can see from the communal officials tasked to do so in the later twelfth century; common land and collective organisation go together, as historians of rural communes know, and Pisa probably had more common land than any other major Italian city except those around the mouth of the river Po.[59] For both these reasons, some collective decision-making has to have long been normal inside the walls of Pisa, and it was not contested (this was not like the civic uprisings of Milan, which got more systematic across the middle third of the eleventh century, but were always, by definition, controversial in the city); war in Pisa, in particular, was a collective and probably widely supported operation from the start, and had (in the building of the cathedral) a considerable collective result as well.

A third point is however this: although I have stressed the formalisation of the city's assembly as a defensive reaction to a crisis in traditional government in the 1080s, one certainly made easier by the sort of collective experience I have just mentioned, the move from that assembly to a city government based on rulers chosen or ratified by that assembly is—as we have seen for Milan—not necessarily the product of the same process. To repeat, we do not actually know exactly when regular consuls appeared, holding at least some of the civic powers we can see attached to them in the 1110s; it may have been, as I have suggested, the mid-1090s; but all we can really say is that it was between 1090 and 1109. We can also say that it was probably a faster development than in Milan, where the first documentation of a *consulatus* in 1097, and thus of an assembly including men called consuls, seems to have been at least three decades before the development of autonomous powers by the successors of those consuls; this probably indicates that the Pisan process was smoother, and less opposed by powerful people, than in Milan. Ronzani tends in his discussions, quite logically, to look for later moments of crisis here to explain the early ruling consuls, and so offers a slightly later dating than I have; perhaps the consuls appeared when there was no bishop in Pisa, in 1098–1106; perhaps they extended their powers because Matilda's last years were ones of relative weakness—perhaps, indeed, their extension of powers is itself a demonstration of that weakness.[60] It is at least not in doubt that the crystallisation of the authority of Pisa's consuls happened without any reference to Matilda; she is not even mentioned, for example, in the *Liber Maiorichinus*— the March of Tuscany is simply absent from it—and it is also the case that she liquidated most of her landholding in and around the city in her major cessions of 1100–1103, and never appears as a protagonist in the Pisano again, unlike, for example, around Florence.[61] But it is also possible that this is the result of the Pisans cutting her out of their politics, not simply reacting to her absence; as we shall see later, we cannot assume that a direct reaction to political crisis explains everything about the crystallisation of consular power.[62]

At least one element of the period, on the other hand, really is clear: the stability of Pisa's ruling élite. Of the 144 consuls documented between 1109 and 1150, 89 came from just sixteen families, nearly two-thirds. Of these families, twelve are already documented as attending the marchesal *placita* of 1063–77.[63] That is a notable continuity. It indicates that the Pisan élite were successful in ruling whatever system came their way; Pisan political power was simply not contested in the same way as it was in Milan. This was not the continuity of 'compromise', which has been seen as a key to communal origins (above, p. 9); there was no need for compromise here—and even if this élite briefly divided between pro-Henry and pro-Matilda families in the 1080s, each side got back together again by 1090, without the need to compromise on anything except the heights of tower-houses. But who were this élite? Fortunately, a generation of Pisan students have devoted their undergraduate theses to exactly this issue, the reconstruction of consular families, under the guidance of some of the University's leading historians, so we can give an answer to that.

The first thing to say here is that in Pisa, as in Milan, there were half a dozen important families who were not particularly interested in consular office. They were in every case castle-owning families, and we could well see them, once again, as families which saw themselves in some way as too important for the commune, until well after our period ends. This is all the more likely in that most of them seem to have lived in the city much of the time; unlike for Milan, purely rural lords were almost non-existent here. Two of them (the da Caprona and the Ebriaci) were also among the *longubardi Pisani*, and thus had close links with other city leaders.[64] But they were far from indifferent to the city: indeed, this group also included some originally non-Pisan families, the da Ripafratta and, above all, the Gherardeschi, hugely powerful rural counts of inland Tuscany, a branch of whom chose to move to the city by the 1110s, and got more and more involved in city affairs as the twelfth century moved on, attesting to a genuine urban pull for them; the Gherardeschi in fact ended up as major figures in the commune of the next century. This set of families anyway did not contain any significant opponents of the commune and of city power over its *contado*.[65]

A second set of prominent families are more important for us, as they were very interested in consular office from the beginning to the end. They included the Visconti families, for sure, as also other *longubardi* families, the Gualandi, Orlandi, and da San Casciano/Lanfranchi; and also, equally prominent, the Sismondi, Dodi/Gaetani, and Casapieri. (Two centuries later, Dante immortalised in his *Inferno* the Gualandi, Sismondi, and Lanfranchi as the emblematic Pisan families.)[66] We could, as I implied earlier, see the *longubardi* families of 1092 as in status terms the Pisan equivalent of Milan's aristocratic *capitanei*, and they do appear acting together later in the twelfth century as well,[67] but it would then be necessary to say at once that, unlike in Milan, absolutely no distinction is otherwise visible between them and other major city leaders, and the word *longubardi* never appears again for them in any text; I shall come back to the question of what resources underpinned such possible parallels. We can then set all these against a third set, families which appear more intermittently in leading positions, the Casalei or the Erizi or the Marignani, or else gained prominence and consular office later, such as the de Curte or the Anfossi or the Federici.[68] We will look briefly at five sample families from this consular group, four from the second set and one from the third, so as to get a sense of their resources and activities, and more briefly still at a few others; but we need to recognise from the start that—as in Milan—the major Pisan families were by no means economically homogeneous, even though they had for the most part acted together since the 1060s and sometimes before. Their very dishomogeneity shows the force of collective political action in the city, but it also makes that collectivity more necessary to explain.

First, the Visconti. For some time, this family, or set of three families, seem to have had it both ways, with consular office very common across all the branches (sometimes there were two at once, and in the Balearic war there were three consuls, plus Viscount Ugo III as a separate figurehead), but every male family member nevertheless calling himself *vicecomes* in texts; the family of Ugo III (the least consular of the three) had one family member called a *vicecomes maior*, whom we might see as the 'real' viscount, until that branch was dramatically expelled from public office—and all the other *vicecomites* lost their residual public powers—in 1153. The families, taken together, were very substantial landowners, particularly in the Valdiserchio north of the city, and also in the city itself, although they—and this is typical of the Pisan consular families when considered as a whole—had no castles, or signorial rights after the arbitration of 1092 and their landholding was also very fragmented (see map 5). They had some archiepiscopal leases and were the archbishop's *fideles*, but such leases were far less prominent than the lands they owned outright. It was not until the thirteenth century that the Visconti became major rural lords, and that was in Sardinia, after wars of conquest there; even then they simply used those lands to support a century-long battle with the Gherardeschi to dominate the city.[69]

The Sismondi had some similarities to this pattern, but also some contrasts. They were both *iudices* and landowners in the early eleventh century and included a marchesal *castaldio* or administrator, Pandolfo Contulino; they appeared in the *placita* as a matter of course. They are also very visible in the years around 1090; Sismondo di Contulino was a military leader, called *consul*, in the Mahdīya poem, and his brother Guinizo's tower was one of those mentioned in Daiberto's arbitration in 1090. Enrico di Guinizo was one of the consuls in the Balearic war, and is much written up in the *Liber*

Maiorichinus, being called *Cinithoniades* and *Sigimundiades*, pseudo-classical epithets taken from his father's and uncle's names; he and his kin were consuls thereafter very often indeed. They moved directly, that is to say, from being major marchesal figures to being major consular figures. Like the Visconti, they owned in both the city and the countryside—in their case in particular at Fasciano in the Valdarno east of the city. But they were not simply urban rentiers. They had a greater interest than usual in Pisa in castles; they had temporarily controlled part of a castle, at Nugola, in the mid-eleventh century (as other judicial families of that period also did) and they bought a lease of part of the major strategic castle of Livorno, not far from Nugola, from the archbishop's tenants there in 1146. This would not have led to significant rural lordship (Livorno was right beside Pisa's main port, slightly south of the city, and was always kept tight hold of in political terms), but the sale certainly showed Sismondi land-holding ambition. Conversely, however, they can be argued equally easily, even if on the basis of more implicit evidence, to have been involved in commerce, for they held a lot of land in the commercial heart of the city—in its southern suburb of Kinzica, along the river edge on both banks, and around Pisa's oldest bridge (see map 4)—and by 1184 were money-lenders to the commune. We would not go far wrong if we saw the Sismondi as being one of the two or three richest landowning families in the city, along with the Visconti and probably the Gualandi; and, more than either of these two, their interests can be tracked in many directions.[70]

The Dodi had a similar public role: they are visible in the *placita*; they were consuls from 1109 onwards, often; they were also close to the archbishop in the early twelfth century; Dodone di Teperto (or *Tepertiades*) is the most prominent

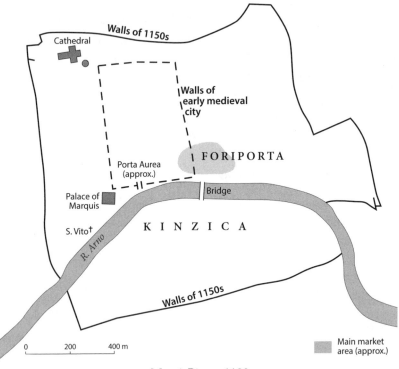

Map 4. Pisa, c. 1100

consul of all in the *Liber Maiorichinus*. Later in the century, they were frequent ambassadors for the commune, they often appear as witnesses to public acts in Sardinia, and they were keen supporters of Pisa's involvement in the Sicilian campaigns of Henry VI in the 1190s. But, unlike the last two, they are not so visible as landowners. Their only substantial landholding was west of the city, in a set of marshy areas running from north to south, between Pisa and the sea, which they began to build up in lease in the 1050s and soon held in full property (see map 5), together with patronage over an important monastery, S. Vito, on the western edge of the city.

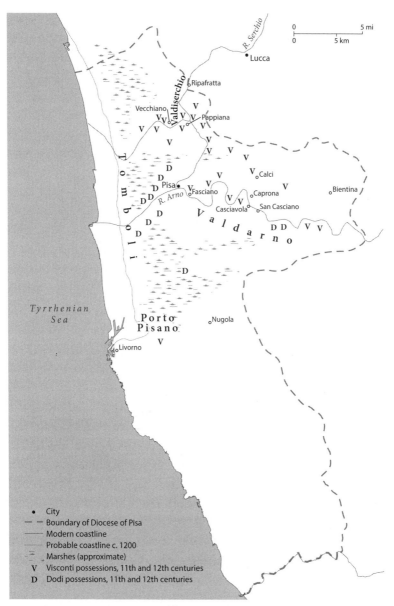

Map 5. The territory of Pisa

On the other hand, to own here was itself significant. Pisa's military strength was in its ships, and to build them the citizens needed timber. The *Liber Maiorichinus* has a grandiloquent passage in which it claims that to build the galleys for the Balearic war the Pisans stripped of their wood the whole of Corsica, the Lunigiana in the mountains of northwest Tuscany, the Mugello valley above Florence, and the seacoast of Lucca. The forested coastal dunes (*tomboli*) of Pisa itself were jealously guarded by the cathedral canons, who extracted rents from (among others) the city's *galeioti*, galleymen, when they needed wood for ship-building, reinforced by violent *silvani* or forest-wardens, as a court case of 1155 tells us. We do not need much hypothesis, then, to suppose that the lands on the edge of the next lagoon, behind the *tomboli*, where the Dodi owned, held similar opportunities; the Dodi, out of all Pisa's major families, can be proposed as particularly associated with ships. And this, and/or the commerce which was consequent on ship-building, made the Dodi rich even in the absence of a lot of land: already by the 1160s, they were frequently money-lenders to the commune, sometimes of very large sums. The long-term stability of their public roles thus becomes easier to explain.[71]

This is even more the case for a fourth important family, the Casapieri, for they had very little land outside the city in this period (they owned above all in Foriporta to the east, which became part of the city when its walls were extended in the 1150s), but they were long prominent. The tower of Pietro di Albizo was another mentioned in Daiberto's arbitration, and a second Pietro di Albizo, probably his nephew, was as we have seen exceptionally visible as a warrior in the *Liber Maiorichinus*, even though he was not a consul—he became that afterwards as well, all the same, four times in all, and so did many of his relatives. There is an interesting sequence in the poem which states that Pietro, for all his military prowess, was also an important mediator between the Pisans and the king of Mallorca in 1114–15, in dealings which put an eventual end to the war. This was because, after the Sardinia war of 1015–16 against ancestors of the king's family, Pietro's own ancestor Ildeberto Albizo had interceded with the emperor Henry II to get the captured son of the then king returned to his father; the kings had been close to the future Casapieri family ever since. We can hardly doubt from this account, whatever its truth value, that the Casapieri were regarded by others as being used to going, or sending ships, across the western Mediterranean for a long time by the 1110s. And indeed the layout of their lands was quite similar to that of the Sismondi, for they stretched along the river to the east of the main bridge, down to a river-bank monastery which they controlled; they also owned several shops in the market area by the 1180s, and not long after they had a *fondaco* or warehouse in the same area: they were even more explicitly attached to commerce that the families we have looked at hitherto, and in the thirteenth century controlled much of Pisa's silk trade. They, like the Dodi, were ambassadors (including, significantly, to Mallorca); and one of their ships was captured and brought to Tunis in 1180. Casapieri wealth clearly came from commerce above all, and that was enough to push them up to the public level of the Visconti and others, or very nearly.[72]

The Marignani were not as prominent as the families discussed hitherto. Azzo di Marignano was a consul at least three times in the 1110s, but then there is a gap, and the family reappears in the 1150s, not as consuls, but as judges in the communal courts (as well as communal *cancellarius* for some years). Unlike in Milan, Pisan communal judges, once they appeared from the 1130s onwards, were not called consuls, and had a less elevated status; so the Marignani turned into a judicial rather than a consular family, with jurists (*causidici*) and notaries among its members on a regular basis. But in fact the family had been a judicial one for a long time. In the mid-eleventh century they were *iudices* and notaries for the marquises, and provided another marchesal *castaldio*; one of them, the notary and *iudex* Marignano di Leone, was one of the arbiters in the Valdiserchio in 1092, and his son Azzo, the consul, arbitrated for the archbishop in 1121. So the fact that his heirs are found as judicial specialists is hardly surprising; what might be more surprising is that they were ever consuls. I think that what we see here is a result of the slow shift in status of judicial specialists in the city—one which has parallels in Milan, and (as we shall see in the next chapter) Rome, and plenty of other cities as well. *Iudices* in the eleventh century were often from wealthy and powerful families, such as the Sismondi, but some families with less status deriving from their landholding could gain (usually via a notarial training) judicial expertise and thus political prominence in *placita* as well, as they certainly did in Milan. The Marignani had land in the city and, east of the city, in Fasciano, which was apparently their village of origin, although land there was certainly shared with other families, again including the Sismondi—who have indeed been proposed to be their relatives, although recent work convincingly doubts this. We never get any sense, however, that this land was substantial; and we also never get any sign, unlike with the Casapieri (to name only one), that they were active in maritime affairs or commerce. I would propose that what happened was that the judicial prominence of the family in the second third of the eleventh century, and perhaps also their genuine political competence, propelled them into the ranks of city leaders for another generation, as the commune was forming; but that after the 1110s they did not have the resources to continue in the city's leadership. By then, judicially trained families were generally from less wealthy and powerful social strata, which fitted the economic position of the Marignani better; willingly or not, they moved into the richest stratum of judicial families rather than remaining in a poorer stratum of consular ones. But, all the same, at the moment of the crystallisation of the commune their legal experience would doubtless have helped to keep them at the centre; Azzo was certainly one of the most influential consuls during the Balearic war (he negotiated the treaty with the counts of Barcelona, for example), even if his heirs could not keep this position later.[73]

Now that we are at this less wealthy level of consuls, we usually have less data to play with, and I shall move faster. The Casalei family seem to be at this level, for, although they were present in *placita* in the eleventh century, they did not come to be consuls until the 1130s, and were at least as often communal judges later. They were another city family with only one real rural base, at Orticaia very close to Pisa to the east; like the Casapieri, they can however be proposed to have been active in commerce, for they appear in several Sardinian public documents, they co-held an island in the Tyrrhenian Sea from the archbishop, and their ancestor Leone de Babillonia had as his nickname, or his father's nickname, the normal Pisan word for Cairo in Egypt. But they do not seem to have been as rich as the Casapieri, and certainly were not as prominent.[74] Very similar were the Anfossi, who were above all jurists and thus judges for the commune, with only two generations who made it to consul (although one of them, Alcherio di Anfosso in the later twelfth century, was certainly very visible in city government); they were also active ship-owners in the wars against Genoa in the same period.[75] We can add the de Curte, who held only a few consular offices from the Balearic war onwards, until they reached a greater prominence in the 1170s. Their property was partly in the city, but also, and above all, in the marshlands to its west; their resource base was thus similar to that of the Dodi in their control of woodland, although on a smaller scale. Significantly, the violent *silvani* of the cathedral canons on the coastal *tomboli* included prominent members of this family, and one of them, Bruno, was a cathedral *silvanus* elsewhere, too. Their toughness may mark a less exalted social position, but Bruno's son Ugo Paneporro was a consul in the 1170s for all that.[76]

What do all these family biographies tell us? One thing must be obvious: we can say rather more about commerce in Pisa than we could in Milan. In the Lombard city, one has to squeeze the documents hard to find any hint at all of a commercial activity and an urban industry which must already have been of major importance; in Pisa, however, even though our documents overwhelmingly concern land, we can say a surprising amount about commercial and maritime activity, and guess a good deal more. This fills out our picture in helpful ways; we have a more rounded view about the sources of wealth of these families. It also shows us that, in Pisa, prominent families could have any kind of resource base as long as they had a lot of it; unusually for this period even in Italy—although we shall see some instances in Rome—one could be rich and influential (as Pietro di Albizo was) without any significant rural landowning at all. But it also shows us, and the point is important for what follows, that the scale of wealth of the consular élite in Pisa was not enormous, even by the relatively modest standards of Milan. None of the major families kept full control of a castle for very long. The da San Casciano did build one in San Casciano, but after the second time it was destroyed, before 1180, they did not try to rebuild it;[77] the Sismondi only had portions of the castles of others; the Visconti, quite strikingly for a set of families with their standing in the traditional marchesal hierarchy, did not control any castles at all—at most they, all three families taken together, were primus inter pares in the city, which is one clear answer why they were never a plausible candidate for the city's rulers on their own, in this age at least. We could put this another way: in Milan, we can see an aristocratic stratum with castles and signorial rights, and a second stratum of rich *cives* (plus a few *valvassores*) without, which sometimes opposed each other (as in the mid-eleventh century), but mostly cooperated later, including inside the commune; some of the first stratum stayed out of the consulate, but others were very active in it. In Pisan communal politics, however, we see only this second stratum, not the first, for the small set of signorial families, the equivalent of the Milanese first stratum but rather fewer in number, were hardly focussed on city politics at all in the early twelfth century.

The other significant point that we gain from these biographies is about the status of judicial expertise. In Milan, from the 1140s onwards, the commune was very largely run by *iudices*, who did not have much land but instead had considerable, and growing, juristic training: not only Oberto dell'Orto, but many of his colleagues as well. I characterised them as a 'medium élite', a third stratum of landowners, who nonetheless came to be accepted as prominent in the Lombard commune. In Pisa, this did not occur, at least after the brief period of centrality of Azzo di Marignano—which is also the period of the consular office of the *iudex* and *operarius* Ildebrando, the only significant consul in our period who cannot be tracked as a landowner at all. Third-level figures after Azzo are only occasional consuls in our period, up to 1150, as we have seen. And prominent judges in the 1130s and onwards, the men who ran the communal law-courts from 1135, and also the men who researched and wrote the city's *Constituta* in the 1150s— men like Carpino and Nerbotto in the 1140s–50s, and Burgundio (documented 1136–93), the man who translated the Greek sections of the *Digest* into Latin—are, like Ildebrando, hardly attested as landowners; and by now they did not become consuls. These judges cannot even be said to be from the 'medium élite', at least in terms of their landed resources; they owed their prominence only to their judicial expertise. If, of their successors, Alcherio di Anfosso could be both a jurist and many times a consul later in the century, this is presumably because he was from a third-level ship-owning family; by contrast, the equally skilled Familiati family, who provided, in Bandino Familiati, a prominent jurist in Bologna itself, who were very often communal judges and minor officials but had decidedly more modest resources, only made it to the consulate once.[78] It is clear, from all the Roman law which the Pisans adopted, that they very greatly respected (and needed) trained lawyers and judicial expertise. Such judicial experts were also evidently very committed to the commune, which gave them a status and a career structure which they would not have managed to gain on their own; it was in effect men like these who most clearly represented the commune in its day-to-day activity in the city, as middle managers do for all organisations. But this did not mean—unlike in Milan—that such people were part of the city's leadership.

It follows that what made men plausible city leaders in Pisa was not so much expertise, as the prominence which was brought by wealth. Such wealth could come from commerce as well as land, for sure; but it had to be available for anyone who wanted to be an active member of the city's ruling élite, and the more wealth one had, the more fully one was part of that élite. This may perhaps have been because élite membership in Pisa, unlike in any inland city, was associated with military and commercial protagonism abroad, for which one needed enough money to run ships; and it is likely that even the land-owning families of the city who are not seen as commercially active in our period (such as the Visconti) at least invested in the ships of others. But this does not have to have been the reason; it may equally have been that the long-term stability of Pisa's leading families, far greater than that of the wider political institutions they operated within, led to an assumption that aspiring new members had to be influential protagonists, in ways that only wealth brings, to be allowed to join, and that a relative lack of wealth (as in the case of the Marignani) would eventually lead to slipping out of the highest level of the élite altogether. This is guesswork; but we must at least recognise that wealth and power were very tightly connected in Pisa, even more than they were in Milan, and also that this connection was not, or not yet, contested in any way that our eleventh- or twelfth-century sources tell us about—even the violence of 1182, which was a real crisis, would be between the same élite families, not against them. And this was so even though Pisa as a commune was dominated by a far smaller group of families than that comprising the city's mounted militia: twelve to fifteen families, from the second élite stratum almost exclusively. The *popolo* did not come early in Pisa, and its activities are not seen before the 1220s.[79]

We have to do, then, with a cohesive and economically defined urban élite in Pisa, wealthy by Pisan standards but not wealthy enough to compete with rural lords on a castle-holding level, and it was that élite, above all, which had to confront the problems of the end of the eleventh century and onwards. In the 1080s, in the civil war period, that élite may have split in two, and thus perhaps had less group protagonism, temporarily; the body that formalised itself to confront the power-vacuum was the city assembly, in which members of the élite, as army leaders and *sapientes* and *consules*, had a relatively informal leadership role. This was the situation which Bishop Daiberto found at his accession in 1089, and which he documented soon after in his tower arbitration. I doubt that Daiberto would have himself found it easy to establish a new centrality for the bishop/archbishop in any stable way; he had no local roots, and the cathedral was not yet as important a landowner as it would become—had the tower document not survived, we would barely have a sense of his Pisan activities at all.[80] But anyway he also left town in 1098 on the First Crusade, and removed an episcopal role from Pisan political trajectories for several years.

In (say) the late 1090s, however, the leading families of Pisa, now probably a coherent group again, must have known that the city still had to be run. The archbishop was still there, but the city had never really focussed itself politically on the bishop and his court, and he would soon leave for Palestine. For centuries, the court of the marquis had been the city's stable focus, and traditional urban hierarchies looked to her or him; but Matilda, although sometimes back in Tuscany by now, was certainly not there very often, and it was in these years that, as we have seen, she handed over her major strategic Pisan lands to the cathedral, and her *palatium* beside the walls of the city itself.[81] Anyone in this situation had to improvise; one sign of this was an alliance, in the Pisa-Lucca war of

1104–10, between Pisa and the Alberti counts of Prato, from a part of Tuscany not hitherto part of the political horizon of the Pisans, and involving a family which fought Matilda herself in 1107. Whether this is the Pisans reacting to marchesal absence, or choosing to separate themselves from marchesal allegiance, matters less in this context; either way, they were reacting to a world which, although the major civil wars were by now over, was configured differently from the past. The new emperor Henry V, who made his own appearances in the 1110s, simply added to a political scene which was gaining steadily in complexity, and also, as can be seen, was turning quickly to periods of localised violence; he, like Matilda, had less effect on Pisa than on Lucca or Florence.[82]

This was not any longer a power-vacuum, but it was certainly one in which traditional hierarchies had lost their automatic attraction. In response to this and to the civil war before it, lords in the countryside, all through Tuscany, turned to constructing traditional hierarchies for themselves, local lordships based on newly defined signorial territories, even if in most of Tuscany (outside the underpopulated south and the eastern mountains) such lordships were fairly weak. Among them, on a small scale, were the former counts of Pisa.[83] But the élites most attached to the city of Pisa were not land-rich enough to do the same, as the half-hearted attempt at a collective signoria north of the city by the *longubardi* in the years before 1092 shows. So the city had to be their political focus; and, inside the city, the only body which had gained any structured, formalised identity was the urban assembly or *colloquium*. That was the body which the leading families found themselves most closely attached to, and which they recognised that they would have henceforth to deal with. It must have been in that context that their dominance of it was regularised by the beginnings of identifiable ruling offices, maybe in the mid-1090s, which by the end of the decade of the 1100s had begun to rotate, for longer or shorter periods, doubtless so as to include enough members of these families. That the office-holders were called *consules* simply reflected the standard terminology of the time for Pisan city leaders. The non-élite members of this assembly might have hardly felt any real change, since these same leaders, or their ancestors, had been the most powerful *cives*, including organising warfare with popular assent and support, for a long time; but it was a change, a major one, for all that. The newly regularised consuls perhaps saw their role as temporary, one which would only last until proper hierarchies re-established themselves. There are certainly signs of that in Genoa, whose political trajectory was very similar to that of Pisa, as we shall see in chapter 5. But they never did, and already by the 1110s the consuls were running a set of affairs—justice, war, diplomacy—which they were unlikely to wish to relinquish.

As we saw earlier (above, p. 12), Pierre Racine, working on Piacenza, called the earliest commune a 'collective signoria'.[84] This phrase has not had fortune in Italy, because it seemed to indicate (and in Racine's argument did indicate) that there was no difference between urban and rural power, which Italians were, rightly, quick to refute. But as a representation of the reaction to the problems of power in parts of Italy in and after 1100, it has its value; consuls in Pisa (although not yet in 1100 in most other cities, we must always remember) were indeed constructing their own power, just as rural lords were doing, bounding it and beginning to regularise it themselves, as a positive—and no longer defensive—response to the failings of the traditional hierarchies around them. This consular power was not fully formalised yet, and it would take decades for it to be so. Dispute settlement in Pisa, in particular, even though the consuls forcefully laid claim to it in 1112, was for the whole of the first half of the century as much based on agreed arbitration and negotiation, on ad hoc practices, as it was on consular justice, including after the latter began to be more regular in the 1130s.[85] An informal commune could certainly be regarded as a temporary expedient. But as it steadily crystallised, it did so in relation to the citizen body as a whole, and not to any external legitimating power. The basis of its authority switched, and the consuls found that their sleepwalking, in Pisa as, not long after, in Milan, had taken them into a world where their legitimacy came from below, not from above.

In Milan, the citizen assembly and its consular leaders were initially only too happy to be close to a traditional aristocratic hierarchy which still existed there, focussed on a powerful archbishop. It was not until the 1130s that a break in its development appeared, with a new set of consular leaders who were in large part less linked to the archbishop and who took the commune in a new direction. In Pisa there was much less of a break: the hierarchies which the assembly and its leaders had to deal with were weaker, and who that leadership was was less contested. I argued that the post-1130s Milanese consuls, even those from judicial families, were still operating inside the thought-world of the feudal aristocracy of the city, and that this helped to explain why they were not fully aware of the implications of what they were doing, and also why the aristocracy did not resist this new political configuration. In Pisa, the situation was different, for that aristocratic world was weaker and further away; there were, for example, some fiefs in the Pisano, as already noted, but they did not loom as large as they did in Milan—out of over one hundred chapters

in the earliest version of the two Pisan *Constituta*, the basic
law of the city by the 1160s, only one concerned fiefs (even if
a long one), and clearly the *constitutores* of the law-codes had
not been 'thinking towards' fief-holders in any way parallel to
the interests of Oberto dell'Orto.[86] In Pisa, indeed, the ruling
families had chosen urban power at least in part because rural
power was *unavailable* to them; conversely, inside the city, if
they could no longer rule a wider collectivity as part of a verti-
cal hierarchy leading upwards to kings and marquises, then at
least they could rule it—with less difficulty than in Milan—
through the assent of its members, through horizontal and
eventually bottom-up links.[87]

As I said, this was a major change, even if, in part precisely
because of that lack of difficulty, it took time for its full implications to become clear. And there are other reasons for
the absence of clarity of the move to the commune in Pisa.
The *Liber Maiorichinus* indeed shows us that Pisans did not
see any major change, at least in the 1110s. The Pisan consuls
are martial heroes in the poem, just as the traditional aristocratic leaders of the *Chanson de Roland* are; and the Pisan
consuls in the *Liber* are also not differentiated in any significant way from their highly aristocratic allies from Languedoc
and Catalonia. Not the consuls on their own, but 'belligerent
Pisa' itself, was in effect a collective lord here, in an imagery of
military legitimacy which had its roots well back in the past.
The rulers of Montpellier and Barcelona may have seen a difference, but for the Pisans there was none. That blaze of pride,
reinforced with every victorious campaign, and probably also
every successful trading voyage, helped further to allow major
changes to take place without any explicit recognition of them.
This is further reinforced by the significant fact that even Pisa's chronicler Bernardo Maragone—as we have seen, active

at the next level down in the hierarchy from the consulate—
retells Pisa's history, in the half-century before his own career
began in the 1150s, as one of the successes of 'the Pisans' or the
'Pisan *populus*': and not of its consuls, who make no appearance in the text at all until 1156.[88] By then, the consuls, and
the Pisans at large, knew full well that they were doing something new, and the ambition of the *Constituta* themselves, also
begun in the 1150s, shows that. But it had been a slow process,
and consciousness lagged behind practice for a long time.

Milan and Pisa cannot be described as typical, for no city
was; but they do, certainly, at least delineate two important
paths away from the failures of the Kingdom of Italy, and, for
all their differences, they have plenty of things in common.
My third example, Rome, brings this further into perspective;
for it had not been part of the Kingdom at all, but for all that,
although it has plenty of unique elements in its development
too, it can be described and analysed in closely parallel ways
to the two more northern cities.

4

ROME

Let us start here once again in the 1110s, in this case in 1118. We have seen that the 1110s were not a good time for the politics of the Kingdom of Italy; Rome was not in the Kingdom, but it was not a good time for the politics of Rome either. Paschal II, who was the city's ruling bishop, that is to say the pope, for most of the decade, faced two humiliating reverses in 1111 and 1116; in the first, in the archetype of an imperial coronation which went horribly wrong, there was an uprising of Romans in Piazza S. Pietro and the pope ended up kidnapped for two months by Henry V; in the second, the Romans rose up against Paschal himself, because he tried unsuccessfully to prevent the son of the urban prefect Pietro 'I', from the prominent Corsi family, from succeeding his father, and the pope had to leave Rome entirely until shortly before his death in January 1118. Then, at the election of the new pope, Gelasius II—who, as Giovanni of Gaeta, had had a successful career as an innovating papal chancellor, but would be an abject failure in his new office—one of the major families of the city, the Frangipane, took exception to the choice of pope and kidnapped him too. We do not know why the Frangipane did this, but it is clear that no-one expected it, since the cardinals had decided to hold the election in a region of the city which the family directly controlled. The response, however, was immediate. A 'multitude' of Romans assembled on the Capitoline hill, the Campidoglio, including representatives of the twelve regions of the city, plus Trastevere and the Tiber island, led by the new urban prefect Pietro 'II', and members of most of the major Roman families apart from the Frangipane themselves; they demanded the release of the pope, and the Frangipane backed down. Not for long, all the same. Henry V reappeared in March with a rival pope to Gelasius, Gregory VIII; Gelasius left the city temporarily; then, after his return, the Frangipane besieged Gelasius when he was saying mass in S. Prassede in July, in another area where the family was influential. They were fought off by the pope's supporters, but shortly after he fled the city finally, and did not return.[1]

Rome does not figure much in accounts of early Italian city communes. It has seemed too 'papal', and the grand narratives of its history in the period 1050–1150, our focus here, have concentrated above all on the story-line of papal 'reform', with Rome as a city seen as little more than an unsympathetic and riotous backdrop to papal efforts.[2] The urban élites which were most prominent in Rome in this century were not, as it happens, at all hostile to papal 'reform', even if they did sometimes differ, quite sharply, over which out of rival popes best embodied it; but above all they had to work out what to do in a period of ever growing crisis in the government of the city, and how best to navigate political waters which were ever more uncertain. They reacted defensively to that crisis, in much the same way as did élites in cities farther north. The events of 1118 show that reasonably clearly: the individual aristocratic families of the city here took sides over who should be their bishop, and they involved the urban 'multitude' to do so—a gathering which was by no means an amorphous mob, if it could be seen as divided up according to the city's regions. We see the same de facto élite protagonism which we saw in Pisa here, and the same invocation of a wider urban community which we saw in both Pisa and Milan. The *multitudo* of 1118 was not, as far as we can see, an organised, still less a permanent, assembly, unlike in the other two cities; this was certainly a difference. But Rome did indeed develop a commune, and a very interesting one. Furthermore, many of the building-blocks of Roman political practice were much the same as in other cities, and the city's specificities were not the ones which people transfixed by the papal story-line might expect. I shall characterise here a political narrative which seems to me to best reflect the realities of Rome.[3] After that, we shall look at those building-blocks a little more closely, so that we can better see how structural elements in the political society of the city on the Tiber, some of which have strong similarities to those we have seen in Milan and Pisa, nonetheless had, in terms of the commune, a quite different result.

We can start with the Tuscolano papacy between 1012 and 1044, a period in which two brothers and then their nephew, from Rome's most powerful family, ruled the city in succession as popes. This was a period of stable government in the city, in fact the longest period of stability for Rome in the next 150 years, until Pope Clement III (second of that name) made a final peace with the Romans in 1188. Rome had a complex bureaucracy, the most complex in Latin Europe (and far more complex than that of any north Italian city in the eleventh century, which was run in effect by a handful of *iudices*, as we have seen). The traditional aristocracy of the city used the offices of state as the basic elements in their jockeying for power and prestige, from the eighth century to the early eleventh, until, under the Tuscolani, this 'old aristocracy' left the city in large part; thereafter they focussed on holding castles in Rome's wide territory in Lazio, although continuing to be loyal to the popes. Rome, although autonomous with respect to the power of the king/emperors of Italy, had also picked up some essential elements of political practice from the Carolingians and their successors, and one important one was the *placitum* assembly, which was attended by papal officials—who thus, increasingly, had a judicial role, just as in northern Italy—major aristocrats, and a substantial audience of less prominent people.[4] Rome thus had a governmental system not at all unlike that of the Kingdom of Italy, even if its official hierarchies were far more elaborate.

What upset this political structure was two events. First, there was a revolt in 1044 against Pope Benedict IX, the least able of his family, by the Romans themselves, probably led by a new élite stratum which is more and more visible in documents in the first half of the century, and which had some similarities to the leading *cives* who revolted against Archbishop Ariberto of Milan in the same period.[5] Then, second, there was a coup by the emperor Henry III in 1046 at the Synod of Sutri and the imposition of popes from outside Rome, in the most systematic external attempt to change the rulers of the city ever to be made, at least up to 1870. The new leading élite can soon be characterised as a 'new aristocracy', for fifteen or so families in the period 1050–1150 were increasingly separate from other leading Romans, and by the end of the eleventh century were often called *nobiles*, distinguishing them from other élite citizens.[6] This aristocracy does not seem to have been opposed to German intervention, and some of its members remained loyal to German-backed popes up to 1100. But it certainly split when the papacy did, that is to say when popes with connections to the marquises of Tuscany began to be elected independently of the emperor, from 1059 onwards. Many of its members were most of all loyal to Archdeacon Hildebrand, a 'reformer' from Tuscany who had spent most of his career in Rome, who ran the city for two successive popes after 1059, and who was elected Pope Gregory VII in 1073, with a wide degree of support from what the sources call the *populus* in the city. For twenty-five years, Hildebrand/ Gregory controlled Rome with little contestation, and, after the failure of the imperially supported pope Honorius II in 1062–64, almost no-one can be seen to have opposed him, except one particularly refractory imperial loyalist, Cencio di Stefano.[7] He ran a fairly traditional government in the city, based on the judicial role of the urban prefect and the last set of grand *placita* which are known for Rome; in that sense, Hildebrand/Gregory was the last heir of the ancien régime, the Carolingian and post-Carolingian papacy, represented most recently by the Tuscolani.[8]

There were elements of instability already in this period, notably the expulsion of Romans from leadership roles in the ecclesiastical hierarchy, which was as complex in Rome as was the secular bureaucracy, and the steady growth in importance of that hierarchy (the college of cardinals in particular), both of which undermined the coherence of the city's public community. But the real crisis in the end was external, and resulted from Henry IV's attacks on the city after the break with Gregory VII, which were constantly repeated in the period 1081–84. Henry bought increasing support in the city with gifts, and in 1084 managed to have his own pope, the first Clement III, crowned in S. Pietro; Gregory, besieged in the near-impregnable Castel S. Angelo, sent word to the Norman rulers in southern Italy to ask for help. They freed Gregory, but also burned down parts of the far north and far south of the city in so doing.[9] This was the last straw for the Romans, and they went over to Henry and Clement almost wholly, leaving again only a handful of equally refractory loyalists to Gregory, notably most of the Frangipane, who were probably the richest landowners among the 'new aristocracy', and what would later be called the Pierleoni family, merchants and financial dealers who had been close to Hildebrand since the 1050s.[10] Clement III ruled Rome for a decade, fending off invasions by rival popes from the Gregorian tradition; although after 1094 he then slowly lost ground, he still was the main pope recognised in Rome until 1099, a year before his death, when the newly elected pro-Gregorian pope Paschal II managed to take the city over.[11] But Clement presided over a government which was losing coherence fast. Just as in northern Italy, *placita* stopped, and disputing came more and more to be dealt with informally, by ad hoc sets of traditional judicial officials and aristocrats, and by the urban prefect, who still played a central role. Under Paschal and his immediate successors, justice was more inchoate still, although, as with the archbishops in Milan in the same period, it increasingly tended to focus on the papal court.[12]

One of the problems was that Rome's papal rulers, from either faction, were by now looking above all to their international role, and most of their main entourage were from Germany (in the case of imperial-backed popes), France (in the case of Gregorian ones), or northern Italy, with little interest in ruling Rome as such. But Rome did need to be ruled as well. That was one of the historic tasks of the bishop of Rome, and one which Gregory VII had not forgotten; but it was one which his successors—again, from both sides— were markedly less able to take on. The urban prefect, who remained Roman (from now on he was almost always from the Corsi family), became more and more crucial to Rome's government, but Paschal, as we have seen, fell out with him too.[13] Hence the difficulties of the 1110s, with which I started, a period in which Paschal may have been sole pope, but he showed little ability to cope with the particular problems of Rome; and nor, even more so, did Gelasius, his successor.

Rome thus faced the same sort of crisis as did northern cities. The vacuum of authority was less acute in Rome on one level, for the city did usually have a ruler who stayed inside the walls for much of his reign, even if his authority was sometimes (as in the 1080s–90s and, later, the 1130s) contested from outside. This, plus the continuity in the role of the urban prefect, is probably why Rome did not develop a formalised city assembly, unlike very many northern cities in this period, to manage some urban affairs. But—as in Milan, where the archbishop remained a central figure—there were problems too; for it is at least clear that, even in Rome, the popes from the 1080s onwards no longer had access to the framing of public authority which was represented by the *placitum*. This presented a problem for the city's élite families, the 'new aristocracy', for being able to run the city was what characterised urban élites everywhere, and the question was how now to do it.

There were two answers to this, in Rome as everywhere else in Italy: to look upwards, to what was left of traditional hierarchies; or else to look to the links between urban leaders and the rest of the city. In Rome—as, again, in Milan—urban leaders did both, in the first decades of the twelfth century. First, they were certainly close to popes. Members of the Frangipane, Corsi, and Pierleoni, plus up to a dozen other aristocratic families such as the Normanni, the Sant' Eustachio, and the family of Cencio di Stefano, in constantly changing groupings, were papal advisors and allies, as well as his deputies when he was away from the city. The Corsi and the Normanni were opposed to Paschal II, but close to Gelasius II; the Frangipane were close to Paschal but opposed to Gelasius; the Pierleoni were close to both.[14] With the new pope in 1119–20, Calixtus II, all the major families came back together, doubtless attracted by Calixtus's ability to amass and distribute money as much as by his charisma—both were part of his well-documented transactional political skills.[15] But the Frangipane seem to have benefited from this less than did the Pierleoni and Corsi; it is probably for this reason that they decided that it was necessary to control, more effectively than in 1118, who was to be the next pope. In 1124, at Calixtus's death, the Frangipane made an irruption into the conclave of cardinals and imposed their own candidate, a second Honorius II, buying off the Corsi and Pierleoni with gifts of rural territories.[16] In 1130, while Honorius was dying, the rivals to the Frangipane were more alert, and there were anxious negotiations as to how to create a united choice of the cardinals; the arrangements were however subverted when the pope actually died, and a self-selected group of them (including the papal chancellor Aimerico, who was very close to the Frangipane) met secretly to elect Innocent II, from a Trastevere family; the other cardinals hastily met the same day and elected Anacletus II, who was a Pierleoni. The papal schism of 1130 has been interpreted by many church historians as an ideological battle between two wings of the 'reform' tradition, with a more traditional 'Gregorian' wing supporting Anacletus and a newer, more 'spiritual', wing behind Innocent (one of his major non-Roman supporters was Bernard of Clairvaux), but this division is not very visible in our data. The input of the Roman families is, on the other hand, very easy to see; Innocent was supported only by the Frangipane and, this time, the Corsi; the others went with Anacletus. Innocent fled the city and did not return except briefly until 1137–38, when Anacletus died, although it was

Innocent who, quite quickly in fact, gained the recognition of the majority of the European powers, including the emperor Lothar III.[17]

The papal elections of 1118, 1124, and 1130 are generally seen as a degrading sequence, which shows up the Roman aristocracy in the worst light (Calixtus's election in 1119, by contrast, had been easier, as it took place in France). It is important to stress that Rome's experience here was not at all dissimilar to that of other cities where powerful bishops coincided with powerful aristocratic families; Milan's experiences during archiepiscopal elections, for example, show close parallels, without historians being very moralistic about them—and in Milan the office of archbishop was more tied to those same families than was by now the case in Rome. (Anacletus is very much the exception here; popes from the established Roman aristocracy did not otherwise begin again until Celestine III and Innocent III at the end of the century.) But it is also clear that the choice of who was to be pope mattered unusually to lay urban leaders in this period, and why this is is more important for us.

This situation links directly back to the failure of Rome's traditional government at the end of the eleventh century, which had until then involved a wide range of aristocratic families in the array of offices available in the city. In the early twelfth century, the main offices of that government, such as the *primicerius* and the *arcarius*, did still exist, but their holders had fewer powers—most of them by now judicial and ceremonial—and they more and more belonged to the ranks of judicial experts who, in Rome just as in Milan and Pisa, were no longer from the city's richest élite.[18] By now, in fact, there was only one stable secular office which had real power attached, the urban prefect, and that was more and more dominated by a single family. So the leading aristocratic families could not expect office-holding from the pope. Nor, however, could they expect much by way of gifts of land, for the period also coincides with that in which the popes, and Rome as a whole, had least control of the countryside around the city and its immediate hinterland; I will come back to this. All they could expect was gifts of money and treasure, for this the pope had a great deal of, the product of dues from the monasteries of half of Europe and some kings, and also often prodigious gifts (we would say bribes, but the term is anachronistic) in return for favourable papal judgements and concessions elsewhere in Europe—a politics in which, as just noted, Calixtus II was particularly skilled, hence indeed his local success.[19] It therefore mattered very greatly indeed who was pope, for popes could turn on and off the tap of financial gift-giving. This structural situation was at its most acute in the early twelfth century, and this explains the unusual tension attached to the papal elections of the period.

Rome as a city, furthermore, was too large and complex to govern easily. The judicial meetings of the *placitum* had created a degree of collectivity, at least among Roman élites, which had worked for a long time; they were not there any more. But the city still needed some way of organising itself as a whole, not least in its relationships with the outside world—and they too were far more complex by now, as the Kingdom of Italy was disintegrating, and the Normans were taking over more and more of the south, which in itself was a menacing development for Rome. This could not easily be subsumed by a papal court which was itself, in this period, not very proactive in the city's own affairs. It is in this context that we find more and more references to wider sets of collective action, run once again by the city's leading families, which had much less to do with popes. A reference to consuls in 1088 may be a forerunner of this; here a set of urban aristocrats calling themselves the 'consuls of the community of the oxen', without doubt an informal grouping, were the judges of a rural monastic dispute along with the urban prefect, a remarkably overt act for an informal group to undertake.[20] The word *consul* was a traditional term for 'aristocrat' in the city, as we have seen (above, p. 83), but it had not been used by anyone except the Tuscolani for seventy-five years, and its return to favour at least indicates a lack of interest in the latter's traditional leadership in the city by now. It was used more often from here on, but, increasingly, not for the aristocracy as a whole but rather for named individuals, who were indeed called *Romanorum consul*, 'consul of the Romans', an apparently honorific title. Members of the Frangipane had the title in 1084–86 and 1139, of the Pierleoni in the early years of the century and then again in 1127, of the Sant' Eustachio in 1141, of the Papareschi (a new family, made powerful by the patronage of their leading member, Innocent II himself, on his return to Rome in 1137–38) in 1148. We do not have many citations of the term—this set makes up half of them, across more than fifty years, up to 1150 or so when the meaning of the office changed—but they are more frequent from the 1120s onwards. They crop up above all in judicial contexts, and it may well be that *Romanorum consul* here was a quasi-judicial title; but it was certainly assigned to aristocrats in large part. It was also, evidently, a title which tied its holders to the Romans as a whole, and not, this time, to the pope.[21]

As we have seen, Rome did not create its own assembly in this period, or at least not one which is recorded in any source. But it is equally true that we find at least informal aggregations of Romans increasingly frequently in the early twelfth century. The uprising against Paschal II over the urban prefecture in 1116 was one such, called a tumult 'of the people' (*populi plebisque*) by Cardinal Pandolfo, who wrote Pascal's biography and clearly saw it as illegitimate; another was the 'multitude' of Romans, divided up regionally as we have seen, in 1118 (Pandolfo again, this time in support of them); a third was a charter of privilege in 1127 for the free passage of the ships of the abbey of Montecassino, which was granted by Leone Pierleoni *Romanorum consul*, three Frangipane, two other aristocrats, 'together with sixty senators and the whole Roman people of the city'; a fourth is a letter to Lothar III in 1130 in support of Anacletus II which went out in the name of the prefect, named aristocrats from five other families, other aristocrats (*potentes*), judges, 'consuls', and 'the whole Roman people' (*plebs*). The last two of these are an explicit invocation of an urban collectivity acting autonomously from the pope, which indeed, in 1127, was granting privileges that popes had previously granted.[22]

Here we are clearly seeing exactly the same sort of mixed and informal but collective grouping beginning to crystallise in the city which we have seen in Milan and Pisa. Those two cities lived through such developments a generation or more earlier, but the format was closely parallel: not least in that it was based on an urban community whose leadership was connected both to the wider city and to an episcopal hierarchy which, although facing a crisis in the structures of government of Rome, still existed. We could assume that the urban collectivity might become more formalised, as a *colloquium* or *concio*; at the same time or later, the 'consuls of the Romans' might soon become an annual office. They then might begin to prise the ongoing management of the city of Rome away from the popes, who in this period were mostly not fully in control of urban politics at all, as we have seen with Paschal and Gelasius—and, indeed, Honorius was not much more impressive, and Anacletus was maybe too embattled to have much effect either, although there, at least, the sources are largely lacking simply because his side in the end lost. The city's aristocratic leadership would thus once again have moved in a communal direction: again doubtless without even intending to, again sleepwalking, for it was hard in Rome not to be fascinated by the long-standing papal attraction.

This did not happen, however. Quite the opposite, in fact. In 1138 Anacletus died, and Innocent II took over the city with no real rival in sight, with full international support, with revenge on his mind, and with no time to lose if he was to make an impact, for he must have been in his sixties (he lasted another five and a half years, as it happens). Innocent deposed all of Anacletus's cardinals, and voided all his acts. He destroyed the church Anacletus had been cardinal of, S. Maria in Trastevere (the region of Rome which Innocent himself came from, in fact), and rebuilt it grandiosely from its foundations, thus simultaneously deleting his predecessor and asserting his own wealth and authority (his mosaic portrait survives in the apse). He went out of his way to assert himself in the city in other ways too, perhaps most overtly by taking the sarcophagus believed to be of the Roman emperor Hadrian, which had been up to then in Castel S. Angelo, Hadrian's mausoleum, and using it for his own coffin—and also, while he was alive, locating it in a prominent position in front of the Lateran palace, the home of the pope, in a piazza which was the location for many civic ceremonies. He built up the wealth and status of his family, the Papareschi, again in a very short time, and without much scruple.[23] Innocent furthermore revived a structured judicial system for the city, based on the trained judicial experts who were increasingly numerous there, whom he attached to his own court and gave annual salaries to; his reign and those immediately following show an array of organised court proceedings for the first time for decades, which were run in many cases with visible professionalism.[24] And Innocent also did something perhaps even more unexpected, given his taste for revenge: he drew into his court not only his long-standing aristocratic supporters, the Frangipani and Corsi, whom he warmly rewarded, but also the leading members of Anacletus's entourage, with the Pierleoni first on the list. He had clearly decided that the divisions between Rome's leaders, whatever he thought of them personally, were structurally damaging, and that it was much safer to wrap them all around himself and his court. They came with alacrity, 'with curled hair and cloaked in silks' as a Flemish visitor to the Lateran wrote in 1141.[25] Innocent had more control over the rest of Lazio than his predecessors had, so he could make this more attractive—and again more stable—by giving his aristocratic entourage land, not just money. The majority of them remained close to the popes for the rest of the century as a result. A monarchical papacy was thus re-created in Rome, with greater effect than at any time since Gregory VII. Innocent took Rome to war in 1142–43 against the city's old enemy Tivoli, and, after initial reverses, won completely in July 1143. The result here was, however, the mirror image of Innocent's purposeful protagonism: the *populus* of Rome rose up against him in August or September (Innocent was by then on his death-bed—he died in September), and established a commune—called a 'senate' in Rome—against both him and his aristocratic supporters, which they located on the Capitoline hill, the Campidoglio, the political heart of the living city (see map 6).[26] There was, definitively, no sleepwalking here; this commune was a fully deliberate creation.

The Roman senate was doubtless called that to mark out the special historic status of the city; other cities could have consuls, but only Rome had ever had senators in the past, and only Rome would do so now. (Pisa, always alert to Roman parallels, later borrowed the term for the counsellors of its consuls in 1160.) The word 'senate' also had a longer currency in Rome, as a term which meant the collectivity of the city's leadership in a generic sense.[27] But it was the confidence of the senate which was its most notable feature. It was originally founded, so say our sources (sketchy and negative ones, however, and also not written by Romans), to 'renew' Roman dignity, 'under the pretense of the utility of the *respublica*', vague phrases which tell us little, and also as appearing in hostile reaction to Pope Innocent's fairly generous terms to the defeated Tivoli, which may indeed have been the spark for the revolt. A year later, in 1144, Lucius II, Innocent's second successor, tried to force the senators out of the Campidoglio, but the Roman *populus* resisted, and one source says that Lucius died in 1145 from a stone thrown by one of the senate's defenders.[28] Whether this is true or not, Lucius certainly failed, and in fact his actions contributed to a further radicalisation of the commune. Senatorial documents, when they begin in 1148, date by the 'era of the renovation of the sacred senate', a quite unparalleled self-consciousness for communes in Italy; that era began in August or September 1144, not in 1143 when the revolt began, which must show that Lucius's intervention was later seen to be when the senate first established itself fully.[29] Then or during the next year, by when the senate was fighting a new pope, Eugenius III, who had refused to recognise it, it also took over the rights (*regalia*) of the pope in the city, abolished the office of urban prefect, and appointed its own *patricius* as its leader, who was Giordano Pierleoni, brother of Anacletus II—he is almost the only aristocrat known to have joined the early commune, however, and his brothers were certainly opposed to it. By then the senators were also destroying some of the houses of the aristocratic supporters of the pope, including the Frangipane and Corsi, and taking over others, including those of the other Pierleoni. Soon after, the senate must have begun the building of its own communal headquarters, a *palatium* on the Capitoline hill, which is first attested in 1151, again not only very fast but well before any other Italian communal palace; it is still part of the buildings of Rome's City Hall, behind Michelangelo's monumental façades on the Piazza del Campidoglio.[30]

Eugenius recognised the senate at the end of 1145, in return for the revival of the prefecture and the abolition of the office of *patricius* (Giordano stayed on, however—he was now called the communal *vexillifer*, 'standard-bearer'), but soon fell out with it again; a lasting peace between pope and senate was not agreed until 1149. In that year the commune swore fidelity to the pope, with four oath-swearers taken from each of the regions of the city, and restored the pope's *regalia*, in return for £500 for the oath. In the meantime, the senate had begun its own judicial tribunals, which are documented from 1148; like those of the popes from Innocent II onwards, they were notably organised ones, and indeed relied on the same judicial experts to run them: one of them was the papal *arcarius* Gregorio, from a family of professional papal judges, who is even attested as a senator in 1151.[31] The senators also began to make direct overtures to the king of Germany Conrad III, to whom they wrote in 1149, before the papal peace, asking him to come and restore the Roman empire with them, and boasting of their occupation of the houses of the king's enemies, the Roman aristocracy. This letter and some of its follow-ups are the first texts which tell us of the views of the senate in their own words. That they are full of classical allusions has excited modern observers, who are keen to see in the actions of the senate a conscious revival of the Roman past, of a type associated with the 'twelfth-century Renaissance'. I do not accept that myself; the rhetoric of *renovatio* studs the whole of the previous three centuries of Roman history, back to Charlemagne's time, and was used by many, often in very conventional ways.[32] But there is no doubt that, once again, the senate had a very high opinion of itself and a very clear sense of its identity, one which in 1149 was otherwise available only to communes like Pisa and Genoa, for which these processes had started decades earlier. The fast institutionalisation of the senate also lasted; it ran the city from now onwards, and indeed in the period 1159–88 ruled it with no contest from outside at all, for in those thirty years the popes were almost never in Rome. That did not change until a later Pope Clement III, himself a Roman, made a final peace with the senate in 1188 and a ceremonial return, heralding a fifty-year sequence of powerful popes of Roman origin with a base in the city.[33]

This, then, is the exceptionality of Rome: that, almost uniquely in Italy, the Romans knew exactly what they were doing when they founded their commune; and that their commune was not, as usual, led or partially led by the city's leading élite families, but actually opposed to them. Before we come on to who did lead the commune, I wish however to step back a bit, and set out some of the other particularities of the city, which will help to explain this dénouement more clearly. Because, given what I have said about Milan and Pisa, and indeed what could be said about nearly every other commune in Italy, these developments certainly need explanation.

───────────

Rome was a large city. It was, around 1050, still the largest city in demographic terms in Latin Europe, with perhaps thirty thousand inhabitants,[34] although Milan, I myself guess, may have overtaken it around 1100. It also stretched across a huge area, the area of the classical Roman city which had reached a million inhabitants in the early empire. The heart of the city was rather smaller than that, but it still extended over a much wider area than did Milan, and its population foci were also interspersed with ruins of monumental classical buildings which were by no means all reoccupied—not to speak of the city's seven hills, some of which were genuinely steep, most notably the Capitoline hill in the centre, between the city's central market and the wide monumental Forum area to its southeast, which was a political focus well before the senate was founded.[35] This geographical dispersal meant that Rome had a regional structure which is very evident in our documentary sources: in sales and leases from the eleventh and twelfth centuries, land and housing is typically located in Rome's *regiones*, which in our period numbered around thirty (see map 6). These regions were not old; the traditional regional divisions of the city, which went back to the classical period, had been only twelve to fourteen in number. They therefore testify to a set of cohesive local identities, which had each built up inside areas of human settlement, probably especially in the eleventh century, and which lasted.[36] In 1177,

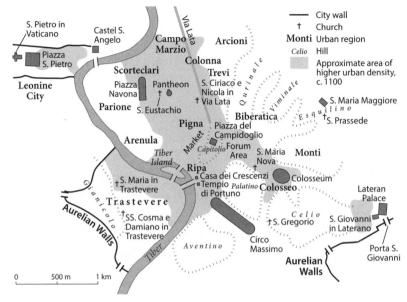

Map 6. Rome, c. 1100

for example, a text from one of Rome's best-documented regions, that situated between the Forum area and the Colosseum, called the region of Colosseo or else of S. Maria Nova, from its major church, shows the *regio* acting as a collectivity with a local leadership, and in control of its own financial resources. We can find a few similar texts from Milan, which was divided into regions by its gates, Porta Comacina or Porta Vercellina, some of which had collective control of common land outside the gate; but Rome's regions are much more visible in our sources, and seem to have been the foci for all kinds of local political action. The thirty-odd regions were in the twelfth century aggregated back into twelve 'super-regions' (plus Trastevere as a thirteenth), which seem to have become the basic set of building-blocks for the city's commune; but local identity was tied up in the smaller units, and the larger ones were called by names like 'Monti, Biberatica and Colosseo', which shows well enough that they were somewhat artificial amalgamations.[37]

Rome was also a rich city. Unlike cities in the north, whose arenas of 'natural' political action were restricted to their dioceses (any extensions beyond these had to be fought for), Rome was at the centre of a large territory, roughly modern Lazio, five times the territory of Milan, over which it was sovereign. This by the late eleventh century was mostly not under the city's real domination—as elsewhere, local lordships were developing which were hard to control—but in every period at least some of the territory looked to the city, and, in the mid- to late twelfth, residual loyalties allowed the popes to re-establish their power more widely again (war was only necessary in the case of really hostile parties, such as Tivoli and, later, Tuscolo), and indeed in many cases give it back out to their aristocratic clients, as we have seen.[38] This gave Rome a starting-point for potential prosperity. But even more important economically was the fact that, uniquely among Italian cities, the whole hinterland of the city, out to up to fifteen miles from its walls—an area the size of some entire dioceses in Italy—was wholly owned from inside the city, with no rural landowners at all until one got quite far out. This meant that all the agrarian surplus from this very large area went straight inside its walls, and unlike in other cities, where peasants from the surrounding areas brought in their grain and wine to sell in the urban market, the surplus of Rome came into the city free, as rent. These landowners were all ecclesiastical; lay landowing is hardly attested at all until the end of our period. They included all the major churches of the city, owning autonomously; this landowning was not controlled by the papacy, which indeed did not, as it seems from the balance of our documents (and it is necessary to say that the archive of the popes themselves is almost entirely lost for this period), hold more than a single sector of these lands, apparently that which extended eastwards from the Porta S. Giovanni, the gate beside the Lateran palace.[39] So the churches of Rome controlled the whole of this huge area, including the land inside the city walls as well. They leased most of it to lay Romans, however: to anyone who could pay the low rent and the normally much higher price for entering into the lease, but of course above all to people who were their own clients, whom they could rely on for political support, in return for leases which could be very remunerative. Most leases that survive from the tenth century are to the city's 'old aristocracy', but from the eleventh they were increasingly to the 'new aristocracy' which succeeded them, and to less prominent people in the city as well. In the twelfth, the churches whose documents survive best can be seen leasing to significant figures in their own regions, whom, as in the previous two chapters, I will call a 'medium élite'—in this case, families who were prominent in a single sector of the city, in Colosseo or Trastevere or wherever, but who did not reach the landed wealth and political status of the *nobiles*, the Frangipane and the others. Very broadly, large tracts of open grain-land were leased to aristocrats, whereas the 'medium élite' are most often found holding urban leases and leases of vineyards in the belt of vines and orchards around the walls of the city. These leases were the basis of the prosperity of all Rome's social and political players.[40]

Grain and wine (and also salt, from Rome's coastal salt-flats, close to what is now Fiumicino airport), coming regularly into the city to feed its inhabitants, also fed a large and complex network of artisans and merchants. Rome's artisans in the eleventh century are better documented than those of any other city in Europe; there were dozens of trades—all the standard trades of a much later medieval city, indeed: workers in textiles, leather, iron, bronze, wood, ceramics, and more, sometimes divided by product, locksmiths as opposed to shield-makers for example; and millers, swineherds, and a variety of food tradespeople, not least in Rome's large pilgrim quarter between Castel S. Angelo and the Vatican, but not only there. They all sold, among other places, in Rome's central market stretching north and west from the Piazza del Campidoglio.[41] Their activities of course added greatly to the value of urban property too. And that reinforced the importance of the churches of each of Rome's regions, which were the owners of that property. To participate in Rome's prosperity, one needed urban leases, and to do that one needed to be close to the churches and monasteries of the regions. For, although there were occasional monasteries whose social network extended farther than a single region—like the female monastery of SS. Ciriaco e Nicola in Via Lata, situated in the *regio* of Pigna three hundred yards north of the Campidoglio, founded by Prince Alberico in the mid-tenth century and hugely rich, whose clients came from a variety of places in the city—most churches had land in a single region of the city and outside the gate nearest to that region, and most churches also had a predominantly regional clientele.[42]

Aristocrats lived in Rome's regions, too, of course; indeed, we usually know where. The Frangipane, for example, lived in S. Maria Nova/Colosseo, and so did the less prominent family known as the *filii Astaldi*; the Corsi lived on the Capitoline hill and also below it on the Tiber bank, in the river-port region known as Ripa, next door to the Normanni and probably the *filii Baruncii*; the Pierleoni lived at the northern end of Ripa and on the Tiber island; the Sant' Eustachio lived near the Pantheon; a variety of families, perhaps slightly less prominent, lived in Trastevere; and so on.[43] When they lived in one's own region, they were also points of reference for their less rich and powerful neighbours, beyond doubt; the Frangipane, in particular, were effectively dominant in the region of S. Maria Nova. But they lived on church land too, and they too were clients of local churches; the Frangipane were very close to S. Maria Nova itself, as also to the monastery of S. Gregorio, situated nearby.[44] Aristocrats were close to the pope, as we have seen, at least from time to time; but they were durably close to churches in their regions.

'Medium élite' families were, by contrast, above all involved with churches in their own regions. They also presumably dealt with the aristocratic families who lived there too, if there were any—but in most cases there were not, for the latter tended to bunch in particular sectors of Rome, and there were anyway too many regions to have a family each. When there was no local aristocratic family, and even sometimes when there was one, the leading figures in the daily practice of regional politics were inevitably members of the 'medium élite', who thus had a rather more important local political role than can be seen in any other city (at least as far as we can see, for the research elsewhere has mostly not been done), and who did not have papal links for the most part—perhaps only some judicial figures had that. The regions of the city were therefore more important for most people, including the relatively rich and prominent, than was the papacy, particularly after the political collectivity associated with *placitum* assemblies ended. This must be why ad hoc aggregations of Romans, as in 1118, were organised regionally, and it is most likely that the senate was too. Regional identity was not all that Romans had, of course. Being part of Rome as a city, and pride in that, was as important here as it was in Milan and Pisa; fighting Tivoli gave Romans as much of a charge as fighting Como and Cremona did for Milan and sacking Palermo and the Balearics did for Pisa. Indeed, the military organisation involved in fighting Tivoli must have brought the regions together very effectively. The regions did not weaken city identity and political practice, then. But they did nothing at all to strengthen the effect the popes themselves had on the city.

Let us pause here for a moment, with a 'medium élite' principally involved in regional, not papal, politics, and look once again at some families: we shall look at three from the aristocracy and three from the 'medium élite'. Once we have got a sense of the kind of leadership the city had, we will return to the city commune, the early Roman senate that is to say, and see what we can say about senators.

The Frangipane are the family of the 'new aristocracy' whom we can track back furthest; they were the descendants of a man called Pietro Imperiola, who appears in 963 as a lay participant in the synod which deposed Pope John XII, and in which he is the only person to be called 'from the people', *de plebe*. His immediate heirs included artisans and merchants, but by the 1010s the family was in the papal entourage and artisans thereafter disappear from its membership. We have seen the scale of the political role the family had in the early twelfth century; this went back to at least the 1080s–90s, when Cencio and Giovanni Frangipane were active supporters of popes of the Gregorian party. They had, as we have seen, a base in the S. Maria Nova/Colosseo area, which is where they housed, for example, Urban II in a 'very strong fortification' in

Map 7. Lazio

1094; they also controlled part of the Colosseum, probably on a papal lease, and they held numerous leases of urban and suburban property. We have less information in this period about their leases of lands in the city's immediate hinterland, but we can assume they were substantial too, for the family can soon be seen elsewhere in Lazio; they were briefly counts of Ceccano in the 1120s, and in the 1140s they began to develop a stable power-base in the territory of Marittima, south-east of the city, certainly as a result of papal cessions, with several castles which they held onto from now on, and a territorial control over the city of Terracina as well (see map 7). The family thus became rich in the eleventh-century city, on leases from a variety of Roman churches, including the papacy; and, later, got even richer.[45]

The Pierleoni were as prominent politically, but all the signs are that they were less rich. They were a family of Jewish converts, who must have converted early in the eleventh century; the family head, Leone di Benedetto Cristiano, a merchant, was very close to Archdeacon Hildebrand in the 1050s, and his sons are later attested as holders of a lucrative lease of an urban mill in their base on the Tiber island. They got a lot of money from their papal connections, which became important again after Paschal II took over the city, and they were also linked to the Norman rulers Roger I and II, who rewarded them generously too. But they are seldom attested as lessees of land. This is partly because documents do not survive from their Roman bases on the Tiber island and in the *regio* of Ripa; but the Frangipani are visible elsewhere in the city too, whereas the Pierleoni are not. They got hold of one castle, Isola Farnese north of the city, in lease from the Trastevere monastery of SS. Cosma e Damiano, shortly before 1107, but that was their only major rural possession. They probably remained a largely commercial family. That was enough to gain them a very considerable political prominence—as with the Casapieri in Pisa (above, p. 105), another mercantile family above all—but the scale of wealth of the Frangipane was certainly greater than theirs.[46]

The *filii Baruncii* were a family of supporters of imperial popes from the 1060s to the 1100s; they turn up as such in narratives throughout the period. They may have provided a senator in 1148, too, although if so they were nearly unique among the aristocracy until as late as 1190. They are even less visible as landowners in our documents than the Pierleoni, and it is probably significant that they had a judicial expert, a *causidicus*, among their members in the late eleventh century, for other aristocratic families did not link themselves to judicial expertise. The *filii Baruncii* were much less prominent in social terms than either of the previous two families, but they are visible enough as political actors to make it quite clear that they were taken seriously as players in the city, and they married into another second-level aristocratic family, the *filii Astaldi*, in the twelfth century. Both families appear, in fact, in 1131 in control of a rural estate, out of the city on the via Appia, which they seem to have been developing as an organised agricultural operation, in a way more common in the late middle ages around Rome; this entrepreneurial streak is notable, and would have been hard to manage if they were not richer than their scarce documentary impression might make us think.[47] The *filii Baruncii* may also have been quite ambitious in other ways, for they are the most plausible candidates for the family who built the so-called Casa dei Crescenzi, a tower house from the mid-twelfth century with a startlingly elaborate architecture, full of reused classical pediments and a set of brick pilasters made to resemble a classical temple (doubtless to match the Tempio di Portuno, surviving today just on the other side of the road); its front window seems, from a boastful inscription, to have had a bust of the builder, Nicola di Cencio, and it has another very long inscription above the door praising the contribution Nicola's 'sublime house' made to 'renewing the decor of old Rome'. This building is unique today in Rome (or anywhere else in Europe in the period), but it was probably less unusual then; it attests, whoever put it up, to some very great self-advertising for an aristocratic family. It is thus striking that we know from narratives that, on either side of the Tempio di Portuno, there were also the tower-houses of two rather more important families, the

Normanni and the Corsi. Nicola di Cencio was in effect defy-
ing these two with his architecture and his inscription. That
was more important than the use of the tower for defence. Although the *filii Baruncii* could not match either in real power
and wealth, they could at least do so in rhetoric.[48]

The signs are, in fact, that the Roman aristocracy was divided into two levels. The richer level was that of the Frangipane, and also the Corsi, who held the prefectural office, and
who had an interest in rural landowning and castle-holding
in the far north-west of Lazio, along the coast and inland,
including the city of Civitavecchia. We can add to them the
Normanni, who were a new family around 1100 but at once
appear as prominent political actors (they were married into
the Frangipane), who were castle-holders west of the city by
the 1190s at the latest and probably before, and were a baronial family in the next century; the Sant' Eustachio, who held
land from the monastery of Farfa right out in the Sabina and
would also have a baronial future after 1200; and the descendants of Cencio di Stefano, Gregory VII's enemy, who by
the 1110s leased half a dozen castles north of the city from
S. Paolo fuori le Mura, which S. Paolo found it hard to keep
control of.[49] All these families gained substantial rural land-
holdings, often well outside Rome's fifteen-mile hinterland,
again through ecclesiastical cessions—although it is necessary to say that none of their castles can be securely attached
to them before 1100, and that they, like the Frangipane, did
not become really rich in lands until close to the end of our
period. This set of families had resources which matched
those of the leading *capitanei* of the city of Milan, and they
indeed in some cases (the Corsi and the family of Cencio di
Stefano after 1100, after 1140 the Frangipane as well) came to
have more castles than any city-based Milanese family; they

were all much richer in land, and certainly in castles, than any of Pisa's consular families, too. This upper stratum was however set against a stratum of families which were less active in landholding, and do not seem to have held anything like the level of resources that the top families did, of whom the Pierleoni were the most prominent and the richest, and the *filii Baroncii* and *filii Astaldi* were others. Here we can add a set of Trastevere families too: notably the family of Giovanni Tignoso and his son Cencio, who had been urban prefects for Hildebrand/Gregory VII until 1077, and who had a set of lands around the city, largely held on lease, which was substantial but by no means enormous—plus quite large sums of money and movables, some of it lent at interest, which indicates at least some activity in commerce.[50] The closest parallels to this second-level stratum in my other cities were the leading consular families of Pisa, and the leading non-aristocratic *cives* of Milan.

There are two points which need to be made about this distinction between two levels of Rome's 'new aristocracy'. The first is that it does not seem to have corresponded to a distinction in political prominence in the city; the Pierleoni appear together with the Frangipane often enough to make that clear, and the *filii Baruncii* were as active as the Sant' Eustachio and the family of Cencio di Stefano on the proimperial side. We can easily suppose that the families on the second level were more active in commerce (as certainly with the Pierleoni and the family of Giovanni Tignoso), but, as in Pisa, this did not impede them at all. Conversely, the less rich families had less staying-power. None of the families at this level can be tracked much after our period ends, except the Pierleoni—and even the latter did not make it into the super-rich baronial families of the thirteenth century, unlike many of the families of the first level.[51] When we find the family of Giovanni Tignoso in Trastevere documents after 1100, they seem to have slipped back to being a purely regional family of 'medium élite', even if at the top of the stratum. All the same, except at the margin, all of them were substantially wealthier than the other 'medium élite' families whom we can track in detail. Let us look at some of the latter now, running slightly later in the twelfth century to pick up some good document sets, so as to make the point.

One example is Galgano *iudex*, who was one of the senior palatine judges, the *primicerius*, between 1138 and 1151. In 1169, his two sons divided their inherited land between them and listed it all; it was largely city land, four and a half houses and two building plots, plus some salt-pans on the coast and a small amount of money. This shows us the sort of scale of land judicial experts had, and it fits that of some others, such as Benedetto di Leone, a highly experienced expert in Justinianic law who appears in court cases of the 1150s, whose grandfather's generation had come from Albano, a town in Rome's near hinterland, with a set of lands there of the same type: enough to live decently, but not enough to compete in any way with the extent of landholding of the families we have just looked at.[52] Jurists had a presence outside their region (in Galgano's case, the *regio* of Scorteclari, between Piazza Navona and the Pantheon), and indeed a link with the papal court, but only because of their judicial training, not their family wealth. Judicial experts in Rome by the twelfth century were thus typically members of the 'medium élite', just as they were in Milan and Pisa. Neither of these two are attested as senators after 1143, but our senatorial lists are full of gaps, and they could well have been senators in undocumented years, as their judicial contemporary Gregorio *arcarius* certainly was.

A second case was the Mancini family of the S. Maria Nova region, who appear across the whole twelfth century. They had land all round the church, and are also very visible in the church's documents as witnesses—they are a good example of ecclesiastical clients, and indeed held S. Maria's land not only in the region where they lived but also in a vineyard area outside the city. They had at least four houses, for these are mentioned in a papal list from 1192 of the houses which had to be reimbursed for putting up temporary arches along the papal processional route from the Lateran to the Vatican, which passed by S. Maria Nova; these or others included one which Giovanni Mancino had pledged in 1160 for a loan of £5, and the family dealt in sums of money on this scale in other texts as well. The Mancini are not documented outside their area at all, but they too could have easily been senators, for, in the list of the leaders of the *regio* of Colosseo in 1177, Giovanni Mancino was the third to be named, so he certainly had a regional-level prominence, and the first two on the same list certainly made it into the senate.[53]

The *filii Grisotti* of Trastevere are a further example. Grisotto di Ingizzello appears first in the 1130s as a creditor of the monastery of SS. Ciriaco e Nicola in Via Lata, holding monastic grain-land at Campo di Merlo on the Tiber some six miles south-west of the city in pledge against repayment of a larger sum this time, £26. The family also appear as tenants farther out of town in the same direction too, and they must have held land in Trastevere, but Campo di Merlo is where their activities are clearest. In 1140 Grisotto took out a lease for part of the same land, which the monastery had now redeemed, but in 1148 the monastery claimed in court, successfully, that this was a phony lease cooked up to prevent Pope Innocent II, who had 'laid his eyes' on the land, from forcing the monastery to lease it to his Papareschi nephews, who were indeed monastic tenants elsewhere in Campo di Merlo. The next year, after Grisotto's death, his son nevertheless got the same land in a real lease, and the next years show the *filii Grisotti* and the Papareschi—who were clearly on bad terms with each other—gaining and losing the same lands in turn. In 1184, Grisotto's grandson Pietro became a senator, and used the position to take over some of the monastery's land illegally; when his co-senators voided this, he ravaged the land. The *filii Grisotti* lost the resultant case, but it cost the monastery a lot of money to win it, and the family had other land in Campo di Merlo still as well, for which in the 1190s they refused to pay rent; they were not got out of their tenures until 1209. This was certainly a badly behaved family, then, but it was operating on the same sort of scale, even if with more liquid silver, as were the ones I have just discussed. This time, as we see, they are attested as holding senatorial office.[54]

This is the sort of scale we are dealing with when we are characterising Rome's 'medium élite'. We have looked at similar families, operating on a similar scale, in Milan, for this is the level of that city's judicial consuls of the 1140s and onwards, men like Stefanardo of Vimercate and Girardo Cagapisto. In Pisa, where judicial expertise did not assure entry into the consulate, we looked at the Marignani, but at no other families on this level in any detail—for Pisa's consuls were for the most part the equivalent of the second level of Rome's aristocracy. In Rome, however, the evidence for senators does not show up more than a tiny handful of people who operated at a larger scale than the three families we have just looked at. Rome's senatorial lists are far less complete than those of Milan of Pisa—between 1143 and 1180 we only have reasonably full lists of senators for seven years out of nearly forty. On the other hand, Rome also had far more senators than either of the northern cities had consuls, fifty to sixty in every year, so up to 1180 we know the names of some ninety senators. Apart from two possible aristocrats, already mentioned, all the identifiable people in these lists are members of the 'medium élite': they are judicial experts, notaries, urban leaders from S. Maria Nova, urban creditors. We can also add two artisans in the early years of these lists, Bentevenga the painter in 1148 and Giorgio the tailor in 1151.[55] Although the latter could have been élite artisans, this profile, taken as a whole, is quite unlike that of either Milan or Pisa.

Conversely, in the context of what we have seen for Rome, it is really what we would expect. In a senate which was deliberately set up against the pope and the city's aristocracy, we would be expecting people to run it who were from the richest non-aristocratic stratum, and this is just what we do get. But the interesting thing is that nearly three-quarters of the names of senators we know are not seen elsewhere at all, even in casual references. Rome might not have the density of documentation that Milan, a city of comparable size, has, but it actually has more texts for the city itself; in Milan, however—and still more in Pisa, a smaller city—we can easily track the great majority of our consuls, and know quite a lot about some of them. Not in Rome. Rome's evidence is more regionally based, and some of our regions have hardly any documents at all, so some of our unidentifiable senators must simply have been based in these undocumented regions; but even then we know very little indeed about too many people. I conclude that it is quite likely that Rome's senators— very numerous in each year, as I said—included not just a 'medium élite' leadership, but also less prominent people still,

at least in some cases: smaller rentiers, less prosperous artisans, people who would be called the *popolo minuto* in later
centuries in Italy. That is supposition, but it seems to me logical. It also fits with one interesting thing about Rome's early
senate, the presence in it by 1148 or so, until his execution in
1155, of the purist anticlerical preacher Arnaldo of Brescia.
Arnaldo's influence in the senate has been exaggerated by
some historians, but a radical wing of the senate can be seen
in a couple of surviving defiant letters to the German kings
Conrad III and Frederick I, and also in one hysterical letter of Eugenius III in 1152, which claimed that Arnaldo had
stirred up a 'rustic mob without nobles or notables' to elect
their own version of the senate and their own emperor.[56] We
need not take this last letter very seriously as evidence of Ar-
naldian activities (the word 'rustic' is already a sure marker of
rhetorical flourish, an attempt at delegitimation of a purely
urban movement), but it certainly shows that the pope could
hear, or think people could believe, rumours of very radical
acts on the part of at least a wing of the senate. Such a wing
is more likely to have been made up of people who were not
members of any élite. And we know of no such equivalent
wing in any other Italian commune.

What was happening in Rome after 1143 was, I think,
twofold. First, the urban aristocracy, which were, in the two
decades prior to Innocent II's victory in 1138, moving steadily
towards acting as leaders of the Roman *populus*, were after
that fully caught up in the attractions of Innocent's court and
abandoned their urban leadership. Innocent had more chutz-
pah than most of his predecessors and also almost certainly
more resources, so could provide the sort of material patronage which the aristocracy needed. Rome's aristocratic families
were active on an unusually wide stage for families at their

financial level; the Pierleoni were dealers in the Norman court, as we have seen, and the Frangipane made some remarkably advantageous marriages outside Rome in the twelfth century, brokered by popes, the most striking of which, in 1170, was to the niece of no less than the Byzantine emperor Manuel I. The families also spent a lot of money in Rome to show off their position—on decorated tower houses such as the Casa dei Crescenzi, and even, in the case of the Frangipane of Innocent's time, on a leopard, which we know about because it 'strangled' an unfortunate woman in their household.[57] They needed papal patronage, if they could get it, as a result. Sometimes they could not get it, when popes were less in control of substantial and transferable assets, and also less good at dealing with their Roman clients—that was when the aristocracy moved towards the city—but, if popes could satisfy these wants, they were a more appealing option.

Secondly, however, we have to look at the same events from the standpoint of Rome's *populus*. That word had many meanings, from the wide participation in Rome's very elaborate processional tradition to a narrower leadership of political players, but it certainly normally included the 'medium élite' as I have defined them here. We can equally say that it also corresponded to the wide stratum of the mounted militia as characterised by Maire Vigueur for the whole of Italy (above, p. 13), which was as much present in Rome as it was anywhere else; indeed, the *equites*, the cavalry, of the city may well have coincided quite closely with the 'medium élite'.[58] They may well have expected to contribute to the slowly developing city collectivity, with aristocratic leadership, as was common in other places; the values of the 'medium élite' do not seem to have been substantially different from those of the aristocracy, for example, with the mixture of military enthusiasm and classical imagery which we have seen, in different ways, in both Milan and Pisa, and which was equally strong in Rome: visible in the aristocratic Casa dei Crescenzi, the anti-aristocratic senatorial letters to German kings, and the aggregation of the war with Tivoli, which doubtless involved aristocracy and 'medium élite' alike. But the aristocracy abandoned them, and returned to the pope. The 'medium élite' responded deliberately and with violence: they seized and later defended the Capitoline hill, and they created a city government for themselves. So, whereas in Milan and Pisa the first consuls were from the city's highest élites, linked into and dominating an assembly-based urban collectivity which represented less prominent social strata, judicial and notarial families, merchants and rich artisans, and so on—the 'medium élite' as I have defined them here—in Rome it was this latter stratum which was in the leadership role at the start, with no aristocrats except the occasional figurehead, as with Giordano Pierleoni. In that situation, the urban collectivity *they* needed to have at their back was of less prominent people still, people who were not part of any élite at all. They needed to have them, not least, because the senate had enemies, more committed and (initially) more bitter enemies than did any other commune: they needed the widest support they could possibly muster, to be able to confront the power of popes like Innocent II.

Rome in the early twelfth century, as I have said, did not develop an assembly, unlike cities farther north. But the senate did. Its rapid institutional stabilisation had space for a *contio*, just as those of Milan and Pisa did, even if it postdated the commune, rather than preceding it: clearly the senatorial leadership felt they needed it, whether for consultation, or formal legitimation, or both. Not insignificantly, Arnaldo of Brescia is reported (even if by a hostile and later observer, John of Salisbury) as having been active in 'public *contiones*'. If, as I have been arguing, Rome's senate had an opening to non-élites, the *contio* is certainly one place where one would expect to have found them. And it is also striking that, in its judicial procedures, the senate acted with a degree of collectivity which one can hardly see elsewhere in Italy. The whole senate, up to sixty people, heard initial pleas, and substantial sections of their number were then told off to consider different parts of judgements, with many people thus directly involved. Although this was a more restricted grouping than the *contio*, it represented a collectivity which had more similarity to the traditional *placitum*, a structured judicial assembly, than to any other legal structure still in existence in 1150 elsewhere in Italy—one which had been allowed to end everywhere, but in Rome could be reinvented.[59] This too was an opening to a wider collectivity, which was, doubtless, to be controlled from the top, by a medium-level senatorial élite, but looked out to more people. Rome's commune thus was uniquely self-conscious, and uniquely open to a wide popular participation. The consciousness was doubtless helped by the fact that Italy by 1143 provided plenty of examples of how cities could be run with success by their own local leaders, without looking to traditional hierarchies, but it was also reactive, not to a power-vacuum this time, but to actual power, the new monarchical papacy of Innocent II. That was enough to set Rome off on a unique route, with a non-aristocratic protagonism which lasted for nearly fifty years: until, in fact, peace with the papacy in 1188 gave space for aristocratic families to come into the senate for the first time. They took it over, indeed, hardly a decade later. Not without trouble; the 'medium élite' fought back; but by Innocent III's death in 1216

Rome's commune was as dominated by aristocrats as was any other, and in fact rather more than some.[60] That is not part of my remit to discuss, however; in 1150 that was very far from the case, and the non-aristocratic commune did not weaken for some time.

Let us leave a Roman focus at this point, and go back to parallels: first of all, parallels between our three case studies, so that we can reprise the similarities and differences between them; then, in the next chapter, we will take a fast tour of other Italian cities to see where they fit in, as we move to a conclusion. I shall be here characterising, in particular, the differences between the political activities of my three urban élite strata, an urban aristocracy with land in the city and the countryside alike, in castles as well; a second leading stratum with a smaller but still substantial rural landholding and more urban (including commercial) wealth, which in Milan was mostly not seen as aristocratic, although in Rome it was; and the third-level 'medium élite' which I have characterised for Milan and, in more detail, for Rome, with enough land to allow its members to be rentiers but no more than that.

In Pisa, the topmost stratum out of these three was very small, and not active in the commune. The consular élite was above all from the second stratum. It was not defined as aristocratic, and was not explicitly separated from the rest of the city; none of its members (not even the Visconti) had the rural wealth and signorial involvement which would have made them parallel to any *capitaneus* of Milan; they would not, that is to say, have made it as even small-scale rural lords, and had to focus on urban power if they were to rule anything.

But, conversely, they were fully dominant in the city already in the eleventh century, and, when their assembly politics crystallised in a communal direction by around 1110, very precociously indeed, the traditional urban élite remained securely in charge of it; they never surrendered that hegemony, with, as it appears, remarkably little reaction from less prominent élite strata. 'Medium-élite' judicial experts and other members of the third stratum were sometimes consuls, but rarely made it to top-rank city leadership here, and jurists with less land were not consuls at all. The internal hierarchy of Pisa thus had an apex of families who were less prominent than in the other two cities, but they had a very secure local hegemony. This was aided, probably, by the absence of effective alternative powers; Pisa's archbishop was less dominant than were his counterparts in either Milan or Rome, and in fact established his power for the first time in the twelfth century in cooperation with the commune itself. The crystallisation of the commune was not perceived as any sort of real break here, partly because the Pisans were first and did not have any models, partly because the people who effectively ran the city did not change, and partly because the Pisans had a sense of the victorious honour of their city which seems to have transcended the details of who actually governed it.

In Milan, however, a contrast between aristocrats and other élites is much more visible; even if the city's aristocrats did not have large numbers of rural lands or more than a couple of castles per family, they certainly had a feudal and signorial interest which was more important than in Pisa. They were distinguished both from the second-level urban élite which did not aspire to this (the leading families of *cives* and probably some *valvassores*, who were the equivalents of the consular élite of Pisa), and from the third-level 'medium élite' of less rich owners, including again judicial experts. This contrast may have gone back to the city uprisings of the 1040s–70s, and it was certainly present in the contrast between aristocratic and judicial consuls in and after the 1140s. The slow crystallisation, out of the city's assembly, of the leadership of something which we can call a commune, took place quite largely inside the archbishop's entourage and in a clearly aristocratic context, beginning to come into focus from the late 1110s, but not fully structuring itself until the 1130s. Then, however, the balance inside the city did shift, and not just to the leading *cives* stratum; here, 'medium-élite' judicial consuls rapidly became very prominent towards the end of our period, in both consular acts and consular policy—in the crucial dealings with Frederick Barbarossa, in particular. The commune gained in self-awareness only very slowly, however, as in Pisa, perhaps because, as I have argued, even the judicial consuls in Milan were unusually interested in aristocratic practices, as we saw for Oberto dall'Orto. This may also help to explain the absence of trouble, in an often troubled city, during the rapid move to centrality of the 'medium-élite' judicial stratum. We might wonder (especially given what happened in Rome) whether it would have been conceivable that the attraction of being close to the archbishop might have kept the first aristocratic stratum wholly out of the commune, had the archbishop wanted to exert direct power in the city; after all, some aristocrats did indeed keep a distance from the judicial-led commune. But it is likely that the power-base of archbishops was rather less solid than was that of popes in Rome; the fact that two archbishops were deposed in Milan in 1111 and 1135, simply because their urban support crumbled, shows that in itself. First-level families like the da Rhò drew their own conclusions, and remained associated with Oberto and Girardo Cagapisto and their 'medium-élite' consular peers.

In Rome, there was a similar contrast between an aristocracy and other citizens, but here the division was between the first two economic strata, both of them called *nobiles* and the like, and a third 'medium élite' stratum which had the modestly prosperous resources which its counterparts had elsewhere too. It would be possible here to imagine a scenario which led the less rich second stratum of Rome's aristocracy to separate themselves from the richest level, that of the Frangipane, as in Pisa, but in actual fact the two consistently acted as a single group, both in the entourage of the local bishop—the pope—and, in the 1120s–30s, when that entourage was a less effective and inviting patronage structure, together with a wider although still informal city collectivity. Around 1140, however, the pope managed to re-establish the centrality of his court, and both levels of the aristocracy attached themselves to it. The 'medium élite' were left without a collective link with the two upper élite strata, and instead established their Roman commune against the latter, in 1143, with a consciousness and indeed a violence which is absent in either Pisa or Milan.

This in itself illustrates the importance which collective action had by now come to have in Italian cities. But it also shows that communes did not all have to be unconscious, and the result of compromise, or else exemplifications of continuity. In Milan we can see signs of compromise, but the rise of judicial consuls marks a visible discontinuity; in Pisa there was less need to compromise, but plenty of continuity; in Rome there was a sharp break, and no real compromise at all, until fifty years after the commune began—and also an awareness of what was going on which the other two cities

lacked. These considerable differences were however the result of a differing dialectic between three social strata which
were in themselves not at all dissimilar from city to city. All
these strata made up the urban mounted militia as described
by Maire Vigueur, as I have stressed, but it should now be
clear that this common military identity only explains part
of the reality of the early communes; how the social strata of
the élite interacted, in different ways in each city, had a major
effect on how each commune turned out. Maire Vigueur certainly shows that there were differences in the detailed social
composition of communal leaderships,[61] but the contrasts I
have just outlined seem to me to have a wider explanatory
power: this is how we might be able to get further with understanding *why* each commune was different, throughout
central-northern Italy.

To flesh this out, in a concluding chapter I will look, very
rapidly, at a rather larger set of other Italian communes, so
that it becomes clearer to what extent my three main case
studies speak for the whole. Other communes are often not
fully studied from the directions I have chosen here; but they
at least allow us to see how a typology of communes can be
understood. We will then be able to return to the problem of
what city leaders thought they were doing when they moved
into the new communal world, but by now on the basis of a
wider range of examples.

5

ITALY

When we enlarge our vision to the whole of Italy—or at least the whole of central and northern Italy, the land of city communes that is to say—the way our analysis can be done has to change. No other city has the complex mixture of data which we have looked at for our three case studies; in particular, no other city (except, in part, Genoa) has really dense narrative sources for the period 1050–1150, so they give us social rather than cultural parallels; and most cities have fewer documents as well. The studies of other cities are also very variable in quality; for the earliest commune, only a handful of cities have really strong accounts.[1] So this chapter will be more structural than the others; it will also be more speculative in some cases. What I want to show here, therefore, is a range of urban experience, focussed on fifteen or so other cities; this will have to be briefer and less dense in each case, but also, where possible, not schematic, for we need always to recognise the uniqueness of each example. I shall group the cities regionally, looking in turn at Piemonte; Lombardy and Emilia; Romagna and the Veneto; and Tuscany, although beginning my discussions with the only two other communes which seem to have developed as early as Pisa, that is to say Genoa and perhaps Asti. The closest parallelisms do not all fit these regional divisions, but some do, and it is in any case a realistic way to set it out, for if, as is generally assumed—and I am sure rightly—that cities regularly borrowed best practice from each other, practice by practice, institution by institution, they are most likely to have done this from their nearest neighbours. The most successful previous attempts to discuss different communal realities as a collective group, by Renato Bordone and Jean-Claude Maire Vigueur, indeed chose a very similar démarche.[2] We will then come to the widest generalising, and back to my three main cities, at the end.

Caffaro of Caschifellone's detailed history of the commune of Genoa, the earliest dedicated *Annals* for any commune in Italy, begins with a flourish: 'At the time of the expedition to Caesarea, just before it, in the city of the Genoese, a *compagna* of three years and of six consuls was begun'. He is referring to the Genoese participation in the First Crusade, and his later datings make it clear that he means 1099 here. The word *compagna* was a synonym of *commune* in later Genoese documents, and this seems a very precise first date for a commune. It can be seen as all the more authoritative because Caffaro in his early twenties actually took part in the crusade, as he says in another historical text he wrote about it, *De liberatione civitatum Orientis*. Caffaro was furthermore himself a consul, several times, from the first year of the single-year consulate in 1122 until the end of the 1140s, and he was already a trusted envoy for the commune in 1120 (as also, in his seventies, to Barbarossa in 1154 and 1158, like Oberto dall'Orto); he was even a (losing) party in one of the first-known communal court cases, in 1111.[3] So he was heavily involved in the commune in its earliest years, and ought to be assumed to know what he was talking about. But he wrote his *Annals* from, as it appears, the late 1140s onwards, decades after—he formally presented it to the commune in 1152 so as to be authorised to continue it as an official record—and it is also by no means a naïve text. It begins with the 1099 *compagna*, as we have seen, certainly a symbolic date for him, but in the *De liberatione* he states casually that that was in reality a renewal, for in 1099 internal strife had meant that the Genoese 'for a year and a half had gone without a *consulatus* or concord'. As we have seen, the first known Genoese consul, Amico Brusco, apparently already holding a rotating office, in fact appears as a witness in a document of 1098. We thus cannot accurately date the earliest Genoese commune, any more than we can date most communes. But we are also entitled to wonder whether, in reality, it was much more organised in its earliest years than the not-quite-communes we have seen for Milan and Pisa in the same decade. Caffaro gives us the names of the consuls for every year from 1099 to the end of his text in 1163, telling us that they were 'all consuls of the commune and of the *placita*' until the two sequences of consuls were separated in 1130 for the first time (he was himself one of the first judicial *consules de placitis*), but he must be using later terminology for the earliest period here. In his account of the First Crusade, he names Guglielmo Caputmalli as a 'consul of the army of the Genoese', who is clearly simply an army leader. Caffaro explicitly identifies the consulate with concord, and his whole text is a manifesto for concord as it is established through institutional organisation, to the extent that he abandoned writing it in 1163, three years before his death at the age of eighty-six, because, his continuator Oberto *cancellarius* surmises, he could not cope with the growing civil disturbance of the period. This ideological charge means, however, that we cannot assume that the commune was really born as institutionalised as he later claimed.[4]

There are not many Genoese documents for the first consuls; one of the two earliest references is an oath of military aid to the king of Jerusalem in 1104–5, which might well be being sworn by army leaders, not city rulers. Similar early documents from Sardinia and Provence in 1107–9—i.e. in the western Mediterranean, and not in a context of warfare—refer, instead, to the *cives* or the *populus* of Genoa, rather than to its consuls, even if a consul witnesses one of these. On the other hand, consuls acting inside the city in a formal way appear already also in 1104–5, in the first known consular judgement anywhere; this is followed by similar texts (written according to the same, fairly succinct, notarial formulary) in 1109, 1110, 1111, 1116, 1117, 1123, 1127 (twice), and then often from the 1130s onwards.[5] The first few of these show the consuls judging before large numbers of people, often called *in parlamento* or *in compagna*, that is to say in the city assembly (the 1117 text is in fact the first reference to the word which came to mean 'parliament' known to me), although later consular judgements do not seem to be in front of any collectivity. And from now on we get a wider range of texts which show an increasingly institutionalised city government: the assignment in 1120 by the *consules et civitas* of enormous sums of money to Caffaro and another envoy to give to the Roman Curia in return for the ending of Pisan ecclesiastical control over Corsica; and, even more notably, the beginning, in 1130, 1133–34 and 1139–40, of consular legislation for the city, the first surviving in Italy, and the *breve*, again the first known in Italy, which lists sworn consular obligations to the *commune* or *compagna*, from 1143.[6]

Caffaro thus would like us to think that Genoa's commune was already organised in 1099, with some antecedents; but the documents allow us to conclude that it was not until around 1105—not so much later, but the half-decade is still significant—that it began to be more formalised as an institution. This is still very early indeed for an Italian city; but, as important, such a dating is closely parallel to that of

Pisa, whose first 'consuls' go back even earlier, to the 1080s, but whose organised commune is first documented four years later than in the Ligurian city, in the period 1109–13. Genoa was similar to Pisa in other ways too, for its consular élite seems to have been long-standing and stable, and urban rather than signorial—Caffaro's own family, with (perhaps) its single castle, was as signorial as it mostly got. Although the number of families supplying consuls steadily grew across the twelfth century, it is in fact most likely that Genoa's consuls were largely from the second élite stratum characterised in earlier chapters; the handful of first-stratum families, such as the Doria and the Spinola, did not dominate the others.[7] Its leadership, judging by our consular lists, indeed did not greatly change from the beginning of the twelfth century to the end (we do not have enough documents to know about the eleventh), by which time, indeed by the 1150s, the uniquely early notarial records of the city show very clearly how much nearly every leading Genoese family was also involved in commerce.[8] Genoa also recognised a prominent but not dominant role for its bishop; consuls were his vassals very often, but this did not have much effect on their political practice. All this had near-exact parallels in Pisa. One major difference was that Genoese consuls ran court cases themselves, as in Milan and Rome but not Pisa; this does not seem, however, to have led to the prominence of a stratum of legal experts, possibly because Genoese legal practice, judging by the surviving cases, was not yet very complex. There is also more evidence in Genoa than in other cities for a belief that the commune might not be permanent.[9] But, notwithstanding that, Genoa's judicial system was regularised two decades earlier than Pisa's, for its early consular court cases are much more numerous, and its first consular legislation is earlier too (the 1130s as opposed to the 1140s). It was not until the next decades that the Pisans caught up and moved ahead in this arena, for Pisa's substantial law-code of the late 1150s, and the Romanisation of its judicial system, well predated anything similar in Genoa.[10]

Pisa and Genoa, rivals and enemies at every step on both land and sea, thus both were, we can be fairly sure, the earliest organised communes. They had fairly similar social structures for their élites and fairly similar military and commercial maritime commitments; and the datings proposed here for the activities of their leaders also reinforce each other, allowing us to recognise a level of at least initial institutionalisation in each case in 1105–10, and developing thereafter at a roughly similar pace, although the Genoese judicial system was routinised rather earlier than that at Pisa. The main way in which they were not parallel was in the vicious internal wars between leading families in the 1160s and 1180s–90s in Genoa, which have hardly any equivalent in Pisa at all.[11] But together these two cities provide one element in a typology of communes, for they were more similar to each other than either was to any other documented city.

Asti, the other Italian city which shows active early consuls, is more of a problem. Asti is tucked away in a valley of the Monferrato, in Piemonte, but was on one of the routes from the western Alpine passes into the rest of Italy, and developed a strong commercial and financial sector fairly early. It was in the area dominated by the marquises of Turin until their effective extinction in 1091, and Asti's bishops, who were very strong in the city, were closely associated with the marquises as well; the Astigiani revolted against both in 1066 and 1091, as brief contemporary narratives say (there are, however, no detailed early narratives for the city itself). The city thus had a certain coherence as a proactive body, and documents of the next decades show it both establishing a sphere of influence with respect to the bishop, who controlled the city's justice and commercial activity, and also extending its power into the countryside. In 1095, the bishop invested the consuls of Asti with the castle of Annone in benefice, 'both for themselves and for all the Astigian citizens', to be held 'to the common *utilitas* of these citizens', in a text witnessed by a set of episcopal vassals; in 1098 the consuls of Asti 'together with the vassals, for the common *utilitas* and for the benefit of the [cathedral] church of S. Maria and the common honour of the Astigian citizens', proposed a military treaty with Count Umberto II of Maurienne, over the Alpine passes into what is now France, which assumed among other things that Umberto would help Asti if asked 'by the common counsel of the consuls of the time (*pro tempore*)', and that Umberto would also agree not to come into Italy (*Longobardia*) for more than eight days at a time without the consuls' agreement.[12]

These are remarkable signs of the early affirmation of a city collectivity, with, as it seems, an established and rotating consular leadership. They are backed up by successful moves into the countryside, with cessions by rural lords which begin in 1108, and an agreement in 1103 between the bishop, the consuls, and a family of rural lords to the west to guarantee free Astigian commercial transit in the latter's region. The property of the *commune* as a body appears by 1123, when the consuls sell some of it to the cathedral canons. The consuls, furthermore, are conceptually separated from the episcopal vassals from the start, and seem (even though a detailed prosopography has not been published) to remain largely separate from the episcopal clientele for the rest of the century. This would then seem to be a commune which had gained a political coherence in opposition to its traditional rulers (in part perhaps for religious reasons; the citizens, or some of them, were pro-Patarene, the marquise Adelaide and her bishop pro-imperial) and, importantly, kept its distance from them thereafter. And it also had a definable consular government so early that it is the earliest attested case anywhere of consuls actually ruling and acting for an autonomous city collectivity—which here as elsewhere took an assembly format, a *comune coloquium* as the 1108 text calls it, a *communi conventus populi* in a text of 1111.[13] This would have implications for my dating of the rulership of the consuls of Pisa (and Genoa too): for, if Asti's consuls had a formalised leadership role already in 1095, we might scarcely doubt that those of Pisa, the city which generated the terminology, and Genoa, linked agonistically with Pisa and not far from Asti, would have done so by then as well.

The problems come with the other signs we have of Asti's political framework. The text of 1111 shows the bishop as more of a power than most of those I have so far mentioned: in it, he imposes a compromise over a contested piece of land between the cathedral canons and the *populus* of Asti, getting the *consules et civitatis sapientiores* of the city to concede the land to the canons in return for a pay-off; and he is also visible as the power most capable of confirming the rights of a local monastery, S. Anastasio, whose documents partially survive, in the years after 1096, with the citizens simply appearing as witnesses alongside his vassals, sometimes called consuls (as in 1096), sometimes simply *cives*.[14] The 1108 text, too, refers to the *cives* of the city, not the consuls. And after the protagonism of the 1090s, the further institutionalisation of the commune of Asti was apparently long delayed; the first surviving court case with consular judges is as late as 1185.[15]

This makes me wonder if the key texts of 1095 and 1098 are not ripe for a rethink. They both appear in a communal cartulary of the fourteenth century, which in fact preserves most of the early communal documents; the first originals with the consuls in are those of 1096 and 1111, which show them in a somewhat more subordinate, and potentially informal, role. Both the 1095 and the 1098 texts have been shown by one of the major experts on Asti, Gian Giacomo Fissore, to have been revised by the later compilers, with some sections of each text omitted; that of 1098, furthermore, is incomplete, and is best interpreted as a draft, not a legally valid text—in effect a wish-list of Asti's rights with respect to Count Umberto, and one which the count would have been highly unlikely to agree to (the idea that the consuls of Asti, which was anyway not the city closest to the Alps, could veto his visits to Italy already in 1098 is particularly implausible). That these are the only early texts which show the consuls in an organised leadership role is thus troubling. It would be easy to propose that the word *consules* was interpolated into the first, and that the second was not just a draft, further revised later, but very heavily reworked indeed, perhaps *verfälscht*, to use the German term. The 1103 text, too, survives only in a nineteenth-century edition with problematic elements to it.[16] More work would have to be done to test this; but I would prefer to see Asti in the 1090s–1100s as a city with an active assembly and a still-informal leadership, and with a consular government only slowly crystallising thereafter, maybe by 1111, certainly by 1123. This is still early, but not so early, which also better fits its even slower development of any known judicial institutions for two generations more. Asti was definitely not a commune dominated by its bishop, all the same. The bishop remained powerful in the city for some time, but the consuls were not 'his', as Landolfo of S. Paolo put it for Milan (above, p. 32).

Asti was without doubt the first city commune in Piemonte, all the same, by any measure. Apart from Vercelli, other cities were in this period still relatively small, and the region, long dominated by powerful marquises, was one in which traditional powers, including bishops, remained strong. Cities were certainly capable of acting as collectivities, as when the bishop of Turin in 1112–18 consulted with the men of Alba, Asti, Vercelli, and Ivrea in a dispute over tithes. Asti, as we have seen, was already developing internal governing structures, but we can conclude nothing from this about the others, for the terminology here could have come from any of the early medieval centuries. In Tortona, consuls with a rotating tenure appear in 1122, in Novara in 1139, in Vercelli in 1141, in other cities even later.[17] Vercelli, which was not only relatively sizable but is also a well-studied commune, had consuls acting autonomously in the 1140s (for the *universitas*, another word for commune, in 1141), but they are largely members of the episcopal entourage; they are urban, sometimes judicial figures, including only one signorial family in that decade, but are nonetheless closely attached to the bishop for the most part. In the period after 1165, when we know more of their names (and when consular tribunals appear), the second-level élite, reasonably well-off landowners, mostly without signorial interests, is overwhelmingly dominant. In 1150–65, however, consuls seem to have ceased to exist, and episcopal government reasserted itself for a period; this is a good example of the 'latent' commune as characterised by Giuliano Milani.[18] Bishops were indeed the key interlocutors of all the Piemontese communes; even if in the south communes (Asti, later Alba, to an extent Tortona) were relatively autonomous of them, in the north (Vercelli, Novara) episcopal entourages extended into the consulate, for all that the families concerned were, at least in Vercelli, essentially urban-focussed. We do not know, for our documentation is too sketchy, how many of the communes were as protagonistic as Asti and how many were as weak, as 'latent', as Vercelli, but the odds are on a predominance of the second type. The work has also not been done (or, at least, published) for any of them that would allow us to determine what economic resources city leaders had, except for Vercelli.

When we reach Lombardy and Emilia, we reach the traditional heartland of royal power in the Kingdom of Italy, where the break-up of the power of the Kingdom in the two decades after 1080 might be expected to be particularly significant, and where cities were often much larger, and had been protagonistic for a long time before 1100. We would expect relatively early communes here, for cities had the demographic weight and the powerful élites which would allow them to react creatively to the power-vacuum of the years around 1100, and we indeed find them. We might also assume that the model of Milan, far and away the largest city in this region, with an archbishop whose authority extended to all the cities except Pavia, would be a dominant one; but actually the cities here did not follow the Milanese pattern of development with any consistency, even though the military *ordines* of *capitanei* and *valvassores* are visible in most of them (as also in Vercelli, not far west of Milan), as Keller established.[19] I will focus on the three best-documented and most fully studied communes, Bergamo, Piacenza, and Cremona, with others relegated to endnotes.

In Bergamo, the consuls are praised for their active judicial and military role in Mosè del Brolo's *Liber Pergaminus* in c. 1120 (see above, p. 53)—as also is the city's aristocratic bishop, Ambrogio Mozzi. In documents, assemblies are referenced from the late eleventh century, after some late *placita* (up to 1091); consuls are first mentioned, uncertainly, in 1108. We have, however, clear evidence for them in 1117 and 1133, and then more regularly from 1144 (the first consular court case), a dating very close to that of Milan. Some of the castle-holding aristocracy kept out of the commune, but some (for instance the da Gorlago, or, soon, the powerful Mozzi themselves) can be seen to have been regular consuls once the lists become denser, along with a larger number of urban notables, who themselves, more and more, gained fiefs and signorial rights from the bishop in the early twelfth century. The consulate was thus very much one of feudal/signorial families in the bishop's *curia*, who had been the city's élite for a century and more, but most of whom had only recently entered the military-aristocratic world. The parallels with Milan remain here too, but it is less clear than in the larger city that the judicial expertise shown in later consular documents is associated with a significant stratum of legally experienced consuls without episcopal connections or rural power: in the consular cases of the 1140s–50s there is only one *iudex* of the Oberto dall'Orto type, prominent in the city but with no documented landholding at all, Arnaldo of Azzano, who is simply flanked in the consular lists by the old and new signorial families. As a result, a continuity of traditional élite dominance is more apparent; we are dealing here with the first and second stratum of the élite almost exclusively.[20]

Conversely, the commune is protagonistic, from the start. In 1117, the first consular document begins 'We, [ten names,] the consuls of the city, [and two other men,] by the word and agreement of almost all the other citizens of Bergamo', before granting land to a rural church; another act of the same month is very similar indeed, and this time specifies that the land concerned belongs *ad cummune civitatis*, the commune as a noun owning its own land, as at Asti in 1123. The word 'almost' is an interesting nuance: this is a city community which has reached a decision against opposition and is happy to record it. The 1117 texts are not followed up for twenty-five years, but this instance of a very clear proactivity (in, unlike at Asti, documents surviving in contemporary copies), plus the invocation of judicial activity by Mosè shortly afterwards, makes me feel that it is less likely that this is a 'latent' commune, with intermittent consuls, like Vercelli—this being my only disagreement with the excellent analysis of it by Gianmarco De Angelis. Bergamo in fact may have been a higher-profile commune than Milan was as yet; only from the 1130s would Milan's new political system become more visible—more than Bergamo's, soon—as we have seen.[21]

Piacenza similarly shows the continuity of an élite, ruling the city both before 1100 and in the period of the consular commune—Pierre Racine's 'seigneurie collective': two-thirds of the eighty-two consuls known from before 1150 are indeed from only six families, all close to the bishop. This time, however, almost all of them are second-level aristocratic families, without signorial involvement. Racine regards this as a sign of rural power over the city and a predominance of rural values, but we have seen for Milan and Pisa that second-level families such as these are in general quite distinct from rural-orientated families; in Piacenza some of the major castle-owning families, such as the dell'Andito, already provided consuls too, but they were in a minority. We do not have contemporary narratives for Piacenza which tell us about values. The thirteenth-century chronicle of Giovanni Codagnello simply gives us a set-piece account of a major conflict between *milites* and *pedites* in the city in 1090 which historians have taken far too seriously as reportage—it can better be seen as a late, highly rhetorical founding charter for a magnate-*popolo* conflict which made more sense after 1200. Conversely, we can say that the city had an assembly by 1093, a *conventus civium*, called a *concio* by 1126 when the first consuls are documented (they appear slightly later than in Milan and Bergamo, although the city fights its own wars by 1117). This was an organised public body by 1135, for it was making law, as in contemporary Genoa, and earlier than any other city; its first known consular court case dates to 1133, too. When the military élites of the city went in a communal direction, then, they moved quite fast in institutional terms. It is not easy to see this in terms of rural power, and the whole pattern of the city's development is not really so very far from that of Pisa a generation earlier, in its long-term dominance by second-level landed families.[22]

Cremona, the last of this set, is in many respects unique in its development. For a start, it existed as an organised body very early indeed; the city's leadership had formed as a political force in struggles (originally over commercial tolls; later, over religious issues as well) against its dominant bishop and his rural vassals, which were unique in their severity, more or less continuously from the late tenth century to the late eleventh; then, for forty years from 1068 to 1110, the bishop, when there was one, failed to keep any foothold at all in this apparently pro-Patarene city. Small wonder then that the *comunum*—the first attestation anywhere of the noun—of the city is documented already in 1097, agreeing military service to Matilda of Tuscany in return for a large tract of territory around Crema in the north-west of the diocese, and this protagonism in the *contado* is fairly continuous from then on, as in well-known texts concerning the submission of the *milites* of the castle of Soncino in 1118 and 1120 and of that of Guastalla in 1127–28. In 1118 and 1120, the city's assembly is invoked too, a *consilium* or *aringum* (some version of this must anyway underlie the *comunum* of 1097); and communal justice begins to be documented in 1138, showing an institutionalisation which was by then well under way. But Cremona does not show much evidence for the public role of an organised consular élite. There are casual references to consuls in 1112–16, and then only three times again before 1150; they are indeed only regularly attested at all in the period 1157–82, before they were substituted by *podestà*. The city will have been entirely aware of the normal usage of the word consul to mean a city leader, first informal, and then with a growing claim to rulership, as we have by now often seen. For 1132, indeed, copies of letters survive between the *consules et universi cives maiores et minores* of Cremona and their opposite numbers in Pavia, which show them fronting for the commune by then, as one would expect for this region. But Cremona's communal leadership remained for long an informal, even if active, body. François Menant in his important study of the city, when he gives us a prosopography of the city's leaders, thus has to include anyone, consul or not, who seems to be a representative of the city in our documentation. As one might expect for a city with such a contestatory tradition, there are few major rural lords among them; if several are episcopal vassals by the twelfth century (when tensions with the bishop had diminished), this is not so significant, for the bishop had many small-scale vassals in Cremona. Some are judicial families with no episcopal links, of a type we have amply seen in Milan. And, very unusually (except in Rome), some are explicitly artisans.[23] There was a continuity of an urban élite in

Cremona from the eleventh century into the twelfth, of lesser rentiers, both second- and third-level families here. But its conflictual origins meant that it was less associated than in Milan with the first élite level, richer landed families with signorial rights, and that it opened politically to a rather wider set of social strata than in either Bergamo or Piacenza. And, to repeat, Cremona's formally organised assembly seems to have been happy to have a relatively informal leadership for an unusual length of time.[24]

The Lombard-Emilian communes have a substantial variety of developments, as we can see from this survey: with the bishop prominent in some (Bergamo, Parma for a time, and of course Milan up to the 1130s) but rather less so in others (Pavia, Cremona); with signorial lords/*capitanei* prominent in the early commune only in a few (again Milan, with some in Bergamo, fewer in Piacenza, and very few in Cremona); with fairly smooth continuities with the past visible in several (Milan initially, Bergamo, Pavia—where the continuities are, unusually, secular), but with a sharp break particularly clear in Cremona, where tensions with traditional powers had long been high. Milan's development from the 1130s away from the purely aristocratic commune, of which it is so often regarded as the archetype, into a commune which not only had a substantial number of signorial families in it but was also largely dominated by 'medium-élite' judicial consuls with few landed resources, has however little parallel in the other cities. This is where the largest city of the region, although in many respects conservative, also showed itself to be the most radical, along with Cremona. Nonetheless, one thing that links all these various cities (and others, not discussed here, Como and Lodi[25]) is that they all show a similar, and early, pacing for communal development, with assemblies and/or consuls usually visible by the 1110s and sometimes earlier, in most cases some clear evidence of the institutionalisation of key elements of the communal ideal type by the 1130s, and in all by 1150 or so. This generalised early development thus does indeed fit the argument, already proposed, that it was the royal heartland, where the failure of the Kingdom was more immediately visible than elsewhere, which necessitated early defensive measures from cities which were themselves in many cases already protagonistic in other ways. It may well also reflect the fact that all these cities (except Piacenza) had to fight the unusually aggressive army of Milan, and thus needed an organisation which could match up to the challenge.

Let us now move east, into the Veneto and Romagna, and also move faster, for there is less to say about the early communes here—of which the main ones with studies are Bologna, Ferrara, Ravenna, Verona, Padua, and Venice, to which we can add Modena, not in the region as now defined but just to the west of it. In all these except Venice, the régime inside which communes formed was episcopal above all, and bishops remained strong for a long time in most of them as well: in Ferrara, Padua, and Modena in particular, where consuls remained episcopal vassals. In Ferrara, in the middle of the Po delta, where there were no major rural families, a consul is casually mentioned in 1105, and the 'commune' is a noun by 1120, quite early; the set of consuls seems to have been focussed around second-level landowners. In Padua, the process is later, with documents not beginning until 1138, even if the first of these already attests to consular justice, with a *concio*, conversely, only documented later, in 1142. Here, episcopal vassals dominated, but also—they were largely the same people—jurists and other legal professionals; these men were sometimes quite substantial landowners (and fief-holders), but in some cases cannot be seen with more than small holdings. They were second- but also third-level owners, and this pairing dominated the early commune; only a handful of (usually) small-scale castle-holding lords appear in our consular lists up to the 1180s. Verona, a larger city, has some contrasts to Padua here. Our evidence starts in 1136, again with a judicial document, again showing an institutionalisation which had already begun, but here the bishop is less predominant, and some of the new consuls are documented as merchants alongside their rural lands and, again, sometimes castles, the first and second levels of the urban élite apparently here acting together. In Ravenna, the most evanescent of this group, consuls from urban élite families (and one *capitaneus*) are known for 1109 and 1115, witnessing formal documents, but then are not directly attested again until the 1160s; this may indeed be another 'latent' commune, for the powerful archbishop and his following of *capitanei* (and, sometimes, *valvassores*) take back centre stage in the intervening period.[26]

Bologna, of all of these, was perhaps the city with the most active commune. It is first visible in a very protagonistic act of 1123 ('We, the consuls of Bologna, for us and our lord bishop Vittore and his successors, with our whole Bolognese *populus* ...'), although consuls are referred to again only four times before 1150. It too had, in the second half of the century when the names of consuls are known, a consulate dominated by twenty families of (mostly) second-level urban landowners, some of them certainly legal experts (as is hardly surprising in as important an intellectual centre as Bologna), and also perhaps less attached to the bishop, who is less visible from now on in Bologna than in other cities in this wide area. Bologna, with Ferrara, seems to have begun to crystallise as a commune by the 1120s, even if not that fast (for the first surviving communal court case in Bologna is rather later, in 1149, and is the work of the *concives*, the assembly—not yet the *iudices comunis*, who only appear in this role in 1157); Verona and Padua by the late 1130s; and a similar shift is slightly later in Modena, where consuls, referred to in 1134, are not named until 1142 (in an episcopal document), and are temporarily replaced in the 1150s (as also happened in Verona, Bologna, and in some other cities) by a single *rector*.[27]

The Veneto and Romagna cities are the classic instances of centres where bishops remained relatively important for some time, even though their urban communities were often substantial, sometimes (as with Verona and Bologna) as large as some of the leading cities of Lombardy. They were not, any of them, cities where new élites appeared to rule the city, although here as elsewhere—and fastest in Verona and Bologna, indeed—episcopal rule was steadily hollowed out and replaced by the political action of laymen, even if they for the most part remained part of the bishop's own entourage. This picture, often regarded as the normal one for Italian communes as a whole, still works particularly well in this region: it is the type-example, that is to say, for the formation of communes inside traditional power-structures, less protagonistically than in Lombardy-Emilia (let alone the port cities) but, by the end of the twelfth century, with much the same eventual results.

Only Venice stands out here: on the Rialto island, the duke remained fully at the head of the city's government. All the same, in the 1140s and onwards his acts come more and more to be performed in front of an assembly, a *colloquium*; by 1143 these are represented, in an already formalised way, by *viri sapientes*, described as *qui preerant consilio*; by 1147 the word 'commune' is a noun; and by 1148 the new duke tells us in a document that he has made an oath at his accession to *cuncto communi Venetico populo,* 'the whole common Venetian people'. The commune thus crystallised quickly here, but without changing the governmental system of the city at all—and, indeed, the *sapientes* and *iudices* of the rest of the century are overwhelmingly from families with visible roots before 1000. Andrea Castagnetti sees this as the élite ('i maggiorenti') of the city taking some power from the dukes, and it is certainly the case that from now, slowly, the complex and often stifling bureaucracy of the city, which constrained everybody into the future, began to develop; this power-sharing with old families has some parallels with the situation elsewhere in the Veneto-Romagna cities, although here ducal power was by no means hollowed out.[28] But for our purposes what it also shows is simply that, by the 1140s, a communal (clearly, not here consular) imagery and collective ceremonial practice was part of the air breathed in the cities of the Po plain, and that it by now seemed logical to adopt it even if nothing else changed—for Venice never became anything much which resembled a bottom-up political system.

Finally, let us look at Tuscany, to give a regional context to Pisa this time, here concentrating on three other well-studied cities, Lucca, Florence, and Arezzo. Here, even more than in Lombardy-Emilia, the civil wars resulted in a fast collapse of traditional powers, in this case the unusually coherent March of Tuscany, and episcopal power had in most cities never been very great either, so we might expect communes to crystallise relatively early; but in fact, apart from Lucca (and, of course, Pisa) this did not occur. Lucca, which was relatively large although not as commercially orientated as Pisa, developed in ways which were not dissimilar to those of its neighbour, at least after the eleventh century, when urban politics was dominated by a single leading landowning and judicial family, the Flaiperti/Avvocati. Its consuls are first mentioned in 1119, apparently in a subordinate position to the local bishop, but in the context of a 'multitude of the Lucchese *populus*', presumably an assembly. Assemblies are otherwise ill-documented in Lucca, but this is a possible sign of their priority in the city, as a formalisation of the more inchoate collectivities which argued about rival bishops in the 1080s. Already by 1120, however, consuls are city representatives, and the commune also from now on developed without reference to the bishop, with a *cancellarius* in 1127, consular court cases starting in 1136 and becoming frequent soon after, and a set of largely successful wars in the same period to control its contado; its institutionalisation was in fact rapid, and pretty complete by the 1150s. Its twelfth-century *consules maiores* were from a wider range of families than at Pisa, however: they could be from first-level and partially signorial families, with close links to the bishop, such as the *filii Malpilii* and the Avvocati (by the 1130s in the former case, after waiting a generation in the latter; but other major signorial and episcopal families stayed out of the commune entirely, until the end of the century); second-level families such as, slightly later, the Antelminelli; and also third-level families such as that of Salomone di Salomone, who only owned substantially in a single village. The last-named is interesting as—like the Pierleoni in Rome—he may have had Jewish origins; he was nonetheless one of the first known consuls, already in 1119, and again in 1123 and 1140; and he also served as a judicial consul in the 1130s. Other third-level families, however, like that of the Roman lawyer Rolando di Guamignano later in the century, only served as judicial consuls, who were in Lucca not as powerful as the *consules maiores*, and who, as in Pisa, could also be men from families with little or no documented land at all. This implies that third-level families tended to drop out of the ruling élite; this too has parallels with Pisa. But the hegemony of that élite, even though more buttressed here by support from signorial families, was less complete than at Pisa; a *popolo*-based resistance broke out in war already in 1203.[29]

If we move inland in Tuscany, however, communal organisation appeared rather later. In Florence, well-studied by Enrico Faini, consuls are first documented as late as 1138, and then only named once more before a series of consular acts (including the first regular court cases) survive from the 1170s; even then, they do not seem yet to have imposed themselves fully as the city's political focus. The city before that seems to have been run very informally indeed, by urban leaders sometimes called *maiores* and the like; nor does the bishop, who was certainly a major landowner, appear with any regularity as a political focus, except briefly in the 1120s. There was certainly a power-vacuum here. Matilda had used Florence as a base in her last years, and several other major aristocratic families such as the Guidi and Cadolingi were active there up to 1100 or so, but they either died out or ceased to be active in the city's political arena shortly afterwards; so too, unusually, did the rest of the castle-owning aristocracy of the eleventh century, which had played a substantial part in eleventh-century urban politics, but which left the city and separated itself out into signorial territories in Florence's large contado after 1100, as Maria Elena Cortese has shown. The city was left to very urban-based families (and rural landowning by city-dwellers had dropped substantially), led by the Caponsacchi, Giandonati, and Visdomini, all three of which could best be characterised after 1100 as second-level élite families; but they and others do not seem to have needed an organised political structure for a long time—it is worth remarking here that Florence was not for most of the twelfth century a particularly large or economically important centre; that development came later. Any communal element before 1170 is described by Faini as 'evanescent' (even an assembly is invisible in our evidence), and he suggests that consular office was only occasional before then, too; this certainly fits the model of the 'latent' commune which we have seen for Vercelli and Ravenna, although there was, here, no traditional power-structure to take over at times in its place. In the 1170s, however, the newly visible consuls included not only members of the Caponsacchi and Giandonati, but also more powerful urban élite families with some signorial rights in the countryside, the Fifanti and Uberti, as well; and also, significantly, a set of families with little land and a documented involvement in credit, and several who cannot be identified at all: third-level families and maybe lesser families again.[30]

We might conclude from this that Florence stayed together as a community, including all levels of urban society, in apposition to the contado (in opposition, too, indeed: the city's takeover of its territory was long and difficult). This collectivity would thus have allowed a much wider set of social strata to exercise authority—although we need not doubt that the families already cited acted as a de facto leadership, and the higher élite strata (and also, now, newly urbanised signorial lords) took over the city's highest offices more fully in later decades. But it is still very striking that this community seems to have crystallised so slowly into any form of organised body. Faini cautiously proposes that part of this is a documentary illusion, and that, in particular, it is only with the 1170s that texts referring to consular judgements were kept in church archives.[31] It is indeed close to impossible to imagine how the city, even if it was not a large centre yet, could have managed with no formalised authority at all for over half a century, in a period in which it was, furthermore, involved in numerous contado wars. I wonder if what is hidden from our documentation is in fact not consuls, but rather an assembly, well-defined and cohesive enough to allow for a durable informality (indeed, incoherence) in its leadership; this would fit with the likely situation in Arezzo, as we shall see in a moment, and has parallels in Cremona too. But it would certainly be hard to say that the city had as yet, by the end of our period in 1150, many communal characteristics.

In Arezzo a consul, Raineri, appears as early as 1098, referred to as a witness, and as the father of another witness, in two private documents. Jean-Pierre Delumeau convincingly doubts that he had any formal role as a ruler—he was doubtless simply another example of the use of the word *consul* to denote members of the urban élite—and consuls are not referred to again until 1142. By then, however, the *universitas* of Arezzo had been involved, twice (in 1110 and 1129), in destroying the *castrum* of the local bishop, who, unusually, had his fortified cathedral outside the city, and was also the city's count. This looks like the city collectivity, presumably in assembly form, both operating as a recognised community and also acting, as in Rome and Cremona, in opposition to traditional powers—and more than to just the bishop, indeed: the 1110 action resulted in Henry V burning the town when he came through at the end of the same year. This political collectivity was thus a relatively early development, even if not as early as 1098; but it was followed by little else for a generation and more. The first named lay city ruler, in 1153, is actually not a consul at all, but a single *rector et gubernator*, as in Modena and Verona, here clearly acting in an assembly context (*in presentia populi in parlamento*); named consuls only begin in the 1160s, the first consular court case (an amateurish text) in 1167, and the first organised tribunals as late as the 1190s. Arezzo's hostility to its bishop had ended by now (no longer count, he now lived in the city, and the cathedral was moved at the end of the century too), and the institutionalisation of the commune seems to have become complete only after the end of the century. The identity of Arezzo's most prominent consuls in the 1160s–80s seems in every known case to be attached to the second level of the city's élite: well-off but non-castle-holding families (one of which, the Bostoli, were from a signorial background, but were themselves by now primarily urban and suburban dealers), unlike the more aristocratic group around the bishop in the previous generation. It is a pattern which we have found elsewhere, but here the lack of linkage to the episcopal clientele is even less surprising, given the events of the 1110s–20s.[32] Anyway, we have here, even more clearly than at Asti, an early collective proactivity, to which however was not added any of the other elements of the ideal-type commune for a very long time.

Tuscany, then, shows us a wide range of solutions to the problems which came from the collapse of the March. Unlike in the Veneto, these solutions did not usually relate very closely to bishops; even in Arezzo, where bishops had been genuinely powerful in the eleventh century, the city's community developed in opposition to them, rather than inside their clientele. They also show cities which were run above all by second-level and sometimes third-level élites, with little involvement of signorial powers; even though some urban families with a connection to the signorial world (notably the *filii Malpilii* in Lucca, and the Uberti in Florence) did commit early to Tuscan communes, these did not dominate in any city—although here we should distinguish between cities like Pisa and Lucca, where signorial families were anyway few and marginal, and cities like Florence and probably Arezzo, where such families had simply chosen not to involve themselves in twelfth-century city society. We can certainly say that the world of military *ordines* and episcopal courts was not strong in any of the Tuscan cities. This fits a region where, at least in the urbanised north, signorial powers were generally weak.[33] We can also say, more tentatively, that consular office was, when it appeared, available to a wider range of people in Florence, where it extended from signorial families (even if probably of the second level) to third-level families, than it was in Pisa; this may mark a community in Florence which felt itself more embattled, with a resultant greater need for inclusivity, than did its counterpart down the Arno on the coast. But it is above all clear that there was a very great difference between the experience of Pisa and Lucca, on the one hand, with communal structures which were fully developed long before the end of our period (very early in the case of Pisa), and the experience of the inland cities, on the other, where in the 1170s and even the 1190s they had only just got started. As in Piemonte, the inland cities were smaller, and could maybe therefore get away with less-defined political structures for longer. In Tuscany, a formalised assembly may have been enough government for two generations and more, as I have hypothesised for Florence, and as is slightly more visible in Arezzo. But it is still striking that cities which were by no means isolated from the rest of what can now be called communal Italy should have chosen to wait so long to follow their peers elsewhere.

———————————

The typology of different patterns of communal development which these different examples show is not a simple one. It is not helped by the wide variation in the density of documentation for each city, and the even wider quality of the studies of the early commune in each. I have tried to add to them with my three case studies, but there is more to be done there too. Only a systematic study of all the documents of north-central Italy across our period would allow us to be really sure that we were comparing like with like, and that huge task is not as yet on the horizon anywhere. But we can say some things, all the same, some of them speculative, but some less so.

The first point is that the chronological pacing of communal development follows some recognisable geographical lines. This is based, as usual, on the chance of our evidence, which only gives us a *terminus ante quem* for any given development (and sometimes not even that); but these geographical homogeneities give us some grounds for belief that the patterns are at least partly reliable. The earliest communes of all were the two ports of Pisa and Genoa, where communes had crystallised by 1110 or so; they each developed more institutional solidity subsequently, and they were also the first communes whose legislation survives (together with Piacenza), already in the 1130s–40s; the complexity of their governing structures remained unusually great thereafter too. After them came the major cities of Lombardy and Emilia, in the old royal heartland—plus Lucca, a key city in the March of Tuscany and intimately opposed to Pisa—where consuls had mostly appeared by 1120, usually preceded by assemblies, and where other elements of the communal ideal type are usually coming into visibility by the 1130s. (Once again, however, we cannot simply use the appearance of consuls as a metonym for the appearance of any fully fledged commune; there are several examples of cities with early 'consuls' but few signs of communal institutions, particularly not regularised communal court proceedings, until well after our period ends, such as Asti, Ravenna, Pistoia, and Arezzo.)[34] The cities of the Veneto and Romagna and part of Piemonte followed Lombardy a couple of decades later, with varying speeds of communal institutionalisation (rapid in Verona and Padua, and in the atypical case of Venice; less so elsewhere); Rome must be added here, with its sudden appearance and super-rapid consolidation inside a year in 1143–44, and so can Provence (also part of the empire), where communes appear in the 1130s–40s. The inland cities of Tuscany and the rest of Piemonte, and also outlying cities in the eastern Veneto and those of Umbria and Lazio, not discussed here, were much later in their development, which is usually hardly visible until after our period ends. It is in these outer areas, too, that we find our most likely examples of 'latent' communes, Vercelli, Ravenna, and Florence, which remind us that communal development does not have to be one-way only—a point reinforced, further south, by the experience of Benevento, where the commune, called here *communitas*, which appeared in 1128 (as often, in a period of political crisis) was reversed by Pope Anacletus II in 1130, and did not re-emerge in that form.[35]

This picture, of—to put it very schematically—the moves towards the commune spreading from the ports to

Lombardy-Emilia and then slowly outwards from there, has however already to be qualified by the sharp differences in other aspects of communal orientation. Bordone and Maire Vigueur have stressed the varying degrees to which communes formed around a signorial element in the episcopal clientele, from Milan, the archetype of the episcopal/signorial commune (but, as we have seen, only in the 1110s–20s), through cities like Padua, where the bishop was important but his urban clients were markedly less signorial, to Asti, Cremona, Rome, and most of the Tuscan cities, where (either because the bishop was too strong or because he was too weak) city leaders were not closely associated with him at all. But we have seen other sorts of distinction which can be made too: for example in the importance in the communal leadership of judicial figures, often not very substantial landowners, which is particularly visible in Milan after the 1130s, but can also be seen—again in varying ways—in Cremona, Padua, Vercelli, Bologna, Pavia, and (but only initially) Pisa and Lucca. The different pacing of the different elements of the ideal-type commune—assemblies, consuls with rotating offices, regularised court proceedings, legislation—also varied very greatly from city to city; only military commitment was there in every case from the start.

The degree to which communes were contested also varied. Setting aside the early eleventh-century uprisings which marked several cities, particularly in the royal heartland of Lombardy, three widely separated cities, Rome, Arezzo, and Cremona, show evidence of often violent hostility between the city's community and traditional powers (in each case bishops), in the decades in which the first elements of communal activity and identity come into vision. It is fairly easy to see why the high-handedness of bishops might have produced this in these cases; it is rather harder to see why it did not in other cities, which often (Milan is only one out of many) had prelates which were just as overbearing, although in the last chapter I offered some explanations as to why Rome, at least, was special here. The three had few other elements in common, too, stretching as they did from a very large and active city, Rome, through a rising commercial hub, Cremona, to the relatively small centre of Arezzo. Two of them seem to have had an early assembly which formed against the bishop and which was also apparently the main focus for collective politics for some time after, but in Rome, where the commune formed in all its main elements in the space of a year, the assembly followed it rather than preceding it. We are not going to get very far with a generalised pattern of causation here, then, but it is worth at least stressing that two of the three, Rome and Cremona, are joined by a result: they each show evidence of an opening to a rather wider array of social strata in the makeup of their early communal leadership, extending in each case not only to the 'medium élite', but to non-élites too. The need to oppose traditional authority could, in some cases, break down long-ingrained assumptions about which sorts of social group could exercise power.

If we want to look for the root causes of communal differences, we run into problems of evidence very quickly. But, as I stressed at the end of the last chapter, one important element seems to me to be the way the different leading strata of each city related to each other, inside a common élite (or militia) identity, in their involvement in the early commune. (And, indeed, not only then, for the interrelationship between these strata—and the membership of each, as families rose and fell—constantly changed thereafter; but this book stops in 1150.) I have stressed the difference between three levels of the élite, a richer and usually more signorial first level, a prosperous second level without castles (and, if with fiefs, only of land or, sometimes, tithes), and a third level of a 'medium élite' with distinctly less land. If we take the cities of communal Italy as a whole in the early twelfth century, we find one clear pattern: the group which made up early consuls was overwhelmingly associated with the second level as defined here.[36] This must have been the political core of the cavalry militia of each city, and this trend fully justifies Maire Vigueur's characterisation of them (above, p. 13) as having a homogeneously 'honest' landed patrimony. The only clear exceptions are two of our case studies, Rome, where the third level dominated, with links to non-élite families, and Milan, where, even if power after the 1130s was held by all three strata, 'medium-élite' judicial families were very prominent indeed. This seems to me an important basis for considering our city élites as a group; the homogeneity visible here seems to me at least as important as the best-studied difference between them, the degree to which this stratum was in each city associated, whether feudally or otherwise, with the local bishop.

All the same, differences come with the more delicate (and usually, less-studied) information we have as to which social strata this second level most closely associated itself. Bergamo, which matches Milan in the signorial feel of the early commune—above all because very many of the families of the second stratum were actively pursuing signorial rights—does not match it in an opening to non-landed jurists on any scale. Here, the second stratum is most easily linked to the first; they may have been rivals, but they are the two groups most visible in the early commune. Lucca offers some parallels here, in that the richest early consular family, the *filii Malpilii*, were not only castle-holders but had quite recently acquired them (they had been a judicial family less than a century earlier[37]), although the commune was here otherwise dominated by less signorially minded second-level, and for a time even third-level, figures. This pattern can be extended to Verona, where the best-documented mercantile family of the early twelfth-century city, the Crescenzi, moved into castle-holding and signorial activity from 1100 onwards while also becoming consuls. One of the signorial (in this case, though, probably not first-level) families in Florence, the Fifanti, was also relatively new to such activity, unlike the long-standing castle-owning families of the contado. But this group should be kept separate from another set of cities in which a small group of older first-level signorial families committed themselves to a commune which was otherwise dominated by second-level families with urban aspirations above all, such as Vercelli (the da Casalvolone), Piacenza (the dell'Andito), or Padua (the da Baona). What the first group shows up is that the crystallisation of the commune hit cities at different stages in the cycle of replacement of rural and urban élites alike which most societies—and, even more, most expanding economies—experience. An ambitious urban family might, as with the *filii Malpilii* in Lucca, the Veronese Crescenzi, and above all the leading Bergamasco families, be just breaking into castellan society at the moment when the urban stage became more autonomous and more collective, and might well want to hold on to the possibilities of both political arenas; whereas in other cities, such as Padua, where second-level élites were not looking to the signorial world, the communal stage could become absorbing enough for them not to want to for some time yet. Even in Milan, although several first-level families, such as the da Rhò and the Burri, committed themselves to the commune throughout, and even more did in its earliest years, there is less sign that second-level families were trying to join them in obtaining signorial power-bases. The commune would be differently constructed in each case as a result.

The same is true for the association between second- and third-level families. Some cities parallel Milan here to an extent: at the moment we can see Padua, Florence, and Cremona most clearly.[38] In Padua, we can track judicial consuls without documented land (as also with a single case in the early commune of Bergamo, Arnaldo *iudex*), and also small-landowner consuls with no other obvious wealth. In Florence, rising but as yet small-scale creditors appear among the early consuls. In Cremona, where we have lists of civic leaders rather than of consuls in the early twelfth century, it is nonetheless striking, as we have seen, that they include several artisans, who otherwise are hardly visible in any city other than Rome.[39] These examples each show a different way that third-level families could become communal leaders: because they had a professional expertise which was socially valued enough for them to be accepted as credible political players (Milan, Padua); because economic expansion was pushing up new families very fast (Florence); or because the commune was opposed to (and by) traditional powers (Cremona, Rome). Padua may also show an openness to ordinary third-level landowners because it had a strong link to a rural area, the Saccisica, where they were very well-organised. I suspect that more cities would emerge in each of these categories if the less prominent consular leaders in each were more concentrated on by historians; although it may equally be that, if research in more cities went beyond the ad hoc data-collection which is all that exists at the present state of knowledge, it might show that in some of these cases such families were less important than I

am implying here—after all, there were some third-level consuls even in Pisa, which was the second-level commune par ex-
cellence. But in all such cases, the specific detail of local social
structures underpinned a greater openness to 'medium élites'
as political leaders than other communes had, which then, if
it lasted, could result in different political directions for each.

To understand why each commune was different: as I said
at the end of the last chapter, this is a key problem for anyone who wants to understand the developments set out in
the preceding pages. The micro-analysis of different internal
social structures which I have just summarised seems to me
the best way forward here. Not so many of the other cities in
Italy, as sketched out in this chapter, however show as clearly
characterised a set of internal contrasts as it was possible to
set out for Milan, Pisa, and Rome. This may be because they
are less fully studied (which as we have seen, with some exceptions, is quite true), or else because their evidence is less
good (which is equally true in most cases); but it also might be
because they were genuinely less differentiated. I find that, at
least, harder to believe, for the communes which we have been
able to say most about here, Genoa, Asti, Bergamo, Cremona,
Padua, or Florence, were certainly as diverse in their overall
development as the three studied in the rest of the book. We
must hope that future work will allow us to say more about
the others; for this seems to me a necessary step to take.

But we must, equally, turn the argument back round to
similarities. We have seen a wide range of difference here; but
it remains true that the early twelfth century was for most cities, except in margins like Piemonte and inland Tuscany, the
period in which most of the elements of the ideal-type commune appeared across northern and central Italy. We therefore need to end this discussion by trying to see how and why,

despite this range of very diverse experience, there were also common trends across so much of the peninsula. Here I will start by focussing on the importance of assemblies; and then move to sketching, with a very broad brush, a chronology of the experience of northern and central Italians as a whole, as the decades proceeded from the 1080s to the 1140s: in order to see, or at least speculate about, what different events could have meant to them, and, once again, what at each stage they thought they were doing.

In previous chapters I have laid stress on assemblies, as the main form of formalised city activity to appear in the 1090s in both Milan and Pisa, well before the development of an organised consular leadership. I argued there that it was assemblies, not 'the commune', which were the main form of defensive reaction to the crisis of the Kingdom of Italy (and, in Tuscany, the March) in the 1080s and onwards, and that defined consular leaderships appeared later, as a more propositive development—doubtless still ad hoc for a long time, but destined as it turned out to develop quite quickly into an institution, the first of many, and, in most places, one which would last.[40] Now that we have sketches of many more cities, we can put that into context. The assembly experience of Milan and Pisa is here matched, with varying degrees of clarity, in several other cities: Bergamo, Brescia, Piacenza, Cremona, Lodi, Parma, Arezzo, as also the anomalous case of Venice. I would cautiously add to that list Genoa, where consuls are attested in active roles of different kinds very early, but the *compagna/consolatus*, which certainly included an assembly element by the 1110s, seems to have been the initial organising body for them. These cities are almost all either port cities or in Lombardy-Emilia, that is to say the locations of the earliest communal experiences as a whole. The Veneto and Romagna did not, by contrast, have obvious examples of assemblies which preceded communes, except for Venice, where consuls never appeared at all and ducal power remained the city's centre. In Tuscany, too, their presence in Lucca and Florence is hardly attested; I argued in both of the latter cases that this might be a problem of our evidence. There seems less reason to do so for the Veneto-Romagna, however, given the homogeneity of our (poor) data, although it is worth at least noting that the first appearance of the consuls of Bologna was together with the whole *populus*.[41]

What emerges here is a fairly clear pattern; the earliest documented communes did indeed, for the most part, have an assembly before—in some cases decades before—they developed a consular leadership in any organised way. The proposition that assemblies formalised themselves out of pre-existing practices of collective action to face a power-vacuum in the Kingdom (and the March of Tuscany) does thus have some wider support. But it above all applies, apart from the ports, to the old royal heartland of Italy. Here the effects of the institutional breakdown of the Kingdom were most pronounced; and it was thus here that cities developed their own deliberative arrangements to make up. In this perspective, we might speculate that the Veneto, which felt that breakdown less fully (some *placita* are still documented there well into the twelfth century, for example), was for the most part copying a slightly later Lombard model which by now included consuls as well, when its cities eventually moved in a formalised communal direction. This may be true for most of Piemonte as well, as also Provence, and must be so for the very late communes of central Italy, even in the highly protagonistic example of Rome.

Thereafter, however, in early developing cities, several developments took place. Cities began at least sometimes to call themselves 'communes', as a noun; as Banti showed, this is unattested at the start of the century except for Cremona in 1097, although he slightly underestimates the speed with which it came in subsequently: by 1110 in Pisa, by 1117 in Bergamo, by 1120 in Ferrara and Brescia, by 1123 in Asti.[42] Communes began to develop regular tribunals for hearing disputes: by the 1110s in Genoa and, more hesitantly, Pisa; by the 1130s–40s in most of the other main early communes and in some of those of the Veneto too. Already by the 1130s–40s at least three communes, Genoa, Piacenza, and Pisa, were legislating (often about marriage gifts, a well-known preoccupation of early city communes).[43] The appearance of rotating city office-holders called consuls, whose remit was to rule the city, was only one among these developments; one of the most important, obviously, but not the only important one—which goes further to decentre its traditional dominance in the historiography. What was happening here was in its essence a steady process of the formalisation of aspects of autonomous city government. First, the assembly became a formal body, in a period when its leaders were still defined fairly casually, as *sapientes* or *boni homines* (or indeed, often, *consules*), and were also uncertain of the nature of their power and of the social status attached to it (this is where Volpe's 'privatistic' image is most useful heuristically). Only subsequently did leaders gain definition, and also clearly defined temporary periods of office (not necessarily yet annual); and then, normally later still, a newly city-focussed legal system developed too—sometimes run directly by the consuls (as in Genoa and Milan and, later, Rome), sometimes assigned to less prominent people (as in

Pisa and Lucca). It was usually then that we begin to find the terminology of the 'public' used by cities, too, although even informal leaders had been in most cases acting for the whole city from the start: informal leadership did not mean incomplete power, still less power which needed to be legally validated from outside.

It is hardly surprising, of course, given its very de facto origins, that this formalisation was differently configured in each city, especially given the differences in the social structures of élites which I have just characterised. Only very slowly, and in different orderings, would the distinct elements of the communal ideal type come into focus in each. But the later developments were not normally defensive in the same way as the formalisation of assemblies was. Rather, the appearance of ruling consuls amounted to élites taking control, in a more organised and proactive way, of urban deliberative bodies which by now already existed, at least in Lombardy-Emilia; and the appearance of regular tribunals is a sign of the increasing institutionalisation of the exercise of power in each city which, in general, marked the beginnings of what can by now be called city 'government'. Legislation and taxation, and the endless reinvention of failing aspects of these (usually fragile) institutions, as also the eclipse of wider participation in deliberative assemblies, followed on from there.

This structural overview can be presented chronologically, as well. Here my story-line will contain a fair degree of speculation—it is what I *think* happened—but it is at least consistent with what has already been argued. Before the 1080s, cities were fully integrated into the Kingdom of Italy. They had sometimes revolted, against king-emperors or bishops, and were occasionally divided by religious conflict, but their leading groups were fully part of traditional hierarchies, as we have seen for Milan and Pisa, with regular appearances in public *placita*, and feudal or clientelar ties to counts and bishops. When the civil wars began, the two great port cities, Pisa and Genoa (the former up till then stably subject to the marquis of Tuscany, the latter part of a distinctly weaker local power-structure) had to respond collectively to political divisions which threatened to pull each city apart, and they could respond relatively quickly, for they were used to organising offensive maritime war; by the 1090s each had an active assembly. Their leading élites were already called *consules*, and the challenges of continuing war (the First Crusade, and then struggles against rural lords and rival cities) allowed these leaders to crystallise into a formalised ruling group with judicial authority, already by 1110. I proposed in chapter 3 that the excitement of successful external war in Pisa allowed this process to be not just smooth, but imperceptible, for there was no-one to stand out against it; this doubtless goes for Genoa as well. That was the ports; inland, in the royal heartland around Pavia and Milan, there was also near-continuous war between the emperor and Matilda of Canossa into the 1090s[44]—more than on the coast, indeed—and also in some cities (Cremona, most notably) an internal power-vacuum, so assemblies had to develop to organise local society in a more formal way. But bishops were here in most places still hegemonic, and urban leaderships were often happy to remain inside their clientele, aspiring as they did to status and power which was figured in very traditional terms.

Here we see city élites making do, probably both through the urban assembly and with the help of bishops, in decades when something had to be done to keep things going in the absence of other, older institutions. By around 1110 however, in Lombardy-Emilia at least, the challenges of ruling a city, the process of making do in a slightly more peaceful period but still one with no wider ruler with a permanent presence, gave urban leaders, here too increasingly called consuls, more need to present themselves as acting politically on behalf of their cities. The 1110s show that Lombard and Emilian consuls could routinely write letters in the name of cities, run wars for them, make formal transactions for them. All the same, they had no real institutional basis, and in a city like Milan they were not separate from the archbishop and his aristocratic entourage; it was indeed not the consuls (or the archbishop) in Milan which began the Como war in 1118, but the city assembly; and it was also city assemblies in the region which made many of the principal deals with rural lords and small towns.

Had a Frederick Barbarossa been able to appear in the 1110s as he did in the 1150s, intent on restoring royal power in a systematic way, it might not have been hard to achieve it. All he would have had to recognise, as a by-now-permanent feature of the urban landscape, would have been local *conciones*, a formalised assembly politics, and above all in Lombardy and Emilia, i.e. as yet only a small part of the Kingdom. Aristocratic urban leaders could have easily folded back into traditional hierarchies which they had usually never left; second-level city leaders, increasingly important everywhere, would perhaps have had to content themselves with running assemblies and trying to rise into the patronage networks of the aristocratic élite, as indeed they had done for centuries. This did not happen, and indeed could not have easily happened for internal German reasons; and probably the institutional bases of the Kingdom had weakened too far to be easily re-established—in particular, the old formal elements of royal government at the city level (represented most clearly by the *placitum*) had, as we have seen, broken down almost completely. But the thought experiment is still worth making, to allow us to see that the permanence of the elements of city autonomy which were in existence in this decade were not yet to be taken for granted—after all, even Genoa, the most institutionally solid commune at the time, still saw its *compagna* as potentially temporary.

From now on, however, particularly in the 1130s–40s, simple routine allowed the rule of consuls to become more institutionalised, and copied in more and more parts of northern Italy. As we have seen, turning the formal assembly and its leadership into a governing structure, with rules and a greater organisation of power, was not necessarily by now in response to any vacuum of power. It was more a question of leaders taking on and regularising the power they had gained. And from now on, too, wars between cities became more and more common, which in itself could make a more solid power for city leaders more necessary. We find our first casual references to fiscal exactions in a city's contado already in the 1120s, in Como and Siena, in the context of war.[45] And the 1130s were a particularly bad time for wars; when a model letter in a north Italian letter collection from this decade says quite casually, among references to family business, 'throughout *Longobardia* [the Po plain] and indeed throughout Italy wars are very dangerous (*infestissima*)', its author was not exaggerating. Whatever one thinks of the virtues of communes, one can hardly deny that the level of violence between cities across north-central Italy was substantially greater in this period, for city leaderships, as prickly in their honour as any signorial lord, showed themselves to be remarkably intolerant of their neighbours, and ever less keen to compromise with them; we indeed see here the start of the hegemony of the war-making mounted militia discussed by Maire Vigueur. The contrast with the relative calm of the Kingdom of Italy must have been only too obvious to at least older contemporaries.[46] The role of consuls was also by now not only political/military leadership, but had extended to cover urban dispute-settlement; when the Veneto cities adopted consular leaderships from this period onwards, they came with a more stable package of communal/public/legal practice, and so did those of the next generation further south.

Even now, however, in most places élites probably still thought they were simply filling gaps in a (possibly temporarily) failing system; only later would it have become clear that they were creating a fundamentally new one. City communes, which are visible by 1150 in most of north-central Italy, were very various indeed, for reasons we have explored; the different elements of the ideal-type commune sketched earlier were emphasised in different ways from place to place. Communes did not have to be very proactive (as those of most of Piemonte were not), or very developed governmentally (as those of inland Tuscany were not, at least yet), or even autonomous (as that of Venice was not). All the same, the 1130s–40s, and not earlier, is where the fulcrum of communal developments comes: where consular government was increasingly stable, increasingly institutionalised, increasingly hegemonic even in cities with strong bishops. So much so that the Venetians could borrow the rhetoric of communal self-presentation wholesale in the 1140s; so much so that the Romans, when they broke with the pope in the same period, had a ready-made framework of political institutions which they could just adopt. And so much so that when Frederick Barbarossa made his own interventions after 1158, he was, as it turned out, too late.

But we are by now, in these decades, a whole generation on from the first formalisation of assembly politics. That was a long period, and one which did not aid conscious self-reflection. Whatever consuls thought they were doing, they did not, in any visible case except Rome, see themselves as contributing to the establishment of a new world. The grand narrative of Italian exceptionalism, focussed on city-states, which generates a triumphalist tone when consuls are at last visible in our documents in even some very recent works, was in reality a sequence of chances, of roads taken by people whose heads were turned in often opposite directions. We saw in chapter 2 how Oberto dall'Orto, though an important Milanese consul and political representative, was fascinated by feudal relationships, and in chapter 3 how the author of the *Liber Maiorichinus* was obsessed with Pisan military glory; as for Rome, as we saw in chapter 4, the senate was certainly a conscious creation, but if the aristocratic consuls of the previous decades had ended up creating a durable city government as they did elsewhere, steadily but far less consciously, such a government would doubtless still have used the same backward-looking, and traditionally Roman, imagery of *renovatio* with the same degree of enthusiasm. We cannot attribute more self-awareness to the leaders of any other Italian city. Mosè del Brolo around 1120, for example, spends far more lines of his praise-poem about Bergamo on the virtues of the local bishop, and even on the city's fountains, than he does on the consuls and their acts; the city annals of later in the century do not even mention consuls before the wars with Barbarossa; and in 'latent' communes such as Vercelli and Florence a consular régime was an element of government which could be abandoned for substantial periods.[47] These people did not know what they were doing; or, to the extent that they did, were cloaking their actions, even to themselves, in imagery which belonged to other political systems. Communal identity came later; and when it did, it had to be created out of whole-cloth, with, in the history-writing of the thirteenth century, entirely invented moments of earlier collective affirmation. In our period, though, communal leaders were sleepwalking.

I would like to underline this point, in conclusion, by using an image which I have used elsewhere, in a very different context:[48] the Mafia in Palermo. The Mafia is there as a parallel political structure: the institutions of the Italian state exist in the city, and run, in their own way, but 'we all know' that the Mafia 'really' rules, informally, as a system of usually profitable patron-client operations, not all violent and not all successful (the state sometimes wins), but almost impossible to eradicate. What would happen, though, if the institutions of the state went away, city government, *polizia*, *carabinieri*, judicial and fiscal system? The Mafia would have to run it on their own. And everything would have, slowly, to become clearer. Those informal, coercive, exploitative, but also problem-solving operations would have to become explicit; people would now need to know who their rulers were, and their subordinates; they would need to know what the rules were, and how far they could count on them. And, it must be added, someone would still have to look after the sewers and pay the sewer-men, not to speak of the electricity system, dull things which the Mafia currently does not have to worry about. So, what would be needed to make this work would be the formalisation of rules and processes: whether the Mafia bosses intended it or not. They would sleepwalk into a new governmental system, perhaps a long way behind the curve of how it was actually working; one day they would wake up and take it on fully, but it might have been effectively in operation for some time, creating their choices for them. This is what happened with the Italian communes and their leaders, many of whose ancestors, too, had 'really' run most of the now-defunct public institutions of previous generations. When they woke up from their sleepwalking and finally took it on consciously, the new world was already formed around them.

NOTES

1. COMMUNES

1. *Landulphi Iunioris Historia Mediolanensis* [henceforth *HM*], c. 44. *Theatra* elsewhere means 'thrones' in Landolfo's Latin, but since Milan still had a Roman theatre to act as a point of reference (it was a popular assembly place), and since the occasion was a major one, we can assume quite large wooden stages or banks of seats.

2. *Gli atti del Comune*, n. 1. See Giulini, *Memorie*, vol. 5, 75–91; Manaresi's institutional analysis in the introduction to *Gli atti del Comune*, xxviii–xxxii; Bosisio, *Origini del comune*, 173–83; Barni, 'Milano verso l'egemonia', 319–21. Landolfo makes clear, *HM*, c. 44, that the meeting on the Broletto and the *arengo* or *concio* of the people, in which pleas were heard (he mentions at least two sessions), were, if not identical, closely following on from each other. In 1117 the archbishop of Cologne wrote to the *consules, capitanei, omnis militia*, and *universus populus* of Milan too: *Monumenta Bambergensia*, 513–14.

3. Cattaneo, 'La città: considerata come principio ideale delle istorie italiane'. Cf. e.g. Bordone, *La società cittadina*, 7, one of many histories which simply start by citing Cattaneo; compare also Tabacco, *The Struggle for Power*, 19–36 (who emphasises German historiography); Wickham, *Community and Clientele*, 1–4, 185–89 (for the parallel rural communal debate). Note that this book does not discuss southern Italy; here, the essential starting-point is now Oldfield, *City and Community*.

4. Lane, 'At the Roots of Republicanism', 403. See Muir, 'The Italian Renaissance' (who quotes Lane at 1106); Molho, 'The Italian Renaissance, *Made in the USA*'.

5. Putnam et al., *Making Democracy Work*, 180 (and more generally 121–37); Skinner, *The Foundations of Modern Political Thought*, 3–22.

6. Otto of Freising, *Gesta Friderici*, 2.13; see for recent comment Zabbia, 'Tra modelli letterari e autopsia'. Cf. *Romualdi Salernitani Chronicon*, 276–77, on the rhetoric of one of the major Milanese consuls, Girardo Cagapisto (see pp. 45–52 in this volume), when ne-

gotiating the Peace of Venice in 1177: this is an external view of the radicalism of the communes, not a local statement (see also Zabbia, ibid., 129–34, who is more accepting of the authenticity of Girardo's words than I would be). It is worth adding that the principle of election of rulers did not, of course, in itself mark out Italian communes; of sovereign rulers, both the emperor and the pope were elected in our period, and so were bishops. But their electorates were very specialised and high-status, with only occasional hints of participation by a wider *populus*; the choice of consuls, which, however orchestrated, was always presented as being by that *populus* directly, was rather different.

7. Both of them also worked on later periods in their extensive writings, but wrote little on the early commune (though for Tabacco see his appendix to *The Struggle for Power*, 321–44, and 'Le istituzioni', which go up to 1100).

8. There is a list of monographic works for individual cities in the historiographical survey in Coleman, 'The Italian Communes' (a sequel will appear in *History Compass* shortly); see further, more recently, Rippe, *Padoue*, 323–79; De Angelis, *Poteri cittadini* (Bergamo); *Vercelli nel secolo XII*; Faini, *Firenze*. Among general works, Tabacco, *The Struggle for Power*, is fundamental; see further Bordone, *La società cittadina*; Jones, *The Italian City-State*, esp. 130–51; Pini, *Città, comuni*; and see the bibliography for Keller's many articles. Recent manuals in Italy—very numerous, which is a sign of movement in itself—are Milani, *I comuni italiani*; Maire Vigueur and Faini, *Il sistema politico dei comuni* (these two books stress most the informality of the early commune, a major argument of this book); Franceschi and Taddei, *Le città italiane*; Occhipinti, *L'Italia dei comuni*. Of non-Italian manuals, Menant, *L'Italie des communes*, is by far the best; the classic in English, Waley and Dean, *The Italian City-Republics*, still repays reading. Grillo, 'La frattura', provides a further important historiographical survey, and also new interpretations; it is developed in idem, 'Cavalieri, cittadini'.

9. The contrast with northern Europe is not always helpful; see for example Scott, 'A Historian of Germany Looks at the Italian City-State'. For Italy, among recent works Menant, *L'Italie des communes*, and Franceschi and Taddei, *Le città italiane*, discuss economics in most detail.

10.   Among many, Franceschi and Taddei, *Le città italiane*, 120; Occhipinti, *L'Italia dei comuni*, 32; Jones, *The Italian City-State*, 141; Pini, *Città, comuni*, 70–71 (who calls it an 'operazione gattopardesca', referring to Tommaso di Lampedusa's *The Leopard*). Cf. Banti, '"Civitas" e "Commune"', 222, who calls the commune an agreed 'soluzione di emergenza'.

11.   Banti, '"Civitas" e "Commune"', 223–32. *Commune* first appears as a substantive in Milan as late as 1158 (*Gli atti del Comune*, n. 45), although in a context which shows that it was a normal word by now; in Pisa it already appears in 1110: see p. 88 in this volume. For other early examples, see chapter 5, n. 42, in this volume.

12.   Cassandro in a very brief article of 1958, republished as 'Un bilancio storiografico', set out the later-accepted model of the public role of consuls, against Volpe's famous image from 1904 of the commune as a 'private association': Volpe, *Medio evo italiano*, 100–104. We will see later (e.g. n. 29) that Volpe's views still have a good deal of relevance; but the public role of consuls is already clear in, for example, Adalberto Samaritano's treatise on letter-writing, from Bologna in the late 1110s, *Praecepta dictaminum*, 60–61: there he shows drafts of possible flattering letters to consuls which invoke their role in conserving the 'vigour and status of your city', and supposes that consuls will, at least in some circumstances, 'examine disputes over the public and private affairs of citizens'.

13.   For judicial continuities, see e.g. Fissore, 'Origini e formazione', 586–88. Note that I will not always translate *iudex* here; 'judge' does not always work well, as *iudex* was often, especially in the eleventh century, simply a title; 'legal expert' would work better, but the content of such expertise varied greatly across our period. Tabacco, *The Struggle for Power*, 321–44, is the best and most subtle starting-point for the role of bishops and their relationships with cities (he also problematised the concept of 'public' back in 1962: 'Interpretazioni e ricerche', 715).

14.   Bougard, *La justice*; Wickham, 'Justice in the Kingdom of Italy', developed in idem, 'Consensus and Assemblies'; idem, 'The "Feudal Revolution"'. One exception is a Pisa consular example: see p. 89 in this volume. Note that the end of the *placitum* assembly does not mean that the term *placitum* dropped out; it continued to be used to mean 'dispute' or 'judgement' in the twelfth century, as with the Genoese or Lucchese *consules de placitis/placito* (*Annali genovesi*, 27 and passim;

Wickham, *Courts and Conflict*, 32), or the Last Judgement referred to as the *universale placitum* in Adalberto Samaritano, *Praecepta dictaminum*, 61; the word did become less common, however.

15. Keller, *Signori e vassalli* (xi–xlviii for his reply to critics; this book did not, however, focus on city communes themselves, for which see his articles as listed in the bibliography—the most wide-ranging is 'Die Entstehung'–many of which are now collected in idem, *Il laboratorio politico*); Jones, 'Economia e società', 210–79, and idem, *The Italian City-State* (143 for the quote; but it is worth stressing that this vast tapestry of a book contains nuances to every argument); Racine, *Plaisance*, 372 (see p. 114 in this volume for Pisa). The word *cives* is ambiguous, for it could include the aristocratic *ordines* too: Rossetti, 'Il comune cittadino', 36; Keller, *Signori e vassalli*, 15–17, made a similar point.

16. E.g. Bordone, 'Tema cittadino'; Rossetti, 'Il comune cittadino'. (Keller did not in fact claim otherwise; he limited himself to saying that cities could not be understood without studying feudal relations in the countryside too: e.g. *Signori e vassalli*, 339–41, cf. xxix.)

17. For local variation, Bordone, *La società cittadina*, 160–182; Maire Vigueur, *Cavaliers et citoyens*, 220–46; *La vassalità maggiore*, passim; and three important articles, Grillo, 'Aristocrazia urbana, aristocrazia rurale'; Castagnetti, 'Feudalità e società comunale'; and Cortese, 'Aristocrazia signorile e città'. For the city-country difference, see all three of these articles; Grillo, ibid., 87–96, is the key starting-point. (Keller did not deny it—see *Signori e vassalli*, 339; but it is true that he did not stress it.) See also pp. 182–83 in this volume, for Florence.

18. Bordone, *La società cittadina*, 34–100, 130–33: here civic culture is eloquence, legal knowledge, war, clothes, processions, and the idea of a civic *libertas*. Not all of these distinguish urban from rural. See pp. 56–57 in this volume.

19. Maire Vigueur, *Cavaliers et citoyens*, esp. 217–19, 337–62; quotes from 341.

20. Or *valvassores*; but they are often difficult to distinguish, and the terms overlap (e.g. *I placiti*, n. 467, a. 1088, in which several leading Milanese figures whose families are called *capitanei* in plenty of other texts are referred to as *vavasores*—cf. Keller, *Signori e vassalli*, 27, who

associates this with the different usage of the royal court). *Valvassor* is rather rarer as a term in texts than *capitaneus*, too. I shall not lay stress on *valvassores* as a separate category in this book; as remarked here in the text, more useful seems to me a set of distinctions inside the aristocracy (and the wider élite) related to wealth. Keller, *Signori e vassalli*, 10–12 and passim, sees the difference between *capitaneus* and *valvassor* as quite rigid, and also tied to wealth, but he shows, equally (e.g. 192–207), that the economic difference between *valvassores* and rich *cives* was not always that great, which for my purposes is the more important point. In our city case studies, an identifiable aristocracy is clearly visible inside the wider élite in Milan and defensible in Rome; less so in Pisa. Indeed, élite social structures were very different from city to city more widely across Italy. On élites, see also Wickham, *Roma medievale*, 222–26. Note that Maire Vigueur himself calls his whole militia an aristocracy or a *noblesse*: *Cavaliers et citoyens*, 281–83 and passim. This is more of a thirteenth-century phraseology, however; it is a valid choice, but I will not use it.

21.   Keller, 'Gli inizi', 56. Two surveys which include initial references to consuls in a wide range of cities, Waley and Dean, *The Italian City-Republics*, 220–32, and Opll, *Stadt und Reich*, 178–480 (a particularly detailed city-by-city study), are unfortunately not up to date.

22.   Ronzani, *Chiesa e "Civitas"*, 194, 226, 253; Delumeau, *Arezzo*, 850–57; Savigni, *Episcopato*, 42–43. See chapter 3 in this volume.

23.   At the back of this characterisation is Volpe, *Medio evo italiano*, 100–104. There is a useful discussion of these structures in Rossetti, 'I caratteri del politico'. The oath is stressed in particular by Dilcher, *Die Entstehung*, 142–58.

24.   Caffaro's *Annali genovesi*; Otto Morena, *Historia Frederici I.*; Maragone's *Gli Annales Pisani* (who stresses, 16–20, the expensive extension of the city walls from 1156, the first act which he records the Pisan consuls as doing); Otto of Freising, *Chronica* and *Gesta Friderici I*. Soon after come, for Milan, the anonymous *Annales Mediolanenses*, which also take consular rule for granted from the start. For the Pisan laws: see chapter 3, n. 14, in this volume. For fiscal exactions, the basic studies are now by Patrizia Mainoni, 'A proposito della "rivoluzione fiscale"' and 'Sperimentazioni fiscali': the 1150s show the first signs of systematic communal direct taxation (the 1140s in Genoa and

Piacenza: ibid., 711, 716, 729)—commercial tolls, however, had been normal for centuries. Grillo, 'La frattura', 685–90, generalises out from Mainoni's work, arguing for rapid institutional consolidation in the decades around 1150, in some cities at least.

25. Wickham, *Courts and Conflict*, 31–38. See further below, chapter 2, n. 21, and chapter 3, n. 51, in this volume. 'Regular' also means recorded in regular formats: see chapter 2, nn. 20, 25, in this volume, for Milan, and chapter 5, n. 5, for Genoa. The formal banishments from cities, first seen in Genoa in 1139 and (more clearly) Bologna in 1149, studied in Milani, *L'esclusione dal comune* (27–56 for our period), also assume a public body capable of ensuring them; the relationship between early communal courts and territorial jurisdiction is further explored in idem, 'Lo sviluppo della giurisdizione'.

26. For Pisa see chapter 3 in this volume; for other cities, see chapter 5 in this volume (pp. 168 and 185 for Asti and Arezzo).

27. Keller, 'Die Entstehung', 206–9; idem, 'Einwohnergemeinde und Kommune', 575–76; idem, 'Die Stadtkommunen', 685–91 (this whole article is a significant contribution to the concept of institutionalisation); idem, 'La decisione a maggioranza', 47–49—although I would argue for the 1130s in the case of Milan, rather than the 1120s (see pp. 33–34 in this volume).

28. Arnolfo of Milan, *Liber gestorum recentium*, 3.11, 18, 23 (an important example, from 1071); cf. Landolfo Seniore, *Mediolanensis historiae*, 2.26, 3.5, 8. The quote is from Keller, 'Gli inizi', 54; other arguments along the same lines are idem, 'Die soziale und politische Verfassung Mailands', e.g. 49–51, 54, 61; idem, 'Die Entstehung'; idem, 'Einwohnergemeinde und Kommune'; idem, 'Pataria' 333–49; idem, 'Mailand im 11. Jahrhundert', 93–98 (in many ways the most developed version). Tabacco, *The Struggle for Power*, 185, is a bit teleological too: 1044 is 'the premise for the future commune'. A good argument against the 1040s as a communal period is Dilcher, *Die Entstehung*, 128–34 and passim, taken up again in idem, 'I comuni italiani', 79–83, even if I do not follow his juridical approach as a whole. I also take my distance from another aspect of Keller's model, in 'Einwohnergemeinde und Kommune', 570 (and elsewhere), on the commune as a religious phenomenon ('Grundlage der Kommune ist letzlich eine religiöse Idee'), perhaps linked to the Peace of God (ibid., 572–74; idem, 'Die Entstehung', 194–97; cf. also Jones, *The Italian City-State*, 148, and see chapter

3, n. 32, in this volume, for Pisa); the development of communes in the twelfth century seems to me to have taken place in a much less fervent context than that of some cities in the mid-eleventh.

29. Milani, *I comuni italiani*, 24–25, for 'latent' (developing ideas of Mary Douglas)—strictly, he uses the term for all early communes, precisely because of their informality and uncertainty, but the image also helps to delineate the communes which can be shown to have been initially intermittent, at least in their consular leadership, and I will use the term in this way here. Vercelli, Ravenna, Florence: see pp. 170, 178, 182–84, in this volume. The opposition between formal and informal is further developed in Wickham, 'The "'Feudal Revolution"'; cf. idem, *Courts and Conflict*, 18–19; and Keller, 'Die Stadtkommunen'. This brings us back, too, to Volpe's image of the 'private association' in *Medio evo italiano*, 100–104, which remains more interesting than much later work, notwithstanding the caveats expressed above, n. 12.

30. See Wickham, *Courts and Conflict*, 24–28.

2. MILAN

1. Arnolfo of Milan, *Liber gestorum recentium*; Landolfo Seniore, *Mediolanensis historiae*; *Landulphi Iunioris Historia Mediolanensis* [henceforth *HM*]. For discussions of them as historians, Capitani, 'Storiografia e riforma', and idem, 'Da *Landolfo* Seniore a *Landolfo* Iuniore', remain basic points of reference; Busch, *Die Mailänder Geschichtsschreibung*, 38–50, is also fundamental if brief.

2. Grillo, *Milano*, 209–34, is the best guide to industry, as also to all socio-economic and socio-political developments after 1183. For a quick and acute economic survey, Castagnetti, 'Feudalità e società comunale', 213–20. Note also the impressive canal and irrigation system which was developed in Lombardy from the mid-twelfth century onwards: Menant, *Campagnes lombardes*, 174–76, 182–200. For the urban hub in Piazza del Duomo, see Spinelli, 'Uso dello spazio', and Salvatori, 'Spazi mercantili'. Archaeology does not help us much for Milan; *Scavi MM3*, which publishes the major set of urban excavations, is conceptually weak, although the finds for our period, especially in Piazza del Duomo (Andrews, 'Lo scavo di Piazza Duomo', 167–79, 188–98), do fit our documentary evidence, as set out in Spinelli and Salvatori.

3. The count in 1045: *I placiti*, n. 364; see Violante, *La società milanese*, 187–88; Tabacco, 'Le istituzioni', 346–48. The supremacy of the archbishop over the city is not formally assigned to him by any surviving imperial document.

4. Violante, *La società milanese*, 209–12 (also for an analytical narrative up to 1045); Tabacco, 'Le istituzioni', 357–64; Maire Vigueur, *Cavaliers et citoyens*, 227; cf. *Sacrorum conciliorum nova et amplissima collectio*, vol. 19, cols. 946–48, at 948 (a. 1067), for the *ordo negotiatorum* as a third *ordo*; this unique reference certainly stresses the commercial stratum. As noted above (chapter 1, n. 14, in this volume), members of the two *ordines* could be described as *cives* too, but the counterposition of *nobiles* and *cives* and similar phrases was very common in Milan, as in other cities. Very sensible on eleventh-century Milan in general are Tabacco, 'Le istituzioni', and Keller, 'Mailand im 11. Jahrhundert'.

5. Arnolfo of Milan, *Liber gestorum recentium*, 2.1 (1018); Landolfo Seniore, *Mediolanensis historiae*, 3.3 (1045), 32 (1075); *HM*, cc. 2 (1097), 7 (1102). Cf. Violante, *La Pataria milanese*, 16–29 (for 1045); and the articles by Keller cited in chapter 1, n. 28, in this volume. See also, in general, Barni, 'Dal governo del vescovo a quello dei cittadini', with idem, 'Milano verso l'egemonia', which, despite its positivism and an outdated communal narrative, is still the most detailed account to take Milan through from 1050 to 1150, although Keller's articles are the structural starting-point for current work. I was unable to take account of the important discussion in Dartmann, *Politische Interaktion*, 33–120, which I only encountered when this book was in production. For earlier bibliography, see above, chapter 1, n. 2, in this volume.

6. Violante, *La Pataria milanese*, 175–213; idem, 'I laici' (still the basic structural analysis); Miccoli, *Chiesa gregoriana*, 127–212 (for Patarene theory); Cowdrey, 'The Papacy, the Patarenes'; Moore, 'Family, Community and Cult', 65–69; Keller, 'Pataria'; Schultz, "*Poiché tanto amano la libertà* . . . ", 32–56. Landolfo Seniore on Erlembaldo: *Mediolanensis historiae*, 3.14. The involvement of Arnaldo da Rhò in Erlembaldo's death is stressed in the 1130s by Landolfo of S. Paolo, *HM*, c. 66: the account is very circumstantial, but more contemporary accounts do not mention it.

7. For oaths, see chapter 1, n. 27, in this volume. Landolfo of S. Paolo was from a Patarene family, but, as we shall see, he does not stress the commune much, and does not link it at all to the political

activities of the last major Patarene leader, his uncle Liprando (d. 1113).

8. See Lucioni, *Anselmo IV da Bovisio*, for the 1090s as a whole; 108–17 for Arialdo, 118–19 for Ambrogio Pagano, 117–39 for lay society. Last *placitum*: *I placiti*, n. 473; Giulini, *Memorie*, vol. 4, 546–48, for the archbishop's court in 1099. Mediolano Ottone was publicly active as a judge between 1053 and 1097, *APM*, nn. 366, 854; like Ambrogio Pagano (see below, n. 40), he is never recorded as a property-holder. [For all abbreviations of document editions in this chapter, see the note on documents in the bibliography of this volume.]

9. *APM*, n. 854. The Gambari were active consuls from 1151 (*Gli atti del Comune*, n. 24; cf. n. 2 for 1119); as landholders, they are only attested in Gudo south-west of the city before 1150 (*APM*, n. 743; *Morimondo*, n. 87), although their prominence and wealth increased substantially later. For the thirteenth century, see Grillo, *Milano*, 346–50. The Stampa: see p. 40 in this volume. On 1097, see Barni, 'Milano verso l'egemonia', 241–44; talked down by Bosisio, *Origini del comune*, 194n; talked up by Fissore (see below, n. 13).

10. *I Biscioni*, vol. 1, part 2, nn. 279–80 (cf. 287), for Biandrate (here *consules* are set up by the counts and *milites* of Biandrate to police the agreement between them and minor disputes); *APM*, n. 852, for Chiavenna (here three *consules de comunis rebus* are in charge of the common lands of Chiavenna, acting *pro comunis iusionibus vicinorum*: such lands were important in the Alpine valleys where Chiavenna is situated). In neither case can we call the consuls local leaders in any developed sense, but each centre is clearly using a by-now-existing vocabulary in different ways. See for the latter Keller, 'La decisione a maggioranza', 28–30; Becker, *Il comune di Chiavenna*, 51–54. Manaresi (*Gli atti del Comune*, xxvii–xxviii) thought that Milan had got its consular vocabulary from Ravenna, where *consul* was also an old élite title (see Franchini, 'Il titolo di *consul* in Ravenna', and Mayer, *Italienische Verfassungsgeschichte*, vol. 2, 532–37—who sees them, unconvincingly, as office-holders; and, with a more up-to-date historiographical framing, Bocchi, "Sul titolo" and Vespignani, *La Romània italiana*, 64–76, 174–78); this seems to me far less likely, given Pisa's 1080s usage.

11. Barni, 'Milano verso l'egemonia', 247 (cf. 245–46), provides a photo of the inscription of 1098 in which the archbishop establishes a market with the *conscilio* quote cited above in the text; for 1100, *Italia sacra*, vol. 4, cols. 124–25, is the most convenient edition.

12. A useful but very traditional conspectus is Fasoli, *Dalla 'civitas' al comune*, 70–76, 85–89.

13. Fissore, 'Origini e formazione', 554–55, argues on diplomatic grounds that the 1097 document is already in effect a communal text, with close analogues to the consular cases of the 1140s. This seems to me mistaken; the document is a standard refutation of rights, and the only link with the consular texts, as with the *placita* before it, is the signatures of powerful people and the three most active *iudices* in Milan at the end, which is what anyone resolving a dispute would want in this (or any) period. For the crusade, *HM*, c. 4; see Lucioni, *Anselmo IV da Bovisio*.

14. *HM*, cc. 9–21.

15. *HM*, cc. 15, 44, 47, 58; see Coleman, 'Representative Assemblies' (with earlier bibliography), and Grillo, 'Una frattura', 692–96, for the *concio*. Grillo, 'A Milano nel 1130', 227, sees Giordano as calling the *concio* in 1118, but Landolfo does not say so. Anselmo V also faced a *publicum interdictum cleri et populi* in 1128 (*HM*, c. 52); Landolfo does not tell us in what context the clergy and people met together. On Anselmo V, Zerbi, 'La Chiesa ambrosiana', 162–84, is basic, although inevitably dependent on the same Landolfo narrative.

16. *HM*, cc. 30–31, 38–41; for Grosolano, Arcioni, 'Grosolano', and Rossini, 'Note alla "Historia Mediolanensis" di Landolfo iuniore', both with some outdated assumptions. It is worth noting that the fall of both Erlembaldo in 1075 and Grosolano in 1111 were precipitated by natural disasters; it may well be that the elaboration of Giordano's public *arengo* after the earthquake of 1117 was to avoid a similar fate.

17. *HM*, cc. 23 (letter-drafter), 44 (1117), 58 (fall of Anselmo), 59, 65–66 (the last two are the da Rhò consuls); 'suis'/'eius' *consules*: 44, 48 bis, both referring to 1117. See Keller, 'Gli inizi', 51–52; and Tabacco, *The Struggle for Power*, 337–38.

18. *HM*, cc. 4, 24, 47.

19. For narratives, contrast the *Annales Mediolanenses* of 1154–77, finished soon after, which are about wars almost exclusively. The 1132 letter is edited in *Die Lombardische Briefsammlung*, n. 80, a currently web-only edition destined in the end for *MGH*.

20. The 1117, 1130, and 1138 cases are in *Gli atti del Comune*, nn. 1, 3, 4; see the whole edition for those following, up to 1216. See in general Padoa Schioppa, 'Aspetti della giustizia milanese', 503–49, the basic

study. The best institutional analyses of the commune in this period are Manaresi's introduction to *Gli atti del Comune*, and Rossetti, 'Le istituzioni comunali a Milano nel XII secolo'. In 1130, however, the standardisation of later cases had not yet developed fully: see below, n. 25.

21. Milanese political power was indeed unusually uncontested inside its diocese: as Bordone notes ('Le origini del comune in Lombardia', 321), the Milanesi fought other cities in the early twelfth century, not rural lords. Some of the consular judicial texts stress the agreement of the parties, and thus open the possibility that these judgements are really private arbitrations—a view popular among traditional legal historians, e.g. Sinatti, *La gerarchia delle fonti*, 18–28, and cf. (more nuanced) Manaresi in *Gli atti del Comune*, xxxiv, who could not accept that consuls claimed full judicial rights, as opposed to de facto powers, before these were granted to the city by the emperor, which was only after Barbarossa's defeat. But the first judgement in contumacy, in the absence of one of the parties, which shows full claims to jurisdiction over the unwilling (here a major rural signorial family, the da Carcano), is as early as 1147, *Gli atti del Comune*, n. 14. Sinatti, ibid., 23, following Manaresi, gets around this by arguing that the fact that consular judges were imperial *missi* gave them delegated imperial power, but there are no signs that this was more than a judicial title, and one particular to Milan, too—other cities acted in the same way without such *missi*; cf. e.g. chapter 3, n. 51, in this volume, for Pisa. Note also *S. Ulderico*, n. 1 (a. 1142), which is a real private arbitration given by Stefanardo, who was a consular judge for preceding and succeeding years: it hardly differs from consular cases, and is written by a consular scribe. I have argued elsewhere that consular judgements were at least modelled on arbitrations, although not the same as them: Wickham, *Courts and Conflict*, 35–38. Behrmann, 'L'atto giuridico', discusses the witnesses.

22. *Gli atti del Comune*, xxi–cxxi. The only other focussed consular/communal publications for our period are *Codice diplomatico del Senato romano* for Rome, and *Codice diplomatico della Repubblica di Genova* for Genoa, re-edited in a different form in *I libri iurium*. The Genoa editions do not, however, for the most part include the city's court cases (for which see chapter 5, n. 5, in this volume); this contrasts strongly with Manaresi's *Atti*. This is doubtless because, in the absence of a surviving *Liber iurium* for Milan, or indeed any of the rest of the communal archive, court cases are all we have for this period.

23. Wickham, 'Justice in the Kingdom of Italy', 220–21, 239. Cf. also chapter 5, n. 21, in this volume, for Pavia in 1112, a late but anomalous *placitum*.

24. *Gli atti del Comune*, n. 1. Cf. also—although it is not strong support for archiepiscopal dominance—*De bello Mediolanensium adversus Comenses. Liber Cumanus*, 407, a text which apparently preceded the *Liber Cumanus* poem in the now-lost manuscript, which states that Archbishop Giordano in 1118 *tunc regebat Mediolanum*. See Grillo, 'A Milano nel 1130', 227.

25. *Gli atti del Comune*, n. 3; Otto of Freising, *Gesta Friderici*, 2.13; see Keller, *Signori e vassalli*, 1–10. The three groups also appear in *Mensa di Lodi*, n. 38, a Milanese document of 1125. Critical are Occhipinti, 'I *capitanei* a Milano', 28; Maire Vigueur, *Cavaliers et citoyens*, 350; and Grillo, 'A Milano nel 1130'. (Grillo however overstates, it seems to me, the diplomatic differences between this text and later consular judgements; it is doubtless transitional, as he says, but I would see it as divergent from them above all because consular formulae had not yet become fixed.) For Landolfo, see *HM*, cc. 38, 53: one is a list of three dead people in a battle in 1113, where the three-fold categorisation seems to act as a metonym for the city community; the other is a formal choice of representatives to meet the archbishop in 1128. Both show that Landolfo in the 1130s, at least, is still thinking in terms of the three *ordines* of the eleventh century, as Keller also pointed out.

26. Archiepiscopal cases: Giulini, *Memorie*, vol. 5, 547–48, 548–54; Zerbi, 'La Chiesa ambrosiana', 207–11 (a. 1123); *Mensa di Lodi*, n. 38. Of the 'quasi-consular' texts, the first is *Gli atti del Comune*, n. 2, of 1119, which has a long set of thirty-five participants; but the source for this is two summaries of the 16th and 17th centuries, and the status of the grouping is unclear—the summaries imply that the original text simply listed the members of the *concio*. The 1129 text is edited in Besozzi, 'Hobedientia de Abiasca e de Clari', 130–32; for analysis see Grillo, 'A Milano nel 1130', 229–30. (Note that the archbishop's own archive does not survive in Milan; the documents which front him all come from other *fondi*, which makes his prominence all the more notable.)

27. E.g. *S. Simpliciano*, n. 5; *S. Dionigi*, nn. 2, 3, 7, 8; *Mensa di Lodi*, n. 42; *S. Maria delle Veteri*, n. 3.

28. *Gli atti del Comune*, n. 1.

29.   Cf. Keller, *Signori e vassalli*, 347–54. See above, n. 26, for the texts.

30.   See the lists in *Gli atti del Comune*, 537–62, with the addition of Vincent of Prague, *Annales*, 675 for 1158 (Classen, *Studium und Gesellschaft*, 50–51—see also 49 for a table of judicial consuls). In the next pages, references to consuls are all to these lists, and to the documents they refer to. It must be remembered that the figures are very unlikely to be complete; as already noted, Milan's communal archive and any formal registers of communal acts are lost, so we are reliant on the court cases for our prosopography. Castagnetti, 'Feudalità e società comunale II', 20–23, notes the same development.

31.   Da Carcano: see Grillo, *Milano*, 288–91, and Keller, *Signori e vassalli*, 186–87 (they provided one consul, in 1196: *Gli atti del Comune*, n. 194). Da Besate: Violante, 'I "da Besate"'. For the urban–rural difference, see Grillo, 'Aristocrazia urbana, aristocrazia rurale', 87–96. Da Rhò and Burri: see below. Da Porta Romana: see Salvatori, 'I presunti "*capitanei* delle porte"', 46–68. Da Settala: they are not well-documented, but the family held fiefs at Coronate south-west of the city, and were close to the nearby monastery of Morimondo: *Morimondo*, nn. 58, 66 (fiefs), 92, 170. Da Soresina: Violante, 'Una famiglia feudale' (which concentrates, however, on pre-1050). For the Crivelli, a relatively rich family in the thirteenth century at least, see the detailed study by Caso, *I Crivelli*. They did not actually provide consuls, after 1117–30, until 1167, but they constantly appear as witnesses to consular acts in between: *Gli atti del Comune*, nn. 5, 8, 13, 25, 29, 46. The same is true of the Visconti, who are not consuls between 1130 and 1159, but witness in between in *Gli atti del Comune*, nn. 5, 7, 8, 13, 17, 25, 30—see for the family Occhipinti, 'I Visconti di Milano', and, earlier, Biscaro, 'I maggiori dei Visconti'. The da Baggio family are on the edge of this group: they were an urban capitaneal family, closely associated with the archbishop (and providing many senior clerics); their first consul after 1117 was already in 1151, but they did not witness for the commune in the 1140s (the first is *Gli atti del Comune*, n. 22, for 1150); see in general Corsi, 'Note sulla famiglia da Baggio'; Keller, *Signori e vassalli*, 182–85. The Grassi are similar: not consuls again until 1160 (*Gli atti del Comune*, n. 48), and close to the monastery of S. Ambrogio, for which they were apparently hereditary advocates (see S. *Ambrogio 3/1*, passim), but witnessing in *Gli atti del Comune*, n. 11 and possibly 23, and linked to consuls in the private arbitration S. *Ulderico*, n. 1 (a. 1142).

32.   Da Pusterla: first consul is *Gli atti del Comune*, n. 121, although they witness consular documents in nn. 27, 30, 42; in the archbishop's entourage in the 1120s in Zerbi, 'La chiesa ambrosiana', 210, and *Mensa di Lodi*, n. 38 (of course, a member of the family was archbishop in these years); *seniores* in *Morimondo*, n. 35; Anselmo da Pusterla is advocate of S. Maria di Aurona in *Chiaravalle* 1, n. 66, and *S. Maria di Aurona*, n. 7; they were also prominent in Lodi. Da Melegnano: after Arialdo (see above, n. 8), they are with the archbishop in Giulini, *Memorie*, vol. 5, 547–48, and *Mensa di Lodi*, n. 38; their first consul is in *Gli atti del Comune*, n. 123. Pozzobonelli: first consul in *Gli atti del Comune*, n. 206, although they sometimes appear as witnesses to consular documents earlier, in nn. 8, 12, 38, and then several times in the 1180s; one of them formally meets Anselmo V in *HM*, c. 53; they hold land and fiefs in Villamaggiore in *Gli atti del Comune*, n. 76, and *Chiaravalle* 2, nn. 13, 102, and are in general better-documented in landholding terms after 1150 than before. Da Tenebiago: very little-documented after 1130, they hold land from the da Landriano and tithes/signorial rights in Villamaggiore (cf. below, n. 35) in *Gli atti del Comune*, n. 169; *Chiaravalle* 1, n. 96; cf. *Chiaravalle* 2, n. 6. Fanti: see Chiappa Mauri, 'A Milano nel 1164', 23–29, and Andenna, 'Le strutture sociali', 266–69.

33.   Biscaro, 'Gli avvocati'. Cf. Keller, *Signori e vassalli*, 180–82. A family member witnessed for the consuls only once, in 1154 (*Gli atti del Comune*, n. 28).

34.   For the late eleventh century, e.g. *I placiti*, n. 467; for the early twelfth, see e.g. *HM*, cc. 19 bis, 53, 60, 63; *Gli atti del Comune*, n. 2 (not a consular text); Giulini, *Memorie*, vol. 5, 552, and *Mensa di Lodi*, n. 25 (for the archbishop). First consul: *Gli atti del Comune*, n. 33; rector of the Lega: ibid., nn. 94, 100, etc. Family members witnessed for the commune in 1140 and 1153: *Gli atti del Comune*, nn. 5, 27. For Villamaggiore, see e.g. *Chiaravalle* 1, nn. 50, 112.

35.   Vassals of S. Ambrogio: *APM*, n. 40, cf. 515, 588; later, *S. Ambrogio* 3/1, n. 45. For the family's public roles, *APM*, n. 854 (witness to the *consulatus* document); Zerbi, 'La chiesa ambrosiana', 210 (a. 1123, with the archbishop); *Gli atti del Comune*, n. 181 (first consul, in 1193). Quinto de' Stampi: *Gli atti del Comune*, nn. 44, 68; *S. Giorgio al Palazzo*, nn. 44, 53, 78; cf. *S. Lorenzo*, n. 31. They also held in Villamaggiore: *Chiaravalle* 1, nn. 7, 41; cf. *Chiaravalle* 2, n. 5.

36. Violante, 'I "da Besate"'. Another example is the da Intimiano, whose lands were spread across Lombardy, but who were not involved in Milanese city politics apart from the famous example of Archbishop Ariberto: see esp. Basile Weatherill, 'Una famiglia "longobarda"'.

37. With the archbishop: *Mensa di Lodi*, nn. 38, 42; *Velate*, n. 123; *Capitolo Maggiore*, nn. 19, 21, 22. Tithes: *Velate*, n. 61; *S. Maria in Valle*, n. 8. Castle at Rhò: *Velate*, n. 61. Other lands: e.g. *S. Giorgio al Palazzo*, n. 32.

38. Archiepiscopal entourage and vassals: Zerbi, 'La chiesa ambrosiana', 210; *Velate*, n. 123 (here Malastreva is explicitly a Burri, which he is not in most consular texts, though see *Gli atti del Comune*, n. 2). Land: *S. Giorgio al Palazzo*, nn. 12–14, 16; *S. Stefano di Vimercate*, n. 51; *Chiaravalle* I, nn. 34, 80, cf. 112; *Morimondo* I, nn. 104, 141, 152. Tithes: *S. Stefano di Vimercate*, n. 25; cf. *Chiaravalle* I, n. 69. Dowry: *Morimondo* I, n. 43. Malastreva also intervened in the bitter dispute between the Capitolo and the monks of S. Ambrogio, in a letter to a cardinal whom he describes as his kinsman: Pflugk-Harttung, *Iter italicum*, 464–65, a reference I owe to the kindness of Katrin Getschmann. For the family in the thirteenth century, see Grillo, *Milano*, 263–66.

39. Fasola, 'Una famiglia di sostenitori milanesi'. For 1143, *Capitolo Maggiore*, n. 12. For *proditor*, *Annales Mediolanenses*, 373, 376.

40. Gualterio in 1109: *Chiaravalle* I, n. 7 (cf. n. 8). Ariprando di Pagano: from *APM*, n. 823 to *Capitolo Minore/Decumani*, n. 2; *Chiaravalle* I, n. 5, for his father. Ambrogio Pagano: from *APM*, n. 509 (notary) and 585, a. 1078 (*iudex*) to *S. Vittore di Varese*, n. 34; see also above, n. 8, and the next note. For the later Ariprando and Barbarossa, *Annales Mediolanenses*, 376. I am not convinced that the Ariprando Corbo of the period 1155–74, a very frequent scribe and *iudex*, is necessarily the same person as the Ariprando *iudex* who was a consul; but if he is (as Chiappa Mauri, 'A Milano nel 1164', 29–34, argues), then these *iudices* were part of the Corbo family who after the 1140s owned some land south of the city and were witnesses for S. Giorgio al Palazzo: medium landowners, probably, like other families of *iudices*, as we shall see.

41. Keller, *Signori e vassalli*, 188–89, briefly sets out the chronological difference. In Lucca, too, *iudices* were very often major landowners in the eleventh-century city: Schwarzmaier, *Lucca*, 309–28; but not in the twelfth-century city: Wickham, *Courts and Conflict*, 56–60. Even in the eleventh, however, *iudex* in Lucca could also be a qualification

one worked up to from the notarial profession, as Ambrogio Pagano did. An Ambrogio Pagano *infantulus* appears as a landowner with a medium-size estate in 1062 (*APM*, nn. 434–35), but this must be a different man; the judicial figure is already a trained notary by 1069.

42.   For Stefanardo's land and Vimercate connections, see *Chiaravalle 2*, n. 30; *S. Stefano di Vimercate*, nn. 20, 78, 85, 114, 119 (land); ibid., nn. 52, 61, 64, 72, 73, 94 (judicial roles)—plus *Gli atti del Comune*, n. 349 (a. 1211), and Grillo, *Milano*, 343, for a 1220s reference. The later thirteenth-century Milan-based historian Stefanardo da Vimercate (see Cremaschi, *Stefanardo*, 1–9, for his life) must have been a descendant. For Vimercate as a rising small town, see Rossetti, *Percorsi di Chiesa*, 186–209. Another immigrant *iudex* is Ottobello of Lodi, consul between 1140 and 1144; we may perhaps also add Arderico Cagainosa, consul in the same two years, for that surname is earlier attested on the Isola Comacina: *APM*, nn. 642, 883; *S. Faustino*, nn. 2, 3.

43.   Andenna, 'Dall'Orto (de Orto), Oberto'; Classen, *Studium und Gesellschaft*, 50–51; and di Renzo Villata, 'La formazione dei "Libri Feudorum"', 666–81, collect most of the references. For 1139, see *Chiaravalle* 1, n. 65. Classen says (50) that 'die Familie scheint aber zu den valvassorischen gehört zu haben'—I can see no evidence for saying so.

44.   For the texts and their study, see below, nn. 57, 59. For Oberto's possible training in Milan, Classen, *Studium und Gesellschaft*, 36–39; for the 1140s for the date of Oberto's letters (other authors assume the 1150s), ibid., 60, 67. For Pavia, see Radding, *The Origins* (the city offered a dense legal training but not a formal school, 97); he cautiously suggests a link with the Milanese jurists, 172–73. Vincent of Prague: *Annales*, 675; Classen, *Studium und Gesellschaft*, 51, cites the necrology.

45.   For 1151 and 1147, see, respectively, *Italia sacra*, vol. 5, cols. 793–94 and 788; the best commentary on the latter is Padoa Schioppa, 'Il ruolo della cultura giuridica', 278–84; see also di Renzo Villata, 'La formazione dei "Libri Feudorum"', 676–77.

46.   See Classen, *Studium und Gesellschaft*, 49–54, for Girardo's legal and consular career (plus Soldi Rondanini, 'Cagapesto [Cacapisti, Pesto], Gerardo'). Andenna, 'Una famiglia milanese di "cives"', is basic for the family. 1154: Otto of Freising, *Gesta Friderici*, 2.16–18. 1177: see chapter 1, n. 6, in this volume. 1170: *Canonica di S. Ambrogio*, nn. 63, 70, 76, 79. 1188: *Gli atti del Comune*, n. 159. Bruzzano: *S. Eusebio*, nn. 1, 2; cf. their witnessing for the same church of S. Eusebio in nn. 3–5.

47. Menant, 'Une forme de distinction inattendue'. 'Pesto', strictly, refers to anything crushed, or pressed solid, both food and non-food; the details of the modern Genoese pesto recipe do not have to be kept in the mind. As a result Cagapisto is translated by Menant, ibid., 452, as 'crush-a-shit'—as also Cagainosa as 'shit-on-the-bones'—these are valid alternatives to my own etymologies.

48. Wickham, *Roma medievale*, 438. For Mala- names, see Collavini, 'Sviluppo signorile'.

49. Otto of Freising, *Gesta Friderici I.*, 2.16–18 (Girardus Niger), 2.13 (*miliciae cingulum*—it is a standard phrase for office-holding in the late Roman empire, as Otto, a highly classicising author, knew, and does not have to mean entry into the military *ordines*. Even if Otto elsewhere in this text, ibid., 1.26 and 2.23, uses it to mean 'knighthood', in his *Chronica*, 4.9, 5.7, 6.2, it clearly means 'office'). Note that Girardo often dropped the 'Caga-' from his surname at the end of his life (Menant, ibid., 445, 452–53); but his relatives did not.

50. See Mohr, *Holy Sh*t*, for an excellent historical survey of taboo and rude words, focussed on English but with wide applicability. For Hildebrand, see e.g. Benzone of Alba, *Ad Heinricum IV. Imperatorem*, 6.6 (562).

51. Shit-names were not restricted to the urban (usually élite, including aristocratic) milieu, but also included some peasants: Menant, 'Une forme de distinction inattendue', 443–44. But they did not extend to the rural aristocracy.

52. 'Il "Liber Pergaminus"', lines 271–92. For Milan, Barni, 'Milano verso l'egemonia', is as good a guide as any to wars. For Como, see below, n. 56.

53. Vincent of Prague, *Annales*, 675; for 1154, above, n. 46.

54. But not all of them: the Zavatari, who had a consul of the *cives* in 1130 (*Gli atti del Comune*, n. 3), had signorial rights in Moirano in 1160: *Canonica di S. Ambrogio*, n. 47.

55. *Annales Mediolanenses*, passim.

56. *De bello Mediolanensium adversus Comenses. Liber Cumanus.* The eyewitness nature of the poem is explicit in lines 6, 1670–74. For consuls, lines 703–4; for *proceres*, lines 752, 1051, 1125, 1602, 1645, and cf. 1995 for *maiores*. Consuls also appear in the 'introduction' to the poem, 407 (cf. above, n. 24). *Iudices* fought in the war, too: e.g. lines 253–56. The only recent discussion of the poem I have seen is Grillo,

'Una fonte', 68–76, focussed on its evidence for early rural communes; Settia, *Comuni in guerra*, 91–114, on Milan, and idem, *Rapine, assedi*, a general survey of medieval warfare in Italy, also cite it with regularity.

57. Anselmo dall'Orto, *Iuris civilis instrumentum*; idem, *De summa Anselmini de Orto super contractibus*. Comment: Classen, *Studium und Gesellschaft*, 55–57 (Verona), 64–66 (Anselmo); Padoa Schioppa, 'Il ruolo della cultura giuridica', 278–89 (Verona); Cortese, *Il diritto*, vol. 2, 122–23, 161–62 (Anselmo; he is very negative about the sophistication of the text on leases). *Gli atti del Comune*, nn. 73–74, a. 1170, is the only Milanese consular case with Roman actions in the century; cf. Behrmann, 'Von der Sentenz zur Akte', 76–78.

58. Edited as *La Summa Trium Librorum* by Conte and Menzinger; for his culture, ibid., li–lxiv; for his career, xxvii–xlii; cf. Wickham, *Courts and Conflict*, 51–53; Savigni, *Episcopato*, 580–81. He is not, however, documented as a *consul maior*, Lucca's term for an annual city leader.

59. Lehmann, *Das langobardische Lehnrecht*, Antiqua 8 and 10 [henceforth *Antiqua*]; quote from 142. Commentary: Classen, *Studium und Gesellschaft*, 59–68; Reynolds, *Fiefs and Vassals*, 215–30, 483–86; and the fullest recent study, di Renzo Villata, 'La formazione dei "Libri Feudorum"'; see n. 63 for earlier literature. The only other named author in the text (*Antiqua* 9) is Ugo of *Gambolado*, Gambolò in the Pavese, who was a *consul* in Pavia in 1112 (di Renzo Villata, 'La formazione dei "Libri Feudorum"', 657, sums up here; see chapter 5, n. 21, in this volume)—what is said here about Oberto largely applies to him too.

60. *Antiqua* 8.1 (Lehmann, *Das langobardische Lehnrecht*, 115); for Milanese law being posed here as superior to Roman law, see among very many Andenna, 'Dall'Orto (de Orto), Oberto'; Classen, *Studium und Gesellschaft*, 63; Padoa Schioppa, 'Aspetti della giustizia milanese', 549.

61. Lehmann, *Das langobardische Lehnrecht*, 114–48, gives the references to the Milanese statutes in the footnotes; for later feudal law, Reynolds, *Fiefs and Vassals*, e.g. 249–57, 286–87, 460.

62. *Gli atti del Comune*, nn. 5, 18, 24 (aa. 1140–51), etc.; the Verona *consilium* concerns feudal law too, above, n. 45.

63. Historians (two out of very many are Castagnetti, 'Introduzione', 20; Keller, *Signori e vassalli*, 3–5, 23–24) tend to assume that

Oberto wrote *Antiqua* 8.16, the section about *capitanei* being defined as the holders of [tithe rights in] *pievi* in fief, and *valvassores* as those who hold fiefs/benefices 'anciently' from *capitanei*—and those who acquire them *noviter*, 'recently', being [only] *plebeii* (note that one of these 'recent' families was the Cagapisto, as Oberto presumably knew). Transalpine legal historians, however, Classen, *Studium und Gesellschaft*, 68, and Reynolds, *Fiefs and Vassals*, 217 and 485, regard this as an interpolation. This goes back to Laspeyres, *Über die Entstehung*, 192–93, who remains the only person, back in 1830, who has seriously investigated the issue; he did so entirely on the basis of the interruption in Oberto's argument caused by this paragraph, and certainly not on any MS evidence (the main MSS, which begin around 1200, all contain the passage)—and Laspeyres, indeed, restricts himself to saying that it is 'sehr bedenklich' that the passage is inserted. In the absence of more detailed study (which might indeed not take us further) I think we simply have to register uncertainty here. For *pievi*, the basic study is Violante, 'Pievi e parrocchie'; 718–21 for the link with the *Libri feudorum*.

64.   Kershaw, 'Working towards the Führer'.

65.   [Otto of Freising and] Rahewin, *Gesta Friderici*, 4.1–10—note that Frederick also legislated about feudal law in the same gathering.

66.   For assemblies, see above, n. 15; see also Celli, 'Il ruolo del parlamento', which gives assemblies their proper weight in the early history of communes, even if his general argument is otherwise alien to me. I discuss the issue further in Wickham, 'The "Feudal Revolution"'.

67.   See for Milan *Gli atti del Comune*, xxxviii, lxxiii–lxxvi.

68.   Mainoni, 'A proposito della "rivoluzione fiscale"'. 35.

69.   See *La Summa Trium Librorum*, 383–84 (cf. Conte, *Servi medievali*, 111–14), for rural oppression; for bad behaviour among aristocrats, Lansing, *The Florentine Magnates*, 165–91, is a good guide.

3. PISA

1.   The figure of three hundred is in *Gesta triumphalia per Pisanos facta*, 6, a text of around 1120. The poem was edited in 1904 as *Liber Maiolichinus* [henceforth *LM*]. Booty: e.g. *LM*, lines 2925 (the king of Mallorca here says the Pisans simply *volunt omnes thesauros tollere nobis*, 'want to take all our treasures from us', and he was not wrong—

this was not an expedition of conquest), 3515–19. Enrico pievano of Calci is widely accepted as the author, on flimsy grounds (e.g. Fisher, 'The Pisan Clergy', 193–95; Ceccarelli Lemut, 'Enrico da Pisa'), but von der Höh, *Erinnerungskultur*, 156–60, 164–78, who also cautiously accepts the standard authorship, has good reasons to say that the author is a cleric (ibid., 155–98, is the fullest recent study of a text which would repay further work). Still, the poem is quite as secular as it is religious in tone.

2.   For the wealth of recent work on Pisa in this period see, among many, the works of Gabriella Rossetti, Mauro Ronzani, and Maria Luisa Ceccarelli Lemut cited in the bibliography; the classic survey is Volpe, *Studi*. For the families, see the articles (partly collected in Rossetti et al., *Pisa nei secoli XI e XII*) and the *tesi di laurea* cited below, nn. 65–77.

3.   Concerning direct evidence for commerce, *Documenti sulle relazioni delle città toscane* contains a good set of private documents for Pisans in late twelfth-century Constantinople; see also, for example, Baldelli, 'La carta pisana di Filadelfia', for an early twelfth-century Pisan naval account in Italian; letters concerning the commercial expeditions of the Ebriaci family in Byzantium, Egypt, and the rest of Italy in the 1130s in *Die Lombardische Briefsammlung*, nn. 56–57; and a reference to a commercial *socius* in a document of 1151 (Puglia, 'Fuori della città', 194); see further pp. 105, 107, in this volume. Pisa as a funnel for goods: Cantini, 'Ritmi e forme'; Baldassarri and Giorgio, 'La ceramica'. Imports are further shown by the Islamic polychrome bowls (*bacini*) which decorate Pisan church façades and campanili: Berti and Tongiorgi, *I bacini*. Pisa produced goods, too, in our period: see in particular Bruni, Abela, and Berti, *Ricerche*, for the Piazza dei Cavalieri excavations, which showed metalworking from the seventh century to c. 1100. For metalwork, see also the variety of sources cited in Renzi Rizzo, 'Pisarum et Pisanorum descriptiones', 1–2, 27–29.

4.   Goldberg, *Trade and Institutions*, sums up for now; Constable, *Trade and Traders*, covers Spain.

5.   A good recent survey is Salvatori, 'Lo spazio economico di Pisa'; a neat synthesis is Petralia, 'Le "navi" e i "cavalli"'. For earlier periods: Tangheroni, 'La prima espansione di Pisa'; Bruce, 'The Politics of Violence and Trade'; Catia Renzi Rizzo is preparing a new analysis.

6.   Malaterra, *De rebus gestis*, 45. Treaties: Banti, *Scritti di storia*, 287–350, and Salvatori, 'Lo spazio economico di Pisa' sum up; texts

are in *Documenti sulle relazioni delle città toscane* and *I diplomi arabi*. For how commerce worked in the twelfth century, Abulafia, *The Two Italies*, is basic. Pisans also attacked Nice before 1119 (Salvatori, *Boni amici e vicini*, 185–87); but in the twelfth century, naval wars were above all with southern Italy and Genoa. For later 'piracy'—i.e. when Pisa was an accepted player, with treaties, and piracy began to be an embarrassment—see Puglia, 'Fuori della città', 183–88, and esp. Salvatori, 'Il corsaro pisano Trapelicino'.

7. For a context, see Ronzani, *Chiesa e "Civitas"*, 11–32, 240–69. Ecclesiastical jurisdiction over Corsica remained fought over between Pisa and Genoa until Innocent II established a division of rights in 1133.

8. Although Genoa did have the best chronicle of the early commune, beginning in 1099, Caffaro's *Annali genovesi*; see pp. 162–63 in this volume. The fullest overall surveys of Pisan self-memorialisation are Fisher, 'The Pisan Clergy', and von der Höh, *Erinnerungskultur*.

9. The basic epigraphical edition is now Ottavio Banti's *Monumenta epigrafica pisana*: nn. 48–50 for Buscheto, 46–47, 51 (the Palermo poem) for the expeditions. The dates of these texts are disputed, often fiercely, between an early dating—eleventh century for the poems—and a later dating, in some cases closer to the date of the current cathedral façade, around 1150; Banti, among others, prefers later dates (see also Banti, *Scritti di storia*, 67–90), whereas Giuseppe Scalia, the other editor of the texts, prefers early ones (see for example, among many articles, 'Tre iscrizioni e una facciata'). Von der Höh, *Erinnerungskultur*, 315–63, in the most recent detailed study, accepts 1135 for the most likely date of the Palermo inscription, following Ronzani, 'La nuova Roma'. I shall not make arguments that assume that they are either contemporary or later.

10. *Roma altera*: *LM*, 133; *Monumenta epigrafica pisana*, n. 9, for the Porta Aurea. See Scalia, '"Romanitas" pisana', 805–6 on *Roma altera*; the whole article is the basic analysis of classical imagery in Pisa in this period, which extended to the wholescale incorporation of classical inscriptions into the cathedral masonry (ibid., 795–802); see further Petralia, 'La percezione'; von der Höh, *Erinnerungskultur*, 399–412.

11. *LM*, e.g. lines 445–48, 717–18, 780, 1184–86; cf. von der Höh, *Erinnerungskultur*, 403–5.

12. Edited in Scalia, 'Il carme pisano'; see below, n. 29, for bibliography. Again its date is contested, although it has to predate 1119, the date of the manuscript.

13. *Liber Guidonis*, ed. Campopiano (see also Fisher, 'The Pisan Clergy', 177–83; von der Höh, *Erinnerungskultur*, 91–103). For Pisa as *belligeras* see *LM*, line 778.

14. *I Costituti*, edited by Vignoli, includes the earliest surviving version of the two *Constituta*, dating to 1186–90 (ibid., lxxvi–lxxvii); 129 for quote. For recent analyses, see Vignoli's introduction; Storti Storchi, *Intorno ai Costituti pisani* (45–48, 69–72 for earlier non-Roman law); Wickham, *Courts and Conflict*, 114–67 (118 for earlier non-Roman law). The best earlier analysis is Classen, *Studium und Gesellschaft*, 68–88.

15. Ronzani, *Chiesa e "Civitas"*, 223–28, sets it out clearly for 1087 (although external patronage for 1064, ibid., 117, is guesswork); 1098 is unproblematic (Matzke, *Daibert*, discusses it in most detail). For 1113, *LM* refs to three flags, of Pisa, of the cathedral, and of the papacy, at lines 1684–88; see p. 88, in this volume, for the archbishop nominally leading the expedition. This sponsorship did not, however, amount to the Pisans raiding only because they had been asked to; 1087 and, later, 1113 were the Pisans' own initiatives.

16. For arguments for crusading-style imagery which seem to me over-interpretative, see e.g. Scalia in *Gesta triumphalia per Pisanos facta*, xl–xlii; Banti, 'La giustizia'; von der Höh, *Erinnerungskultur*, is more balanced.

17. See in general Ronzani, 'Dall'*edificatio ecclesiae*'. Buscheto was an early *operarius*; Ildebrando was the most prominent—see p. 91 in this volume.

18. Volpe, *Studi*, 1: 'Il comune pisano, nato dalla organizzazione privata degli armatori e dei mercanti di mare ...'.

19. Maragone is edited in *Gli Annales Pisani*. See Ceccarelli Lemut, 'Bernardo Maragone', for his career.

20. *I placiti*, nn. 414, 421, 428, 433, 436, 445; for a context, Goez, *Beatrix von Canossa*, 89–99, 106–7; Ronzani, *Chiesa e "Civitas"*, 109–90—the whole book is basic for the period 1060–92.

21. The first hard-to-control communal trouble related by Maragone is in 1182: *Gli Annales Pisani*, 73–74. But we must add the 1153 Visconti crisis too, although we do not know how serious it was: see below, n. 50.

22. *I placiti*, n. 445; cf. inquisitio, n. 14 (*I placiti*, 451–52), in which Ugo acts in a case at Beatrice's command, but again in 1077, after her death.

23. *Die Urkunden und Briefe der Markgräfin Mathilde von Tuszien* [henceforth *DM*], n. 23.

24. Ronzani, 'L'affermazione dei Comuni cittadini', 5–10; Cowdrey, 'The Mahdiya Campaign', 16–18. For the 1081 Pisa privilege, see below, n. 27; for other diplomas of Henry and Matilda, see below, nn. 26, 43.

25. Ronzani, 'Le tre famiglie dei "Visconti"', separates out not only two but three vicecomital families. This separation is not quite conclusive genealogically, but the political differences between the separate vicecomital branches are pretty clear, and I am happy to accept the argument. For pro-imperial families, see also Struve, 'Heinrich IV', 516–23. For Matilda, see the list of acts and locations in Overmann, *La contessa Matilde di Canossa*, 127–43.

26. *Heinrici IV. diplomata*, nn. 359, 362, 404, are the emperor's gifts, to the cathedral and the Orlandi family (for whom see also 346, a *placitum*); the last is from 1089, by when Henry's support in Tuscany had waned (cf. also Matzke, *Daibert*, 59–60). Matilda re-gave the land in 404 in *DM*, n. 74, and also confirmed Orlandi lands in n. 125.

27. *Heinrici IV. diplomata*, n. 336, re-edited in Rossetti, 'Pisa e l'impero'; 163, 168–70 for the interpolation. (This argument is convincing, but there are problems about interpolation-hunting, in that once started it is difficult to stop: see Puglia, 'Reazioni alla dominazione canossiana', 41–46, who adds more interpolations, and contrast Struve, 'Heinrich IV', 514–16, who defends the text as a whole.) Henry did not create this civic collectivity, for Matilda in 1077 (*DM*, n. 23) had referred to the Pisan *cives* as in effect the guarantors of the communal life of the cathedral canons; but this is to me less significant a citation.

28. The most recent edition of the text is in *I brevi dei consoli*, 107–8. For the text as a forgery: Wolf, 'Il cosiddetto "Privilegio logudorese"'. Blasco, 'Consuntivo delle riflessioni', and Ronzani, *Chiesa e "Civitas"*, 190–99 (which also argues for the tighter dating of 1080–81), successfully defend its authenticity. Blasco's detailed argument that the text should be redated to 1121 has not yet been comprehensively countered (even if he is not in the end convincing to me: he finds it hard to argue away the citation of Bishop Gerardo, and the list of *ammicos* fits the 1080s better than the 1120s), and it would be wrong to put too much weight on the date; my interpretation here does not do so, however.

29.   Scalia, 'Il carme pisano', 43, for the quote. See above, n. 12, for the uncertainty of dating here too. Commentary, apart from Scalia: Fisher, 'The Pisan Clergy', 183–93; Cowdrey, 'The Mahdiya Campaign'; the best analysis is in von der Höh, *Erinnerungskultur*, 120–54. Scalia argues that all four are consuls; it may be so (the phrases would then be separated for reasons of scansion), but it does not alter the argument.

30.   See in general Ronzani, *Chiesa e "Civitas"*, 229–33, 245–46; and Matzke, *Daibert*.

31.   Rossetti, 'Il lodo del vescovo Daiberto', gives the text and the basic analysis; see also Ronzani, *Chiesa e "Civitas"*, 233–40, 247–55. See Redi, *Pisa com'era*, 200–11, and plates at the back for surviving towers; Garzella, *Pisa com'era*, 62–63 and passim, for a documentary context.

32.   Rossetti, 'I caratteri del politico', goes further than I would here. Matzke, *Daibert*, 64–65, following Hagen Keller (see chapter 1, n. 27, in this volume), says that the oath is like those of the Peace of God; this does not seem to me helpful. For the consular oaths, see *I brevi dei consoli*, 60, 88.

33.   *I brevi dei consoli*, 105–7, 108–10, is the most recent edition of both; for commentary, see among others Rossetti, 'Società e istituzioni', 320–37; Ronzani, *Chiesa e "Civitas"*, 252–55, with different views. Wickham, 'Property-ownership', 227–29, translates the texts; the focus there is on rural signorial rights, however, not the city.

34.   William, etc.: see in general Niermeyer, *Mediae latinitatis lexicon minus*, 260–61, s.v. *consul* 5. Note that early ruling consuls in Italy were not by any means always annual. Caffaro's *Annali genovesi*, 5–17, shows that consuls changed every three or four years in Genoa between 1099 and 1121; in Pisa, the consuls of the Mallorca war served for three years, and several consuls into the 1120s held office for several years at a stretch, which does not have to have involved annual re-elections: see the data in Ceccarelli Lemut, 'I consoli'.

35.   Wickham, *Roma medievale*, 236–37; cf. *LM*, line 51, referring to the Pisan consuls of 1113 as *consules atque duces*.

36.   Hiestand, 'Iudex', for the *iudices*; Wickham, *Courts and Conflict*, 118–21, for borrowing from Rome.

37.   *Codice diplomatico del monastero di Santo Stefano*, n. 96. See pp. 162–70 in this volume, including for Asti's consuls in 1095–98, which create more problems than do those of Genoa.

38.   See again Keller, 'Gli inizi', 56.

39.　See *LM*, line 343, for 1113; and *I brevi dei consoli*, 117–19, for the *publica contio* in 1153—see below, n. 50.

40.　*LM*, lines 449–50; cf. pp. 13–14 in this volume.

41.　For Pietro, Ceccarelli Lemut and Garzella, 'Optimus antistes'.

42.　See pp. 27–29, 195–96, in this volume, for more on this; and also Wickham, 'The "Feudal Revolution"'. Note that in Tuscany such assemblies are, outside Pisa, much less well-documented in our period: see pp. 000, 000, in this volume.

43.　*DM*, nn. 61–63, 74, 124, 125 (the last being to the Orlandi family, who had been the beneficiaries of diplomas of Henry IV in 1082–84: see above, n. 27). Matilda is documented outside Lucca in 1099 (*I placiti*, n. 479). Note that King Conrad, the pro-Matilda rebel son of Henry IV, was also in Pisa in 1097 (*Die Urkunden König Konrads*, n. 4, edited in *Heinrici IV. diplomata*), we do not know with what effect on the city's régime.

44.　Savigni, *Episcopato*, 42–50, tracks the period.

45.　*Carte dell'Archivio arcivescovile di Pisa* [henceforth *AAP*], vol. 2, nn. 10–17 (14 for the commune). See Ronzani, 'Le prime testimonianze', for the fullest analysis; idem, 'L'affermazione dei Comuni cittadini', 20–27. For the *comunum* in Cremona in 1097, the first reference, see p. 174 in this volume.

46.　See below, n. 48.

47.　*LM*, 137–40 (a. 1114); *AAP*, vol. 2, nn. 49, 55. For 1111, *Documenti sulle relazioni delle città toscane*, n. 34 (pages 43–45 for the Greek, 52–54 for the Latin)—the archbishop and cathedral get gifts from Alexios, though; cf. the Nice treaty, probably 1118–19, which has Archbishop Pietro together with consuls and viscounts acting for the city (Salvatori, *Boni amici et vicini*, 185–87). For the scribe (*scriniarius*) in 1126, see Banti, *Studi di storia*, 58.

48.　*AAP*, vol. 2, nn. 20, 19. I myself earlier wondered (Wickham, *Courts and Conflict*, 111n) if the former text, with its unique *placitum* format, might indicate that the archbishop really presided over the case, as he did in the parallel 1117 episcopal *placitum* from Milan, discussed earlier (pp. 1–2, 34, in this volume); but it has to be said that there is not a trace of any such episcopal protagonism in the document, and we cannot assume it.

49.　*Regesto della chiesa di Pisa* [henceforth *RCP*], n. 300. The first phrase could be 'of the commune of the Pisan *populus*'. Ronzani, 'L'affermazione dei Comuni cittadini', 36, argues that this was to raise money to pay for a favourable papal decision over the powers of the Pisan church in Corsica, recently successfully contested by Genoa. In *RCP*, n. 311 (a. 1129), Ruggero complains about consular neglect of an earlier archiepiscopal cession.

50. For 1138, *AAP*, vol. 2, n. 124. For 1153, *I brevi dei consoli*, 117–19, is the most recent edition. The other families of viscounts were soon back in power, although not with formal vicecomital rights, so it is by now easiest to call them Visconti as a family name (one of the other families, that of the Pietro who was consul in 1153 itself, was explicitly excluded from the 1153 decree anyway, and Guittone Visconti, not from Pietro's family, was a consul in 1158); Alberto's family, however, were not again consuls until 1183. See in general Pratesi, 'I Visconti'; Ceccarelli Lemut, 'I consoli'.

51. *AAP*, vol. 2, n. 20; Ceccarelli Lemut, 'Terre pubbliche', for the archbishop's signorial rights. For Volpe, *Studi*, 9–18, cf. 178–82 (critiqued in Ronzani, 'L'affermazione dei Comuni cittadini', 35–36). Rossetti, 'Costituzione cittadina', the fullest analysis of the cessions of castles to the archbishop, gives an updated Volpean reading at 108–11, 158–60. For the general issue of the juridical legitimacy of early communes, see chapter 2, n. 22, in this volume. Judgements in contumacy (which begin in 1142: D'Amia, *Diritto e sentenze*, n. 2), the expulsion of the viscounts in 1153 (see the previous note), and the decision to construct the city's two *Constituta* in 1155 are even clearer examples of the assumption by the commune of a public role; all these predate the formal granting of rights to the commune by Frederick Barbarossa in 1162 (*Friderici I. Diplomata*, n. 356).

52. Ex-consular arbitration: *AAP*, vol. 2, nn. 61–62 (Azzo di Marignano, who was consul in 1120: ibid., n. 55; two consuls witness n. 62 too). A lay case before the archbishop, *AAP*, vol. 2, n. 89, has him as a party as well, and he may here be acting as a signorial lord (cf. below, n. 54)—as he certainly is in nn. 141–42, which however also involve the consuls. The archbishop did judge canon-law cases, however: up to 1150, *AAP*, vol. 2, n. 67; D'Amia, *Diritto e sentenze*, n. 1; *RCP*, n. 367. Archbishop Ruggero, note, was also bishop of Volterra, and in that diocese (one with a very weak and small city) he is found in 1128 running a very late *placitum*, *AAP*, vol. 2, n. 72: it is significant that there are no equivalents to this for Pisa.

53. *AAP*, vol. 2, nn. 105, 124; Ronzani, 'Dall'*edificatio ecclesiae*', 29–42, for Ildebrando.

54. See for example the data in Rossetti et al., *Pisa nei secoli XI e XII*. Note that fiefs were much rarer in Tuscany than in Lombardy (cf. chapter 2 in this volume), although the Pisan archbishop did certainly concede some (and some of the consular families held episcopal fiefs), and he also had a court, a *curia*, for his feudal dependants—see e.g. *RCP*, n. 654 (a. 1137). That text, however, also clearly shows how the archbishop in that period had little control over many of his tenants (cf. Wickham, *Courts and Conflict*, 292–96).

55. See e.g. Rossetti, 'Ceti dirigenti', xxxi, for the traditional weakness of episcopal power in Tuscany. For Lucca, see the discussion in Osheim, *An Italian Lordship*, 10–25. For the lasting force of marchesal power, the absence of early signorie is one sign (Wickham, 'La signoria rurale in Toscana', 361–70), plus the late survival of *placita* in the March (*I placiti*, vol. 3, passim). Arezzo is the exception; there, the bishop was a real public and tenurial focus: Delumeau, *Arezzo*, esp. 525–28; see p. 184 in this volume.

56. In 1050–1150, at least Gerardo, Pietro, Uberto, and perhaps Baldovino were Pisans, but not visibly from major urban families.

57. *LM*, lines 72–81 (the pope), 86, 1209, 1391–92, 1575–89 (Pietro preaching, etc.), 1404 (Dodone quote), 760–61 (the first reference to Ugo), 971–72 (Pietro di Albizo quote: see p. 104 in this volume). The role of Archbishop Pietro is in fact much clearer in the Pisa-Barcelona treaty of 1114 (*LM*, 137–40) than in the poem. Ugo is said in his first citation to 'preside over the city of Pisa', but he does not do much 'presiding' in any document, although in 1111 he ratifies a transaction by a woman in his *curtis*, a judicial role which doubtless still belonged to him as viscount (Guastini, 'Le pergamene', n. 42; cf. Nardi, 'Le pergamene', n. 10, a. 1116, the last reference to this role, for a viscount from another family): see Pratesi, 'I Visconti', 57–8.

58. See pp. 162–66 in this volume; cf. also Wickham, 'The "Feudal Revolution"'.

59. For common land and officials, see Giardina, *Storia del diritto*, vol. 1, 135–85; see, in general, the evidence about the delta area presented in *La pianura pisana*, ed. Mazzanti. The issue is well set out in Rao, *Comunia*. Cf. also, for rural communes, the survey in Wickham, *Community and Clientele*; for Italy, the keenest proponent of the

relationship between rural communes and common land was Bognetti, *Studi sulle origini del comune rurale*, 1–262.

60. Ronzani, 'L'affermazione dei Comuni cittadini', 18–22.

61. Around Florence, Matilda besieged Prato in 1107: see *DM*, nn. 102–3; her last known *placitum* is in the county of Volterra in 1107, n. 104. Her last Pisa act is from 1112, n. 125, issued from Massa, on the coast some thirty miles north of Pisa and well out of the diocese.

62. It might be also thought that we need to explain why Pisa did not simply become a city run by its viscounts, traditional holders of local power as they were too, which it by no means did—the vicecomital families were indeed among Pisa's consuls from the first, in 1109 and onwards. But we will see later, p. 109 in this volume, that this was never a likely possibility.

63. I base myself here on Ceccarelli Lemut, 'I consoli', an invaluable article. See n. 20 for the *placita*. I count each annual office separately; many consuls, as in Milan, served several times. The families are the Baldovinaschi, Gualandi, Casapieri, Sismondi, da San Casciano, viscounts/Visconti (for ease of counting I have regarded the three branches of the Visconti as one family here), Dodi/Gaetani, Orlandi, Casalei, Casalberti, Azzi/Marignani, Erizi, Federici/da Parlascio, de Curte, Ricucci, Anfossi. Only the last four are not attested before 1080, and indeed before 1100; these four are also relatively minor families. The family names used here are in most cases attested as the names of what in Pisa were called 'houses', *domūs*, by c. 1200—rarely in our period, however, even if there are some exceptions; but the names are anyway by now established in the historiography.

64. Luglié, 'I da Caprona'; Ceccarelli Lemut, 'Pisan Consular Families', 128–39, for the Ebriaci; members of each family were occasionally consuls after 1150, and once (the Ebriaci in 1135) before.

65. Delfino, 'Per la storia', 84–98 (da Ripafratta); Pescaglini Monti, *Toscana medievale*, 547–51 (da Ripafratta); Ceccarelli Lemut, *Medioevo pisano*, 163–258 (Gherardeschi). The Pisan branch of the Gherardeschi were city ambassadors by 1158 (ibid., 202–5), and podestà from 1190 (for all the ambiguity of that office as a sign of urban identity); see Cristiani, *Nobiltà e popolo*, for the thirteenth century. The descendants of the counts of Pisa of the tenth century were also rural/signorial-focussed powers by now, although they lived in the city at least in part, submitted to the city consuls already in 1109, and provided

one consul in 1167: Ciccone, 'Famiglie di titolo comitale'; Ronzani, 'Le prime testimonianze'. The only family with no links at all to the commune in this period was the (rural-based) Upezzinghi, based in lands the Pisans moved into, east of the Pisan diocese: Pescaglini Monti, *Toscana medievale*, 449–91.

66.   References to families not discussed later can be found in Tiné, 'I discendenti' (Baldovinaschi); Martini, 'Per la storia' (Gualandi); Ticciati, 'S. Casciano' (da San Casciano); for the Dante citation, *Inferno* 33, lines 29–30.

67.   See Ronzani, 'Nobiltà, chiesa, memoria', for the 'seven houses' from now to the fifteenth century (the seven families of the later middle ages were however slightly different ones).

68.   For the Federici, not discussed later, see Iapoce, 'La famiglia Federici'; for the Erizi see below, n. 73.

69.   Pratesi, 'I Visconti'; 39–56 for the lands. See further Ronzani, 'Le tre famiglie dei "Visconti"', who not only disaggregates the families (cf. above, n. 25) but also, convincingly, changes some of the genealogies around. See above, n. 50, for 1153. For the thirteenth century, see in general Cristiani, *Nobiltà e popolo*; Poloni, *Trasformazioni della società*.

70.   For the family, see Farina, 'Per la storia' (whose genealogical reconstructions are replaced by later work, but whose work on the family's rural landowning, 39–51, is unsuperseded); Puglia, 'L'origine', 85–93; Ronzani, 'La "casa di Gontulino"'. Pandolfo Contulino as *castaldio*: *I placiti*, n. 414. Enrico's epithets: *LM*, lines 1405, 1879. Nugola: *AAP*, vol. 1, n. 132; Livorno: *AAP*, vol. 2, n. 154.

71.   Sturmann, 'La "domus" dei Dodi'. They got their first land in lease from the da Caprona (ibid., 300–301), who may have got it from the marquis. Tangheroni, 'La prima espansione di Pisa', 10, already saw the wood connection. *LM* and wood: lines 98–104. *Tomboli*: Sgherri, 'Le pergamene', nn. 1–6; cf. Wickham, *Courts and Conflict*, 144–50.

72.   See for the family Ticciati, 'Strategie familiari'. For 1016/1114, *LM*, lines 962–74, 2812–14, 2912–36.

73.   See Garzella, 'Marignani' (72–73, 112–13, for Azzo di Marignano); *LM*, 137–40, for the Barcelona treaty. 1121: see above, n. 52. Fasciano as origin: *I placiti*, nn. 421, 433. For the Sismondi as not kin, Ronzani, *Chiesa e "Civitas"*, 84n. The Erizi were similar to the Marignani, as eleventh-century *iudices* and early consuls, but with fewer consuls later, and relatively little land: see Guzzardi, 'Erizi'.

74. Rege Cambrin, 'La famiglia dei Casalei' (179–99 for properties). See e.g. *I diplomi arabi*, n. 2, for *Babillonia*.

75. Ceccarelli Lemut, 'Pisan Consular Families', 124–28.

76. Rovai, 'La famiglia de Curte' (3–9 for the *silvani*, 76–90 for properties).

77. Ticciati, 'S. Casciano', 125–26; Garzella, 'Cascina', 73–77. Note also Vecchiano, a castle which certainly was partly controlled by the da San Casciano, and conceivably shared with the other *longubardi* families, but it did not last either: Ticciati, 'S. Casciano', 126–27 (with reference to another partial castle); Ronzani, 'Nobiltà, chiesa', 760–61.

78. There is almost no trace of these figures in document collections except in judicial roles. See for some of them Classen, *Burgundio*; Ceccarelli Lemut, 'I consoli', for Ildebrando Familiati as consul in 1166; Angiolini, 'Familiati, Bandino' (which is only, however, informative on his Bolognese career).

79. 1182: *Gli Annales Pisani*, 73–74. Lucca is a close parallel: see p. 180–82 in this volume. Early Pisan *popolo*: Poloni, *Trasformazioni della società*, 38–42. Contrast Milan, where a *popolo* was active at the latest in 1198: Grillo, *Milano*, 644–57.

80. Matzke, *Daibert*, 61–74, sets these activities out; there is not a lot.

81. *DM*, nn. 63 (a. 1100), 74 (a. 1103). Strictly, Matilda gave two tracts of land beside the *palatium* (as the 1100 text says), and not the palace itself; but by 1111 the consuls and *populus* had adopted the location as the *forum Pisane civitatis*, and the marquise had no further role there (see p. 89 in this volume); one could suppose either that the second donation in fact included the palace as well, or else that the marquise's land was appropriated de facto by the city, but the transfer of rights happened either way. See Garzella, *Pisa com'era*, 85–88, 109–11.

82. Ronzani, 'L'affermazione dei Comuni cittadini', 20–30, describes this situation best. Alberti alliance: *Chronicon pisanum*, 102n, early Lucchese additions to a text of this short Pisan chronicle.

83. See in general Wickham, 'La signoria rurale in Toscana'. Ceccarelli Lemut, 'Terre pubbliche', discusses the counts of Pisa (103–5) and is basic for the rural signorie around Pisa; for the counts, see also above, n. 65.

84. Racine, *Plaisance*, 372.

85. Wickham, *Courts and Conflict*, 111.

86. *Constitutum usus*, c. 44, in *I Costituti*, ed. Vignoli, 288–301;
it makes some use of the Milanese *Libri feudorum*, in fact (Classen,
Studium und Gesellschaft, 86), in a rapid transferral of knowledge.

87. As indeed happened also to leaders of rural communes, who
were in many places the leading local stratum which did not have
access to militarised lordship: Wickham, *Community and Clientele*, e.g.
231–34.

88. *Gli Annales Pisani*, 16. Cf. Wickham, *Land and Power*, 301–2.

4. ROME

1. *Liber Pontificalis*, ed. Přerovský, 727–41.

2. I will use the phrases 'reform' and 'reform papacy', in inverted
commas, for ease of reference to the period after 1046. They are problematic phrases, in that they take the standpoint of Leo IX, Gregory
VII, and their successors for granted, but they are convenient labels.

3. This will not resemble very greatly the traditional papal grand
narrative, for which see my *Roma medievale* (which covers the period
from 900 to 1150), 36–37; that narrative, quite apart from its intrinsic
flaws, gives almost no consideration to the history of Rome as a city.
More detailed analyses of many of my characterisations in this chapter
will be found in that book. The basic account of the period after 1143 is
now Maire Vigueur, *L'autre Rome*.

4. Toubert, *Les structures*, esp. 1191–1257, 1314–48; idem, 'Scrinium
et *palatium*', 440–55.

5. *Le Liber Pontificalis*, ed. Duchesne [henceforth *LP*], vol. 2, 331,
for Rome; cf. p. 23 in this volume, for Milan.

6. For discussion of the 'new aristocracy', see Wickham, *Roma
medievale*, 266–300. For documentary citations of *nobiles*, see for general uses of the term *Codice diplomatico della Repubblica di Genova*, n.
32; *Patrologiae . . . cursus latina* [henceforth *PL*], vol. 129, cols. 699–
700, n. 9, cols. 706–7, n. 18; *S. Gregorio*, n. 7. [For all abbreviations of
non-papal document editions in this chapter, see the note on documents in the bibliography of this volume.] For the Frangipane family, *S. Prassede*, n. 26; *Acta pontificum romanorum inedita* [henceforth
Pflugk], vol. 3, n. 245; *PL*, vol. 200, col. 178, n. 103; *Le Liber Censuum*
[henceforth *LC*], vol. 1, n. 64. For the Pierleoni family, *Papsturkunden
in Italien* [henceforth Kehr], vol. 4, 157. See further Kehr, vol. 2, 348–

50 (Corsi family); *Epistolae*, ed. Loewenfeld, n. 282 (Sant' Eustachio family).

7. For Hildebrand/Gregory, see Cowdrey, *Pope Gregory VII*, 37–58, 71–74, 314–29, 213–29. For Cencio di Stefano and his family, see Borino, 'Cencio del prefetto Stefano', and esp. Whitton, 'Papal Policy', 223–26, 233–36, 244–52. Basic texts: *LP*, vol. 2, 336–37; Beno, *Gesta*, 1.8 (372); Bonizone of Sutri, *Liber ad amicum*, cc. 6–8 (595, 603–6, 610–11).

8. For *placita*, *RF*, nn. 906, 1006, 1013. See in general Toubert, *Les structures*, 1316–19.

9. See for the Norman attack Hamilton, 'Memory, Symbol, and Arson'.

10. For the Frangipane, see Thumser, 'Die Frangipane', 113–16; the Pierleoni are less prominent in this period because there was a generation change, but see *LP*, vol. 2, 334, 336, for the period around 1060, and p. 125 in this volume. The Corsi were certainly initial supporters of Gregory but may have changed sides by 1088: see *RF*, n. 1115, a Clementine text presided over by Pietro the urban prefect, plausibly already a Corsi family member.

11. Ziese, *Wibert*, 275–79, and now esp. *Framing Clement III*, ed. Longo and Yawn.

12. See for these ad hoc cases *SMVL*, nn. 120–21, 139; *RF*, n. 1115; *Chronicon farfense*, vol. 2, 232–33; ASR, SCD, cassetta 16, n. 109; *RS*, n. 212; *S. Gregorio*, n. 34; Andenna, 'Documenti di S. Paolo', 35–38.

13. See for the prefecture Halphen, *Études*, 16–27, 147–56; Toubert, *Les structures*, 1208–9. For Paschal and the Corsi, see *Liber Pontificalis*, ed. Přerovský, 711–14, 717–21.

14. See in general *Liber Pontificalis*, ed. Přerovský, 705–44.

15. See Laudage, 'Rom und das Papsttum'; Stroll, *Calixtus II*.

16. *Liber Pontificalis*, ed. Přerovský, 750–54, a very one-sided account however.

17. For 1130, the best accounts are Palumbo, *Lo schisma*, and Stroll, *The Jewish Pope*; the latter discusses alternative bibliography.

18. See p. 148 in this volume for examples.

19. For gifts and money/treasure, see Wickham, 'The Financing of Roman City Politics'.

20. *RF*, n. 1115.

21. *Chronica Casinensis*, 3.39, 66, 68; *SMN*, n. 42 (a. 1126); *Codex diplomaticus Cajetanus*, n. 312; Kehr, 'Il diploma purpureo'; *SMN*, n. 49;

S. Gregorio, n. 7; *SMVL*, nn. 165, 178. See Moscati, *Alle origini*, 138–41; Vendittelli, 'Romanorum consules', the best guide to the continuing changes of meaning of the title.

22. *Liber Pontificalis*, ed. Přerovský, 717–20, 734; *Codex diplomaticus Cajetanus*, n. 312 (a. 1127) with Moscati, '"Una cum sexaginta senatoribus"'; Petersohn, 'Der Brief', 505–7. For previous papal grants, see *PL*, vol. 143, cols. 831–34, 1305–9.

23. Doran, 'The Legacy of Schism', 75–78 for cardinals; for voiding acts, Kehr, vol. 5, 14–15, vol. 2, 348–50, *SMCM*, n. 42; for the church, Kinney, 'S. Maria in Trastevere'; for the sarcophagus, Herklotz, *Gli eredi di Costantino*, 19–28; for the Papareschi, see p. 150 in this volume.

24. Salaries: *LP*, vol. 2, 383–84. Court proceedings: an emblematic professional case survives in an eighteenth-century manuscript edition in Biblioteca Apostolica Vaticana, Codices Vaticani Latini 8044, ff. 4–16, a case begun in 1143 and ended in 1145.

25. See, for the Pierleoni, *S. Gregorio*, nn. 7, 89; Bernard of Clairvaux, *Epistolae*, n. 317; *Chronica Casinensis*, 4.130. For 1141, see Müller, 'Der Bericht', 102.

26. Traditional surveys are Fedele, 'L'êra del senato'; Rota, 'La costituzione originaria', 41–53.

27. For the Pisan *senatores*, see *Documenti sulle relazioni delle città toscane*, n. 7 (a. 1160); *I brevi dei consoli*, 48 (a. 1162); for the earlier uses of the term 'senate' in Rome, the best guide is Arnaldi, 'Rinascita'.

28. For sources, see *LP*, vol. 2, 385–86; Otto of Freising, *Chronica*, 7.27, 31; Romualdo of Salerno, *Chronicon*, 228; Godfrey of Viterbo, *Pantheon*, 261; *Carmen de gestis*, 1.808; John of Salisbury, *Historia pontificalis*, c. 27; *Annales Casinenses*, 310. For secondary literature, see Fedele, 'L'êra del senato'; Bartoloni, 'Per la storia'; Brezzi, *Roma*, 317–39; Frugoni, 'Sulla '"Renovatio Senatus"'; Rota, 'La costituzione originaria'; Moscati, *Alle origini* (a key text); Schultz, 'Poiché tanto amano la libertà . . .', 136–62; Doran, 'The Legacy of Schism', 85–178; Petersohn, *Kaisertum und Rom*, 80–109.

29. Bartoloni, 'Per la storia', 24–27. For a Provençal parallel, however, see chapter 5, n. 35, in this volume.

30. For this period, see Otto of Freising, *Chronica*, 7.31, 34; *LP*, vol. 2, 386–87; John of Salisbury, *Historia pontificalis*, c. 27; Wibald, *Epistolae*, nn. 347, 214, 215. For the palace, see *Codice diplomatico del Senato romano*, n. 11; cf. Maire Vigueur, *L'autre Rome*,

3II. Two named senators in the first decade of the senate may perhaps also have been aristocratic, Grisotto di Cencio in 1148, who
might well be linked to the *filii Baruncii*, and Stefano di Cencio di Stefano di Tedaldo in 1150, who was probably linked to
the family of Cencio di Stefano: see *Codice diplomatico del Senato
romano*, n. 12, and Wickham, *Roma medievale*, 280–81.

31. Otto of Freising, *Chronica*, 7.34 (agreement); *Codice diplomatico del Senato romano*, nn. 12, 13, are the first cases. Gregorio *arcarius*: *Codice diplomatico del Senato romano*, n. 13, set against Halphen,
Études, 120–22.

32. Wibald of Stablo, *Epistolae*, nn. 214–16, 347; for Renaissance
imagery see e.g. Benson, 'Political *renovatio*'; Strothmann, *Kaiser und
Senat*, 78–216; and the rather more nuanced Petersohn, *Kaisertum
und Rom*, 80–109. For the long tradition of *renovatio*, the classic is
Schramm, *Kaiser, Rom und Renovatio*.

33. *Codice diplomatico del Senato romano*, nn. 41–44; see for the
succeeding period Thumser, *Rom*.

34. I derive this population assessment from Meneghini and Santangeli Valenzani, *Roma nell'alto medioevo*, 21–24; Hubert, 'Rome au
XIVe siècle'; Maire Vigueur, *L'autre Rome*, 36–38: these focus on both
before and after 1050.

35. Krautheimer, *Rome*, esp. 271–326, modified by Hubert, *Espace
urbain* (these two are the basic texts for Rome's *urbanistica*) and Wickham, *Roma medievale*, 147–55.

36. Hubert, *Espace urbain*, 70–74, 83–84, 86–96, 365–68.

37. Augenti, *Il Palatino*, 188 for 1177; for the commune, Hubert,
Espace urbain, 92–93. For Milan, *Gli atti del Comune*, nn. 22, 97 (Porta
Vercellina common land); Barni, 'Dal governo del vescovo a quello dei
cittadini', 221–22 (Porta Comacina; he further postulates, cf. 100, 375,
that the Milanese gate communities might also have been the bases
for military organisation and have elected consuls; this is a common
view in Milanese historiography, as for example in *Gli atti del Comune*,
xxxviii, xlii, but the evidence for it is weak).

38. Toubert, *Les structures*, 938–1081.

39. Wickham, 'La struttura della proprietà fondiaria'.

40. For the basic analysis of leases in this period, see Lenzi, *La
terra e il potere*.

41. See for a survey Wickham, *Roma medievale*, 173–90.

42. Compare the S. Ciriaco documents preserved in *SMVL* to those in *SMN*, *SMCM*, and *SCD*, for churches and monasteries with a more evident regional remit.

43. See pp. 142–47 in this volume, for most of these.

44. For Frangipane dominance in S. Maria Nova/Colosseo, see esp. Augenti, *Il Palatino*, 188 (a. 1177); for links to S. Maria, see *SMN*, passim; for S. Gregorio, *S. Gregorio*, nn. 7, 16, 21–22, 82, 135, 152.

45. For the Frangipane, Thumser, 'Die Frangipane', is basic. For 963, Liutprando of Cremona, *Historia Ottonis*, c. 9; for 1094, Bernold, *Chronicon*, 509, with Geoffroy de Vendôme, *Œuvres*, 288–90.

46. The best account of the early Pierleoni is Whitton, 'Papal Policy', 185–202; Fedele, 'Le famiglie', is the only fully published study but is often problematic. Leone: *SCD*, nn. 56 (a. 1051), 73 (a. 1072); for Roger II's 1134 diploma, Kehr, 'Diploma purpureo', 258–59; for Isola, ASR, SCD, cassetta 16, nn. 109, 118, 137.

47. For references, *LP*, vol. 2, 336, 345; *RF*, n. 1097 (a.1084); *SMVL*, nn. 121, 122, 123, 200; ASR, SCD, cassetta 16, n. 109; *S. Gregorio*, nn. 34, 137 (a. 1131, for which see Carocci and Vendittelli, *L'origine della Campagna Romana*, 95); *RF*, n. 1115; *LC*, vol. 1, n. 123.

48. For descriptions and analyses, the best studies are Barbanera and Pergola, 'Elementi architettonici'; Pensabene, 'La Casa dei Crescenzi'; Montelli, 'Impiego dei mattoni'; eadem, *Tecniche costruttive*. For the inscriptions, *Iscrizioni delle chiese*, vol. 13, nn. 1339–41; for the other families, *Liber Pontificalis*, ed. Přerovský, 738–39. See Wickham, *Roma medievale*, 280–84, for the link to the family, which is indicative only; but the boastful defiance of the Normanni and the Corsi is there no matter who put it up.

49. Normanni: *LP*, vol. 2, 345–46; *Chronica casinensis*, 4.38; *Liber Pontificalis*, ed. Přerovský, 734–41; *Codice diplomatico della Repubblica di Genova*, n. 31; [Otto of Freising and] Rahewin, *Gesta Frederici I.*, 4.77, 80; *S. Gregorio*, n. 24; for the thirteenth-century family, see Carocci, *Baroni di Roma*, 381–86. Sant' Eustachio: *RF*, n. 1115; *Codex diplomaticus Cajetanus*, n. 312; *SMVL*, n. 165; *LL*, nn. 1187, 1221; *RF*, nn. 1278, 1085, 1095; *Epistolae*, ed. Loewenfeld, n. 282. For the castles of Cencio's descendants, *S. Paolo*, nn. 4, 5, 7–11.

50. For the family as prefects: see Halphen, *Études*, 149–51; D'Acunto, 'Il prefetto Cencio'; with, as texts, *LP*, vol. 2, 335; Bonizone of Sutri, *Liber ad amicum*, cc. 7–8 (603, 611); Pier Damiani, *Epistolae*,

nn. 145, 155, and cf. n. 135. For lands: *SCD*, nn. 24, 25, 35, 41; *SMT*, n. 7; *S. Gregorio*, n. 14; *SMVL*, n. 63; ASR, SCD, cassetta 16, n. 120 (a. 1132).

51.   Thumser, *Rom*, 182; for the baronial families in general, see Carocci, *Baroni di Roma*.

52.   Galgano's sons: *SMVL*, n. 205; Galgano's sister Bonella also owned, not on an enormous scale, in Arcioni east of the Trevi *regio*: nn. 217, 221. For his career as *primicerius*, see Halphen, *Études*, 100–101. Benedetto: for his career, Chiodi, 'Roma e il diritto romano', 1228–39; for his family, see *SMN*, nn. 15, 33, 38.

53.   Mancini: *SMN*, nn. 30, 33, 35 verso, 41, 43, 44, 46, 51, 53, 54, 56, 79, 91, 109, 118, 119, 125, 133; as actors, nn. 47, 82, 99; plus Augenti, *Il Palatino*, 188 (a. 1177); 'Documenti per la storia', n. 19; *LC*, vol. 1, 300. See for a brief discussion Moscati, *Alle origini*, 118.

54.   *SMVL*, nn. 160–62, 172, 175, 176, 178, 194, 216, 225 with 228 (= *Codice diplomatico del Senato romano*, nn. 34–40, which refers to Pietro as a senator), 258, 266; Baumgärtner, 'Regesten', n. 66; elsewhere, ASR, SCD, cassetta 16, n. 143. See for commentary Carocci and Vendittelli, *L'origine della Campagna Romana*, 127–30; Wickham, 'Getting Justice', 108–11 (110n for other possible references to the family).

55.   For lists, see Bartoloni, 'Per la storia'.

56.   For the letters, see Wibald, *Epistolae*, nn. 216, 404, 403. See for Arnaldo Frugoni, *Arnaldo da Brescia*, still the best study; Thumser, 'Die frühe römische Kommune', 128–46; Schmitz-Esser, *'In urbe, quae caput mundi est'*, 33–42.

57.   For 1170, Thumser, 'Die Frangipane', 136; Petersohn, *Kaisertum und Rom*, 272–73; with the main source, *Annales Ceccanenses*, s.a. 1170 (286); for the leopard, Fedele, 'Il leopardo e l'agnello', 215.

58.   Maire Vigueur, *L'autre Rome*, 306–10.

59.   John of Salisbury, *Historia Pontificalis*, c. 31; Wickham, 'Getting Justice'.

60.   See Thumser, *Rom*, 239–56; Moscati, 'Benedetto "Carushomo"'.

61.   Maire Vigueur, *Cavaliers et citoyens*, 220–46, 341–46.

5. ITALY

1.   Vercelli, Bergamo, Cremona, Padua, Florence, and Arezzo are most of the best: see below, nn. 18, 20, 23, 26, 30, 32. Maire Vigueur, *Cavaliers et citoyens*, 339–41, has made similar critical points.

2. Bordone, *La società cittadina*, 160–82; Maire Vigueur, *Cavaliers et citoyens*, 220–46, cf. 339–49. These two, however, used different criteria to create typologies of cities, focussed on the presence of episcopal vassals and signorial interest among consuls (Bordone) or among the urban cavalry militia more widely (Maire Vigueur); I shall focus more on the wealth of consuls, insofar as it can be determined, and on the pacing of communal institutionalisation. For incisive article-length comparisons, see further chapter 1, n. 17, in this volume. Opll, *Stadt und Reich*, 178–480, also collects a large body of information about most of the cities of Italy in the twelfth century (in particular to illustrate their relationship with emperors), city by city; his data are useful but not always reliable for our period.

3. See for Caffaro's career, Petti Balbi, *Caffaro e la cronachistica genovese*; eadem, 'Caffaro'; Schweppenstette, *Die Politik der Erinnerung*, 51–96. The latter work, esp. 83–153, together with Placanica, 'L'opera storiografica di Caffaro', are currently the basic guides to the structure and strategies of the *Annals*; see also the English translation in Hall and Phillips, *Caffaro, Genoa*. For Caffaro's initial phrases, his 1150s embassies, and the *De liberatione*, see *Annali genovesi*, 5, 39, 51, 99; for 1111, *Le carte del monastero di San Siro di Genova*, n. 73; cf. also Wickham, *Land and Power*, 295–98. For consular lists, see Olivieri, 'Serie dei consoli'; but his data are largely taken from Caffaro.

4. *Annali genovesi*, III (*consulatus*), 25 (1130), 11 (Guglielmo), 155–56 (Oberto); *Codice diplomatico del monastero di Santo Stefano*, n. 96 for 1098 (the date is not certain but very probable). For the origins of the commune into the 1120s–30s, by far the best analysis is Bordone, 'Le origini del comune di Genova'; see now also Filangieri, 'Famiglie e gruppi dirigenti a Genova', 63–85. Bordone follows Pavoni, 'Dal Comitato di Genova al Comune', 162–63, in dating the first *compagna* to 1100 not 1099; Pavoni engages in a contorted argument to allow Caffaro to be right about the eighteen months without consuls even though we have the 1098 document. A straight reading of Caffaro's *Annals* still gives 1099 as far as I can see; we need to recognise that he may have confused the chronology, intentionally or not. The 1098 document is important for the dating of Pisa's consuls: see p. 84 in this volume.

5. For the international agreements of 1104–9, see *Codice diplomatico della Repubblica di Genova*, nn. 16, 20, 22, 24. Consular court cases to 1140, by archive, with dates before 1130: ibid., nn. 45 (a. 1127), 49,

50, 77, 93; *Codice diplomatico del monastero di Santo Stefano*, nn. 104 (a. 1109), 110, 115; *Le carte di Santa Maria delle Vigne*, nn. 3 (a. 1109–10), 6; *Le carte del monastero di San Siro di Genova*, n. 73 (a. 1111); Belgrano, 'Il registro della curia arcivescovile di Genova', 27–28, 56–60 (aa. 1117, 1123; this edition includes many more cases for the 1140s, esp. at 60–73); *I libri iurium*, vol. 1.3, n. 524 (a. 1127); *Le carte del monastero di Sant'Andrea della Porta*, n. 2. The earliest of all, from 1104–5, is unpublished: mentioned by Petti Balbi, *Governare la città*, 71n, it is contained in the late thirteenth-century *Liber instrumentorum Monasterii Sancti Fructuosi de Capite Montis*, *Codice 'A'*, in the Archivio Doria Pamphilj in Rome, bancone 79, busta 12, fol. 8rv (cf. fols. 7v, a. 1116, 7v–8r, a. 1131, 8v–9r, a. 1161) concerning rights to the falcons of Capodimonte, on the sea near Portofino. (The text says 1104, but the indiction is for 1105; the consuls who judged are said by Caffaro to have held office for the whole period 1102–5, so would fit either date.) That the history of communal justice in Italy begins with a judgement about falcons is fascinating in itself. See Vallerani, 'La riscrittura dei diritti', 153–60, for a discussion of some of these amazingly neglected texts.

6. For the *parlamentum*, the 1117 text is in Belgrano, 'Il registro della curia arcivescovile di Genova', 56–57. Caffaro, too, refers to *parlamenta* in 1101 and 1123 (and later), *Annali genovesi*, 10, 19; but he of course, even though an eyewitness here, is writing at a later date; all the same, these early citations converge to mean that, in all probability, the word is initially a Genoese one. *E-mgh* turns up no earlier reference; the *Patrologia latina* database records one possible earlier citation, a letter of Pope Urban II to the inhabitants of Velletri in 1089, *Patrologiae . . . cursus latina*, vol. 151, col. 304, n. 22, but the context seems different. For 1120–43, see *Codice diplomatico della Repubblica di Genova*, nn. 31, 53, 67, 68, 96, 102, 128. Peri, 'Ordinamento del comune consolare', is still the fullest survey of the institutions of the commune, although it is abstract and legalistic, and uses few documents.

7. The two most substantial recent studies on family groups in Genoa, both doctoral theses, are Filangieri, 'Famiglie e gruppi dirigenti a Genova', 1–189 (6–19 for a good guide to earlier bibliography; 49–52 for the Spinola); Inguscio, 'Reassessing Civil Conflicts in Genoa' (142–45 for the Doria, 198–201 for Caffaro's family). That Caschifellone was actually a castle is not, it should be noted, explicit in any source I have seen.

8. See Inguscio, 'Reassessing Civil Conflicts in Genoa', 78–103, 112–34, 154–59, 187–235. Genoese documentation does not however allow us a full sense of the landowning activity of these families, for it hardly appears in the notarial registers; this limits our certainties here.

9. *Codice diplomatico della Repubblica di Genova*, nn. 97, 205, envision the impermanency of the consuls or the *compagna*. Cf. for parallels in other cities Faini, *Firenze*, 271–72 (who downplays the phrase); Grillo, 'Il comune di Vercelli', 166 (that being a city where consuls actually did stop for a time). Another unusual feature of Genoa is that the *compagna* explicitly did not include all Genoese: *Codice diplomatico della Repubblica di Genova*, n. 128, at 155–57. The separate *consules de placitis* after 1130 do not seem to constitute an office open to a significantly wider social stratum. The episcopal role in early communal documents is not huge, even given the fact that many early consular judgements survive in a register of archiepiscopal documents, but most of those judgements were made in the cathedral or the bishop's palace, indicating some at least ceremonial importance for the bishop (from 1133, archbishop).

10. See chapter 3, n. 14, in this volume, for Pisa; cf. Wickham, *Courts and Conflict*, 122–67, for the Romanisation of practice in Pisa.

11. See above all Inguscio, 'Reassessing Civil Conflicts in Genoa'.

12. *Codex Astensis*, vol. 3, nn. 635, 707. See Fissore, *Autonomia notarile*, 11–34; idem, 'Problemi'; Bordone, *Città e territorio*, 352–77, for discussion; and ibid., 311–51, for the previous political context. I am very grateful for a critique of this Asti section from Luigi Provero.

13. See *Codex Astensis*, vol. 3, nn. 890–91 (a. 1108); for 1103, Adriani, *Degli antichi signori di Sarmatorio*, 314–15 (for the problems of this text, see Bordone, *Città e territorio*, 304n, and below, n. 16); *Le carte dell'Archivio capitolare*, nn. 3, 6–7 (aa. 1111, 1123). For the social composition of the consuls, see Bordone, *Città e territorio*, 365–66, 373–76: authoritative, but not a detailed account.

14. Cognasso, 'Pergamene', 13–17, 18–19, overlapping with the edition in Fissore, 'Problemi', 500–507.

15. *Le carte dell'Archivio capitolare*, nn. 95, 97; *Codex Astensis*, vol. 2, n. 117, may also refer to a consular judgement of 1171.

16. See Fissore, *Autonomia notarile*, 13–25, followed by Bordone, *Città e territorio*, 355; the 1098 text is also accepted by Sergi, *Potere e territorio*, 154, and by Provero, *Dai marchesi del Vasto*, 66–67. There are

too many circumstantial details in the 1098 text (such as the citation of Marquis Bonifacio of Vasto) for it to be a complete forgery. For 1103, see above, n. 13; to be added to the problematic details in the text is the repeated use of the word *commune* as a noun, which has no early parallels at all.

17.　Bordone, "'Civitas nobilis et antiqua'", gives a survey of the Piemontese cities, not all of which have detailed studies; 29–32 for the 1112–18 text, 38 for Novara. For Tortona, the cited document is *Il Chartarium Dertonense*, n. 2.

18.　For Vercelli, the basic works, excellent analyses, are Panero, 'Istituzioni e società'; Degrandi, 'Vassalli cittadini'; Barbero, 'Vassalli vescovili'; and Grillo, 'Il comune di Vercelli'. For Milani, and my minor modification of his terminology, see chapter 1, n. 29, in this volume. Judicial figures from the third-level élite are by contrast little-attested among the consuls of the commune of Vercelli: Barbero, 'Vassalli vescovili', 299.

19.　Keller, *Signori e vassalli*, esp. 6–30.

20.　Menant, 'Bergamo comunale', 17–27; idem, *Campagnes lombardes*, 633–55, for the *capitanei* and the many urban families around the bishop (606 for the da Gorlago, 639–42 for the Mozzi, 651 for assemblies). For earlier work on assemblies, Mazzi, *Studi bergomensi*, 8–25, 264–65; the whole book (which is difficult to find) is a good analysis of the early commune by the standards of the period. See now the important recent study of De Angelis, *Poteri cittadini*, 262–324 (269–70 for assemblies), with 341–67 for the texts of early consular documents, 236–43 for Arnaldo of Azzano—parallel is his contemporary Lanfranco (ibid., 236, 243–44), another publicly active jurist with no documented land, who died too early to get into the surviving consular cases, but might well have been a consul too. Late *placita* are in *I placiti*, nn. 459, 467, 470–71.

21.　De Angelis, *Poteri cittadini*, 341–46 for the 1117 documents; 282, 293–94, 295–99 for the uncertain nature of the early commune; 288–92 for 'almost'.

Pavia can be added here; it seems to have had consuls acting as early as 1112 in a court case, although the dispute text also indicates that the holder of basic judicial powers here was still the count of the palace, who apparently held an old-style *placitum* after the consular judgement; the count thus seems to have had the sort of role here that bishops had in other cities (for the text, a late copy, see Solmi, 'L'Amministrazione finanziaria', 254–58). Only two other references to consuls survive here before 1150, and *consules iusticie* are first seen only in 1157. Judicial figures are nonetheless prominent among the earliest consuls here, as befits the old political/legal centre of the Kingdom; the senior figure in 1112 was in fact Ugo of Gambolò himself, author of part of the *Libri feudorum* (see chapter 2, n. 59, in this volume). See Lane, 'The Territorial Expansion', 71–123; he is more suspicious of the 1112 text than I am. This is the first consular case known for Lombardy; the second is from Como—see below, n. 25.

22.   Racine, *Plaisance*, 204–36, 358–75; Bulla, 'Famiglie dirigenti'; Fugazza, *Diritto, istituzioni*, 6 (for the 1093 text), 20 (for the 1133 text), 19–29; eadem, '"In palatio episcopi"', 21–34, an important analysis, which stresses how the assembly predates the consuls. For 1090, *Johannis Codagnelli Annales*, 1–3. For 1126 and 1135, *Il Registrum Magnum*, vol. 1, n. 53; vol. 3, n. 804.

Parma can be added here (see Schumann, *Authority and the Commune*, 211–40, for an inadequate survey): it had consuls soon after 1115 (Adalberto Samaritano, *Praecepta dictaminum*, 60–61), but its assembly is rather more visible in the early twelfth century, with the *cives* acting as a body already in the 1100s (Schumann, *Authority and the Commune*, 226–32).

23.   See *Le carte cremonesi*, vol. 2, nn. 242, 273, 279, 296–98, 316; for 1132, see *Die Lombardische Briefsammlung*, nn. 34–35; for a full analysis, Menant, 'La prima età comunale' (248–60 for the prosopography); see further Coleman, "Bishop and Commune". Banti, '"Civitas" e "Commune"', 225–27, is more critical of the 1097 citation than I would be.

24.   Brescia can be added here (see Bosisio, 'Il comune', 569–99, for an inadequate survey): it had both a *concio* and a *commune* in c. 1120 (*Liber Potheris*, n. 2—the dating is not fully certain), and consuls with rotating offices in 1127 (ibid., n. 3). (Its urban collectivity was well-defined already in 1038 if ibid., n. 1, is genuine, but see Menant, *Campagnes lombardes*, 586, for doubts.) The *concio* here, or at any rate the urban community, was apparently strong enough to expel the city consuls themselves in 1135 or 1139: *Annales Brixienses*, 812; few consuls are known by name thereafter until the 1150s.

25.   Como had consuls in 1114, running another early dispute (*Liber statutorum consulum Cumanorum*, 379–80; see Faini, 'Le

tradizioni normative delle città toscane', 474n; the text shows a consular sentence based on oath-helping in front of an assembly); Lodi an *aringo* in 1117 (*Gli atti del Comune*, n. 1).

26. Castagnetti, *Società e politica a Ferrara*, 57–78, 127–69; Rippe, *Padoue*, 323–79 (the fullest study in this region); Castagnetti, 'L'età precomunale', 57–63, with idem, 'Da Verona a Ravenna', 370–74, for Verona. For Ravenna, see Pini, 'Il comune di Ravenna', 209–19; Vasina, *Romagna medievale*, 171–83, 229–44, with 201–9, 246–47, for key documents (and cf. idem, 'Consoli e mondo comunale'); Castagnetti, 'Da Verona a Ravenna', 459–86, also available at slightly greater length in 'Feudalità e società comunale II', 24–54 (the most rigorous, but focussed on a different problematic). A well-known text of 1138, edited by Vasina and discussed by all the above, features the three *ordines* of *capitanei et valvasores et populus*, acting for the city without mediation, and envisages future joint consuls of Ravenna and Forlì who are to be elected by a complex procedure, but this agreement had no visible permanent result: see also Maire Vigueur, *Cavaliers et citoyens*, 352–53. In Ravenna, the consuls in their few documented actions are not associated with the archbishop. Note also that *consul* is, as in Rome, an old word for 'aristocrat' in Ravenna (see chapter 2, n. 10, in this volume), and the 1109–15 references thus may not show much change from the past at all.

27. Bologna: Wandruszka, *Die Oberschichten Bolognas*, 28 (quote), 57–70 (his consular lists are corrected by Paola Foschi at http://badigit.comune.bologna.it/governo_bologna/consoli.htm); Milani, *L'esclusione dal comune*, 27–28, for 1149; Fried, *Die Entstehung*, 73–87 (84–87 for *iudices*); cf. Ferrara, 'La scuola', 605–7. Modena: see Rölker, *Nobiltà e comune*, 121–52; here, the consuls are episcopal vassals (including castle-holders and similar) in 1142; again mostly episcopal vassals (including two *iudices*) at the next citation of them in 1167. For *rectores*, not discussed here, see e.g. Banti, *Studi di storia*, 20–47; they are most usefully seen as proto-podestà, although their precise political context is ill-understood. In this period they were mostly aristocrats (cf. e.g. Rölker, ibid., 146–47; Castagnetti, 'Feudalità e società comunale', 230–32; Delumeau, *Arezzo*, 1144–45).

28. See Castagnetti, 'Il primo comune'.

29. See Savigni, *Episcopato e società*, 47–97; Wickham, *Courts and Conflict*, 22–40, 51–61, 85–88 (40 and 240 for the 1203 war); for

Rolando, see chapter 2, n. 58, in this volume. Cf. p. 20 in this volume for the Avvocati. I have here separated out the Antelminelli from the first level of the élite, contrary to the implications of *Courts and Conflict*, 60. Even non-communally-orientated lords were not very powerful in the Lucchesia, however, and few resisted the commune in any way. For the 1119 text, see Blomquist and Osheim, 'The First Consuls'; for the 1080s, Rangerio, *Vita metrica*, lines 5249–5646, a text of the 1090s.

30. Faini, *Firenze*, 137–40, 150–54, 243–79 (275 for 'evanescent' and 'occasional'), 297–320, 332–63; plus 18–19, 21–22, 27–28, 37–45 of the appendix (for the Cavalcanti, Fifanti, Importuni, Squarciasacchi, Tornaquinci, Uberti, and Visdomini families: the Fifanti had relatively little linkage to castles and signorie, the Uberti rather more and for rather longer); Cortese, *Signori, castelli, città*, esp. 209–58.

31. Faini, *Firenze*, 362.

32. Delumeau, *Arezzo*, 847–61, 1109–24, 1142–58; idem, 'Des Lombards de Carpineto aux Bostoli', 82–99; cf. Wickham, *Courts and Conflict*, 175.

Siena had a fairly similar trajectory, although without hostility to a bishop: Cammarosano, *Tradizione documentaria*, 35–47; Delumeau, *Arezzo*, 1113–15. So did Pistoia, where consuls are documented at the very early date of 1105 (*Libro Croce*, 350), but whose judicial records and well-known statutes do not appear before the 1170s: Lütke Westhues, 'Beobachtungen'; cf. Wickham, *Courts and Conflict*, 173n, including for other bibliography with alternative dates. So did Perugia, doubtless the most powerful commune in Umbria, but hardly documented as such at all (after its first consuls in 1139) until the 1180s; here we can at least say that it had few links either to the bishop or the signorial world—see Grundman, *The Popolo at Perugia*, 12–18; Cammarosano, *Studi di storia medievale*, 151–57; cf. Fiore, *Signori e sudditi*, 170–72, for Umbria in general. The evidence for all three is too poor for this period to justify fuller analysis here.

33. Wickham, 'La signoria rurale'.

34. But not Viterbo: contra Opll, *Stadt und Reich*, 474–75, the inscription which records the building of part of the city walls of Viterbo *ex precepto consulum et totius populi* does not date to 1099 (or even to the actual date cited in the inscription, 1095), but to the reign of Pope Eugenius III, around 1150: see Bottazzi, 'Tra papato e impero', 326–40.

35.   See for Umbria, Lazio, and Marche Maire Vigueur, 'Comuni e signorie', 383–96; for Benevento, see Falcone, *Chronicon*, cols. 1202–6 for the key moment and Oldfield, *City and Community*, 51–54, 59–60, 65–66, 77–80. For Provence, Poly, *La société*, 310–17, is the best quick survey; most communes (called *consulats* in French) are first attested in the 1140s, but Arles had them from 1131, in a document (unpublished, but cited in ibid., 310n) which dates by *anno primo consulatus Arelatensis*, demonstrating a striking self-consciousness which is otherwise only matched in Rome, although there is no evidence of social contestation in this aristocrat-dominated commune.

36.   This fits the conclusions, arrived at from a different direction, in Cortese, 'Aristocrazia signorile e città'.

37.   Schwarzmaier, *Lucca*, 326–27.

38.   We might perhaps also include Asti, given its careful separation from the power-networks of the bishop and its fast-developing commercial sector which will have brought along many new families; Bologna, where jurists were so influential, although we do not know much about their personal wealth; and also, after c. 1180, Pavia (Lane, 'The Territorial Expansion', 111–15).

39.   Rippe, *Padoue*, e.g. 368 (Jonas), 373–74 (Nicolò), 375–76 (Raimondo)—cf. also Vallerani, 'Tra astrazione e prassi', 138–40, for their expertise; Faini, *Firenze*, appendix, 18–19, 27–28, 37–39; and see above, n. 23 for Cremona.

40.   These points about assemblies are further generalised in Wickham, 'The "Feudal Revolution"'. The basic analyses for Italy remain Coleman and Grillo, as in chapter 2, n. 15, in this volume.

41.   In Verona, the collectivity which made a treaty with Venice in 1107, thirty years before the first documented consuls (Castagnetti, 'Feudalità e società comunale', 226–30, 232), may have been a formalised assembly, but the text does not say so, and Castagnetti (ibid., 227) sees it as 'occasionale'.

42.   Banti, '"Civitas" e "Commune"', 229–32; see above, nn. 13, 21, 23, 24, 26; see also n. 16 for a more problematic example; and chapter 3, n. 45, in this volume.

43.   See most recently Faini, 'Le tradizioni normative delle città toscane', 463–65, 471–79; cf. Bellomo, *Ricerche*, 8–25.

44.   Hay, *The Military Leadership*, 76–167.

45. Siena: Cammarosano, *Studi di storia medievale*, 232–33; for Como, see p. 65 in this volume.

46. *Die lombardische Briefsammlung*, n. 43; cf. Otto of Freising's less neutral complaints along the same lines, *Chronica*, 7.17, 19, 27, and esp. 29. The inescapable parallel is Thomas Bisson's work on the greater local violence of the period after the fall of the post-Carolingian state in West Francia and elsewhere, summed up most recently in *The Crisis*, 41–68. See also Fiore, 'Dal diploma al patto', on ever more formal rural pacts to establish local peace in this period.

47. 'Il "Liber Pergaminus"', lines 87–126 (bishop), 205–62 (fountains), 271–92 (consuls); for the annals, Wickham, *Land and Power*, 298, 307–8.

48. Post-Roman Britain, that is to say: Wickham, *Framing*, 330–31.

BIBLIOGRAPHY

ABBREVIATIONS

ASLSP Atti della Società ligure di storia patria
ASRSP Archivio della Società romana di storia patria
BISIME Bullettino dell'Istituto storico italiano per il medio evo
BSP Bollettino storico pisano
DBI Dizionario biografico degli Italiani, Rome, 1960–
MGH Monumenta Germaniae Historica (SS: Scriptores; SRG:
   Scriptores rerum Germanicarum)
QF Quellen und Forschungen aus italienischen Archiven und
   Bibliotheken
RIS² Rerum Italicarum Scriptores, 2nd edition

PRIMARY SOURCES: A NOTE ON DOCUMENTS

The documentary collections for the three cities which form the case studies in this book are published in very diverse and, sometimes, confusing ways. A very brief guide follows for each, citing collections by their short titles.

For Milan, most documents for the eleventh century are published in *Gli atti privati*, cited in the text as *APM*; the main exceptions are *placita*, published in *I placiti*, and some archiepiscopal documents, which are published, badly, in appendices to each volume of Giulini, *Memorie*. For the twelfth century, communal documents are edited in *Gli atti del Comune di Milano*, cited in the text as *Gli atti del Comune*. For private documents, the basic print edition is *Pergamene milanesi*, in twenty volumes, continuing, which arranges the Milanese documentary collections by church archive (*fondo*). This is for the most part, however, now most easily consulted via the *Codice diplomatico della Lombardia medievale*, a fully searchable online collection at http:// cdlm.unipv.it/ [last accessed 14 August 2013], which covers (or will cover) the whole of Lombardy up to 1200 and beyond. That online edition includes by now some editions which are not (yet) available in print, notably, for Milan in our period, *Le carte del monastero di S. Ambrogio di Milano*, vol. 3/1, cited in the text as *S. Ambrogio 3/1*, and *Le carte del monastero di S. Maria di Chiaravalle*, vol. 2, cited in the text as *Chiaravalle 2*; and also (to cite non-Milanese editions used in this book) *Le carte della Mensa vescovile di Lodi*, cited in the text as *Mensa di Lodi*, and *Le carte del monastero di San Faustino dell'Isola Comacina*, cited in the text as *S. Faustino*. It also collects others which were published separately, of which those used here are *Le pergamene della canonica di S. Ambrogio*, cited in the text as *Canonica di S. Ambrogio*; *Le carte del monastero di S. Maria di Morimondo*, vol. 1, cited in the text as *Morimondo*; and *Le carte della chiesa di S. Maria del Monte di Velate*, vol. 1, cited in the text as *Velate*.

Most of the major *fondi* for Milan are thus now published for our period, although there are some exceptions, notably the early twelfth-century documents for the Canonica of S. Ambrogio, the Monastero Maggiore, and the Capitolo of Monza. The online edition does not, however, supersede *Pergamene milanesi*, in part because the electronic transfer has introduced some typographical errors, not (yet) corrected, and in part because it does not (yet) include vols. 1, 8, 11, or 12 of *Pergamene milanesi*. The print edition is most easily cited by volume, but the electronic edition is most easily cited by *fondo*. I cite by *fondo* in the text, in italics, but include here a correspondence between the *fondi* cited in this book and the relevant volumes of *Pergamene milanesi*.

Pergamene milanesi, vol. 1 (edited by Maria Franca Baroni): *S. Maria di Aurona*.
Vol. 4 (edited by Maria Franca Baroni): *S. Maria in Valle*.
Vol. 5 (edited by Luisa Zagni): *S. Giorgio al Palazzo*.
Vol. 7 (edited by Maria Franca Baroni): *S. Lorenzo*.
Vol. 8 (edited by Maria Franca Baroni): *S. Simpliciano*.
Vol. 9 (edited by Luisa Zagni): *S. Vittore di Varese*.
Vol. 10 (edited by Maria Franca Baroni): *S. Ulderico, S. Maria delle Veteri*.
Vol. 12 (edited by Liliana Martinelli): *S. Dionigi, S. Eusebio*.
Vol. 14 (edited by Liliana Martinelli Perelli): *S. Stefano di Vimercate*.
Vol. 15 (edited by Maria Franca Baroni): *Capitolo Maggiore, Capitolo Minore/Decumani*.
Vol. 16 (edited by Anna Maria Rapetti): *Chiaravalle 1*.

For Pisa, there are four main archives in the city, each of which is edited in some form for our period. The Archivio Arcivescovile is fully edited to 1200, except for some smaller *fondi*, in *Carte dell'Archivio arcivescovile di Pisa. Fondo arcivescovile*, cited in the text as *AAP*. The smaller *fondi* and some important archiepiscopal texts which are not in this archive are registered in full in *Regesto della chiesa di Pisa*, cited in the text as *RCP*. The Archivio Capitolare has been edited until 1120, the Archivio di Stato until 1100, and the Archivio della Certosa di Calci until 1200. These editions are not cited in this book, but in the case of the first two the later documents have been edited (until after 1200 for the Archivio di Stato, until 1176 for the Archivio Capitolare) in undergraduate *tesi di laurea* of the University of Pisa, some of which I do cite, in normal short title form in the text, and in full in the bibliography.

For Rome, there are a large number of different church archives in the city, about a third of which are now in the Archivio di Stato. A good guide to them can be found in Hubert, *Espace urbain*, 9–22, plus the relevant editions. The documents used in this book are all published for our period, with the exception of the twelfth-century charters of SS. Cosma e Damiano in Trastevere, and the *fondo* of S. Maria in Trastevere. They are published by *fondo*, whether from single-sheet parchment originals or (as for Farfa and S. Gregorio sul Celio) cartularies. Ten of these editions and the above-mentioned two unpublished *fondi* are used in this book, here listed with the abbreviations used in the text (other abbreviations are given with the first reference in each chapter):

LL Liber largitorius vel notarius monasterii Pharphensis.
RF Il Regesto di Farfa.
RS Il Regesto sublacense.
SCD Fedele, 'Carte del monastero dei SS. Cosma e Damiano'—for the eleventh century; for the twelfth, see the next abbreviation.
ASR, SCD Archivio di Stato di Roma, fondo Benedettini e Clarisse in SS. Cosma e Damiano.
S. Gregorio Il regesto del monastero dei SS. Andrea e Gregorio ad Clivum Scauri.
SMCM Cartario di S. Maria in Campo Marzio.
SMN Pietro Fedele, 'Tabularium S. Mariae Novae'.
SMT Archivio Storico del Vicariato, Archivio del Capitolo di S. Maria in Trastevere, n. 532.

SMVL   *Ecclesiae S. Maria in Via Lata tabularium.*
S. Paolo   Trifone, 'Le carte del monastero di S. Paolo di Roma'.
S. Prassede   Fedele, 'Tabularium S. Praxedis'.

PRIMARY SOURCES

UNPUBLISHED

Archivio di Stato di Roma, fondo Benedettini e Clarisse in SS. Cosma e
Damiano, cassette 16–16 bis–17. [Photographs of the documents are
available online on the archive's website, at http://www.cflr.beniculturali
.it/Pergamene/pergamene.php?lar=1024&alt=768.]

Archivio Doria Pamphilj [in Rome], *Liber instrumentorum Monasterii
Sancti Fructuosi de Capite Montis Codice 'A'*: ADP, bancone 79, busta 12.

Archivio Storico del Vicariato [in Rome], Archivio del Capitolo di S.
Maria in Trastevere, n. 532.

Biblioteca Apostolica Vaticana, Codices Vaticani Latini 8044.

PUBLISHED

Acta pontificum romanorum inedita, edited by Julius von Pflugk-Harttung,
3 vols. Tübingen, 1881, Stuttgart, 1884–86.

Adalberto Samaritano. *Praecepta dictaminum*, edited by Franz-Josef
Schmale. *MGH, Quellen zur Geistesgeschichte des Mittelalters*, 3. Weimar, 1961.

Andenna, Giancarlo. 'Documenti di San Paolo fuori le mura, fra cui un
placito papale del 1113, nel codice XXXIV (71), ora trafugato, della
Biblioteca Capitolare di Santa Maria di Novara'. In *Scritti in onore di
Girolamo Arnaldi*, edited by Andrea Degrandi et al., 25–39. Rome, 2001.

Annales Brixienses, edited by Ludwig Bethmann. *MGH, SS*, vol. 18, 811–20.
Hannover, 1863.

Annales Casinenses, edited by Georg Heinrich Pertz. *MGH, SS*, vol. 19,
303–20. Hannover, 1866.

Annales Ceccanenses, edited by Georg Heinrich Pertz. *MGH, SS*, vol. 19,
275–302. Hannover, 1866.

Annales Mediolanenses, edited by Georg Heinrich Pertz. *MGH, SS*, vol. 18,
357–78. Hannover, 1863.

Annali genovesi di Caffaro e de' suoi continuatori dal MXCIX al MCCX-CIII, edited by Luigi Tommaso Belgrano, vol. 1. Rome, 1890.

Anselmo dall'Orto. *De summa Anselmini de Orto super contractibus emphyteosis et precarii et libelli atque investiture*, edited by Rudolf Jacobi. Weimar, 1854.

Anselmo dall'Orto. *Iuris civilis instrumentum*, edited by Vittorio Scialoja. In *Bibliotheca iuridica medii aevi*, edited by Augusto Gaudenzi, vol. 2, 87–116. Bologna, 1892.

Arnolfo of Milan. *Liber gestorum recentium*, edited by Claudia Zey. *MGH, SRG*, vol. 67. Hannover, 1994.

Baumgärtner, Ingrid. 'Regesten aus dem Kapitelarchiv von S. Maria in Via Lata (1200–1259)'. *QF* 74 (1994), 42–171, 75 (1995), 32–177.

Belgrano, Luigi Tommaso. 'Il registro della curia arcivescovile di Genova'. *ASLSP* 2.2 (1862).

Beno. *Gesta Romanae aecclesiae contra Hildebrandum*, edited by Kuno Francke. *MGH, Libelli de lite*, vol. 2, 366–422. Hannover, 1892.

Benzone of Alba. *Ad Heinricum IV. imperatorem libri VII*, edited by Hans Seyffert. *MGH, SRG*, vol. 65. Hannover, 1996.

Bernard of Clairvaux. *Epistolae*. In *Sancti Bernardi Opera*, vols. 6–8, edited by Jean Leclercq and Henri M. Rochais. Rome, 1974–77.

Bernold of Konstanz. *Chronicon*, edited by Ian Stuart Robinson. *Die Chroniken Bertholds von Reichenau und Bernolds von Konstanz 1054–1100*, 383–540. Hannover, 2003.

Bonizone of Sutri. *Liber ad amicum*, edited by Ernst Dümmler. *MGH, Libelli de lite*, vol. 1, 571–620. Hannover, 1891.

Carmen de gestis Frederici I. imperatoris in Lombardia, edited by Irene Schmale-Ott. *MGH, SRG*, vol. 62. Hannover, 1965.

Cartario di S. Maria in Campo Marzio (986–1199), edited by Enrico Carusi. Rome, 1948.

Carte dell'Archivio arcivescovile di Pisa. Fondo arcivescovile, edited by Antonella Ghignoli (vol. 1) and Silio P. P. Scalfati (vols. 2 and 3). Pisa, 2006.

Chronica monasterii Casinensis, edited by Hartmut Hoffmann. *MGH, SS*, vol. 34. Hannover, 1980.

Chronicon pisanum, edited by Michele Lupo Gentile. In *Gli Annales Pisani di Bernardo Maragone*, 99–103.

Codex Astensis, vols. 2 and 3, edited by Quintino Stella. Rome, 1880.

Codex diplomaticus Cajetanus, vols. 1–2, = *Tabularium Casinense*, vols. 1–2. Montecassino, 1887–91.

Codice diplomatico del monastero di Santo Stefano di Genova, vol. 1 (965–1200), edited by Marta Calleri. Genoa, 2009.

Codice diplomatico del Senato romano dal MCXLIV al MCCCXLVII, vol. 1, edited by Franco Bartoloni. Roma, 1948.

Codice diplomatico della Repubblica di Genova, edited by Cesare Imperiale di Sant'Angelo, 3 vols. Rome, 1936–42.

Cognasso, Francesco. 'Pergamene di sant'Anastasio di Asti'. *Atti della Reale accademia delle scienze di Torino* 76.2 (1941), 3–24.

Constitutiones et acta publica imperatorum et regum, vol. 1, ed. Ludwig Weiland. *MGH*, 4th series, vol. 1. Hannover, 1893.

Dante. *Inferno*, various editions.

De bello Mediolanensium adversus Comenses. Liber Cumanus, edited by Giuseppe Maria Stampa. In *Rerum Italicarum Scriptores*, edited by Ludovico Antonio Muratori, vol. 5, 405–58. Milan, 1724.

Die Lombardische Briefsammlung, edited by Heinz-Jürgen Beyer. Available online at http://www.uni-saarland.de/verwalt/praesidial/LuSt/Lomb/Lo.html.

Die Urkunden und Briefe der Markgräfin Mathilde von Tuszien, edited by Elke and Werner Goez. *MGH, Diplomata*, 5th series, vol. 2. Hannover, 1998.

'Documenti per la storia ecclesiastica e civile di Roma', edited by Emil von Ottenthal. *Studi e documenti di storia e diritto* 7 (1886), 101–22, 195–212, 317–36, and continuing.

Documenti sulle relazioni delle città toscane coll'Oriente cristiano e coi Turchi, edited by Giuseppe Müller. Florence, 1879.

Ecclesiae S. Maria in Via Lata tabularium, edited by Ludo Moritz Hartmann and (for vol. 3) Margarete Merores, 3 vols. Vienna, 1895–1913.

Epistolae pontificum Romanorum ineditae, edited by Samuel Loewenfeld. Leipzig, 1885.

Falcone of Benevento. *Chronicon*, in *Patrologiae . . . series latina*, vol. 173, cols. 1151–1262.

Fedele, Pietro. 'Carte del monastero dei SS. Cosma e Damiano in Mica Aurea, secoli X e XI'. *ASRSP* 21 (1898), 459–534, 22 (1899), 25–107, 383–447, republished as a book with the same title, edited by P. Pavan, *Codice diplomatico di Roma e della regione romana*, vol 1. Rome, 1981.

Fedele, Pietro. 'Tabularium S. Mariae Novae ab an. 982 ad an. 1200'. *ASRSP* 23 (1900), 171–237, 24 (1901), 159–96, 25 (1902), 169–209, 26 (1903), 21–141.

Fedele, Pietro. 'Tabularium S. Praxedis'. *ASRSP* 27 (1904), 27–78, 28 (1905), 41–114.

Friderici I. diplomata, ed. Heinrich Appelt. *MGH, Diplomata*, vol. 10. Hannover, 1975–90.

Geoffroy of Vendôme. *Œuvres*, edited by Gérard Giordanengo. Turnhout, 1996.

Gesta triumphalia per Pisanos facta, edited by Giuseppe Scalia. Florence, 2010.

Gli Annales Pisani di Bernardo Maragone, edited by Michele Lupo Gentile. *RIS²*, vol. 6.2. Bologna, 1936.

Gli atti del Comune di Milano fino all'anno MCCXVI, edited by Cesare Manaresi. Milan, 1919.

Gli atti privati milanesi e comaschi del sec. XI, edited by Giovanni Vittani, Cesare Manaresi, and Caterina Santoro, 4 vols. Milan, 1933–69.

Godfrey of Viterbo. *Pantheon*, edited by Georg Waitz. *MGH, SS*, vol. 22, 107–307. Hannover, 1872.

Guastini, Maria. 'Le pergamene dell'Archivio di Stato di Pisa dal 1100 al 1115'. Tesi di laurea, Università di Pisa, relatore Cinzio Violante, 1964–65.

Heinrici IV. diplomata, edited by Dietrich von Gladiss and Alfred Gawlik. *MGH, Diplomata*, vol. 6. Hannover, 1941–78.

I Biscioni, edited by Giulio Cesare Faccio and M. Ranno, vol. 1. Turin, 1934–39.

I brevi dei consoli del Comune di Pisa degli anni 1162 e 1164, edited by Ottavio Banti. Rome, 1997.

I Costituti della legge e dell'uso di Pisa (sec. XII), edited by Paola Vignoli. Rome, 2003.

I diplomi arabi del R. Archivio fiorentino, edited by Michele Amari. Florence, 1863.

I libri iurium della Repubblica di Genova, edited by Dino Puncuh et al., 8 vols. Genoa, 1992–2002.

I placiti del 'Regnum Italiae', edited by Cesare Manaresi, 3 vols. Rome, 1955–60.

Il Chartarium Dertonense ed altri documenti del comune di Tortona (934–1346), edited by Erwig Gabotto. Pinerolo, 1909.

Il Chronicon Farfense di Gregorio di Catino, edited by Ugo Balzani, 2 vols. Rome, 1903.

'Il "Liber Pergaminus" di Mosè de Brolo', edited by Guglielmo Gorni. *Studi medievali* 11 (1970), 409–60.

Il regesto del monastero dei SS. Andrea e Gregorio ad Clivum Scauri, edited by Alberto Bartola, 2 vols. *Codice diplomatico di Roma e della regione romana*, vol. 7. Rome, 2003.

Il Regesto di Farfa, edited by Ignazio Giorgi and Ugo Balzani, 5 vols. Rome, 1879–1914.

Il Regesto sublacense del secolo XI, edited by Leone Allodi and Guido Levi. Rome, 1885.

Il Registrum Magnum del Comune di Piacenza, edited by Ettore Falconi and Roberta Peveri, 4 vols. Milan, 1984–88.

Iscrizioni delle chiese e d'altri edifici di Roma dal secolo XI fino ai giorni nostri, edited by Vincenzo Forcella, 14 vols. Rome, 1869–84.

Italia sacra, edited by Ferdinando Ughelli, vols. 4 and 5. 2nd edition, edited by Nicola Coleti. Venice, 1719–20.

Iter italicum, edited by Julius von Pflugk-Harttung. Stuttgart, 1883.

Johannis Codagnelli Annales placentini, edited by Oswald Holder-Egger. *MGH, SRG*, vol. 23. Hannover, 1901.

John of Salisbury. *Historia pontificalis*, edited by Marjorie Chibnall. Edinburgh, 1956.

Kehr, Paul Fridolin. 'Diploma purpureo di re Roggero II per la casa Pierleoni'. *ASRSP* 24 (1901), 253–59.

La Summa Trium Librorum di Rolando da Lucca (1195–1234), edited by Emanuele Conte and Sara Menzinger. Rome, 2012.

Landolfo Seniore. *Mediolanensis historiae libri quatuor*, edited by Alessandro Cutolo. *RIS²*, vol. 4.2. Bologna, 1934.

Landulphi Iunioris Historia Mediolanensis, edited by Carlo Castiglioni. *RIS²*, vol. 5.3. Bologna, 1934.

Le carte cremonesi dei secoli VIII–XII, edited by Ettore Falconi, 4 vols. Cremona, 1979–88.

Le carte del monastero di S. Ambrogio di Milano, vol. 3/1 (*1101–1180*), edited by Marta L. Mangini. Available online at http://cdlm.unipv.it/edizioni/mi/milano-sambrogio-mon3–1/.

Le carte del monastero di S. Maria di Chiaravalle, vol. 2 (*1165–1200*), edited by Ada Grossi. Available online at http://cdlm.unipv.it/edizioni/mi/chiaravalle-smaria2/.

Le carte del monastero di S. Maria di Morimondo, vol. 1 (*1010–1170*), edited by Michele Ansani. Spoleto, 1992. Also available online at http://cdlm.unipv.it/edizioni/mi/morimondo-smaria1/.

Le carte del monastero di San Faustino dell'Isola Comacina (1011–1190), edited by Rita Pezzola. Available online at http://cdlm.unipv.it/edizioni /co/comacina-sfaustino/.

Le carte del monastero di San Siro di Genova (952–1224), edited by Marta Calleri, vol. 1. Genoa, 1997.

Le carte del monastero di Sant'Andrea della Porta di Genova (1109–1370), edited by Cristina Soave. Genoa, 2002.

Le carte dell'Archivio capitolare di Asti (830, 948, 1111–1237), edited by Ferdinando Gabotto and Nicola Gabiani. Pinerolo, 1907.

Le carte della chiesa di S. Maria del Monte di Velate, vol. 1 (922–1170), edited by Patrizia Merati. Varese, 2005. Also available online at http://cdlm .unipv.it/edizioni/mi/velate-smaria1/.

Le carte della Mensa vescovile di Lodi (883–1200), edited by Ada Grossi. Available online at http://cdlm.unipv.it/edizioni/lo/lodi-vescovo/.

Le carte di Santa Maria delle Vigne di Genova (1103–1392), edited by Gabriella Airaldi. Genoa, 1969.

Le Liber Censuum de l'église romaine, edited by Paul Fabre and Louis Duchesne, 3 vols. Paris, 1905–10.

Le Liber Pontificalis, edited by Louis Duchesne, 2 vols. Paris, 1955.

Le pergamene della canonica di S. Ambrogio nel secolo XII (1152–1178), edited by Annamaria Ambrosioni. Milan, 1974. Also available online at http://cdlm.unipv.it/edizioni/mi/milano-sambrogio-can/.

Lehmann, Karl. *Das langobardische Lehnrecht*. Göttingen, 1896.

Liber Guidonis compositus de variis historiis, edited by Michele Campopiano. Florence, 2008.

Liber largitorius vel notarius monasterii Pharphensis, edited by Giuseppe Zucchetti, 2 vols. Rome, 1913–32.

Liber Maiolichinus de gestis Pisanorum illustribus, edited by Carlo Calisse. Rome, 1904.

Liber pontificalis nella recensione di Pietro Guglielmo OSB e del card. Pandolfo, edited by Ulderico Přerovský, 3 vols. *Studia gratiana* 21–23. Rome, 1978.

Liber Potheris communis civitatis Brixiae, edited by Francesco Bettoni Cazzago and Luigi Francesco Fè d'Ostiani. *Historia patriae monumenta*, vol. 19. Turin, 1899.

Liber statutorum consulum Cumanorum, edited by Antonio Ceruti. *Leges municipales*, vol. 2, part 1, 1–503. *Historiae patriae monumenta*, vol. 16. Turin, 1875.

Libro Croce, edited by Quinto Santoli. Rome, 1939.

Liutprando of Cremona. *Historia Ottonis*. In *Liudprandi opera*, edited by Joseph Becker. *MGH, SRG*, 159–75. Hannover, 1915.

Malaterra, Gaufredo. *De rebus gestis Rogerii Calabriae et Siciliae Comitis et Roberti Guiscardi ducis fratris eius*, edited by Ernesto Pontieri. *RIS²*, vol. 5.1. Bologna, 1928.

Monumenta Bambergensia, edited by Philipp Jaffé. *Bibliotheca rerum germanicarum*, vol. 5. Berlin, 1869.

Monumenta epigrafica pisana saeculi XV antiquiora, edited by Ottavio Banti. Pisa, 2000.

Müller, Ernst. 'Der Bericht des Abtes Hariulf von Oudenburg über seine Prozessverhandlungen an der römischen Kurie im Jahre 1141'. *Neues Archiv* 48 (1929), 97–115.

Nardi, Rosalba. 'Le pergamene dell'Archivio di Stato di Pisa dall'8 novembre 1115 al 13 febbraio 1130'. Tesi di laurea, Università di Pisa, relatore Cinzio Violante, 1964–65.

Otto Morena. *Historia Frederici I.*, edited by Ferdinand Güterbock. *MGH, SRG*, n.s., vol. 7. Berlin, 1930.

Otto of Freising. *Chronica*, ed. Adolf Hofmeister. *MGH, SRG*, vol. 45. Hannover, 1912.

Otto of Freising and Rahewin. *Gesta Friderici I. imperatoris*, edited by Georg Waitz and Bernhard de Simson. *MGH, SRG*, vol. 46. Hannover, 1912.

Papsturkunden in Italien, edited by Paul Fridolin Kehr, 6 vols. Rome, 1977.

Patrologiae cursus completus, series latina, edited by Jacques-Paul Migne, 220 vols. Paris, 1844–55.

Pergamene milanesi dei secoli XII–XIII, edited by Maria Franca Baroni et al., 20 vols. and continuing. Milano, 1984–.

Pier Damiani. *Epistulae*. In *Die Briefe des Petrus Damiani*, edited by Kurt Reindel. *MGH, Briefe der deutschen Kaiserzeit*, vol. 4, 4 vols. Munich, 1983–93.

Rangerio. *Vita metrica S. Anselmi Lucensis episcopi*, edited by Ernest Sackur, Gerhard Schwarz, and Bernhard Schmeidler. *MGH, SS*, vol. 30.2, 1152–1307. Leipzig, 1934.

Regesto della chiesa di Pisa, edited by Natale Caturegli. Rome, 1938.

Romualdi Salernitani Chronicon, edited by Carlo Alberto Garufi. *RIS²*, vol. 7.1. Città di Castello, 1919.

Sacrorum conciliorum nova et amplissima collectio, edited by Giovanni Domenico Mansi, vol. 19. Venice, 1774.

Sgherri, Rosalia. 'Le pergamene dell'Archivio Capitolare di Pisa dall'agosto 1155 al 18 febbraio 1176'. Tesi di laurea, Università di Pisa, relatore Ottorino Bertolini, 1963–64.

Trifone, Basilio. 'Le carte del monastero di S. Paolo di Roma dal secolo XI al XV'. *ASRSP* 31 (1908), 267–313, and continuing.

Vincent of Prague. *Annales*, edited by Wilhelm Wattenbach. *MGH, SS*, vol. 17, 658–83. Hannover, 1861.

Wibald of Stablo. *Epistolae*, edited by Philipp Jaffé. In *Monumenta Corbeiensia*, 76–622. *Bibliotheca rerum germanicarum*, vol. 1. Berlin, 1864.

SECONDARY SOURCES

Abulafia, David. *The Two Italies*. Cambridge, 1977.

Adriani, G. B. *Degli antichi signori di Sarmatorio Manzano e Monfalcone*. Turin, 1853.

Andenna, Giancarlo. 'Dall'Orto (de Orto), Oberto'. *DBI* 32 (1986), 145–50.

Andenna, Giancarlo. 'Le strutture sociali in età signorile e feudale'. In idem et al., *Comuni e signorie nell'Italia settentrionale: la Lombardia*, 191–314. UTET *Storia d'Italia*, vol. 6. Turin, 1998.

Andenna, Giancarlo. 'Una famiglia milanese di "cives" proprietari terrieri nella pieve di Cesano Boscone: i Cagapisto'. In *Contributi dell'Istituto di storia medioevale*, vol. 2, 640–86. Milan, 1972.

Andrews, David. 'Lo scavo di Piazza Duomo'. In *Scavi MM3*, 163–209.

Angiolini, Hélène. 'Familiati, Bandino (Bandino Pisano)'. *DBI* 44 (1994), 517–18.

Archetti, Gabriele. 'Grosolano (Grossolano)'. *DBI* 59 (2003), 792–96.

Arnaldi, Girolamo. 'Rinascita, fine, reincarnazione e successive metamorfosi del senato romano (secoli V–XII)'. *ASRSP* 105 (1982), 5–56.

Augenti, Andrea. *Il Palatino nel medioevo*. Rome, 1996.

Baldassarri, Monica, and Giorgio, Marcella. 'La ceramica di produzione mediterranea a Pisa tra XI e fine XIII secolo'. In *Pensare/classificare*, edited by Sauro Gelichi and Monica Baldassarri, 35–51. Florence, 2010.

Baldelli, Ignazio. 'La carta pisana di Filadelfia'. *Studi di filologia italiana* 31 (1973), 5–33.

Banti, Ottavio. '"Civitas" e "Commune" nelle fonti italiane dei secoli XI e XIII'. In *Forme di potere e struttura sociale in Italia nel Medioevo*, edited by Gabriella Rossetti, 217–32. Bologna, 1977.

Banti, Ottavio. 'La giustizia, la guerra giusta e la "missione storica" di Pisa in tre epigrafi del secolo XII'. *BSP* 70 (2001), 43–52.

Banti, Ottavio. *Scritti di storia, diplomatica ed epigrafica*. Pisa, 1995.

Banti, Ottavio. *Studi di storia e diplomatica comunale*. Rome, 1983.

Barbanera, Marcello, and Pergola, Stefania. 'Elementi architettonici antichi e post-antichi riutilizzati nella c.d. Casa dei Crescenzi'. *Bullettino della Commissione archeologica comunale di Roma* 98 (1997), 301–28.

Barbero, Alessandro. 'Vassalli vescovili e aristocrazia consolare a Vercelli nel XII secolo'. In *Vercelli nel secolo XII*, 217–309.

Barni, Gian Luigi. 'Dal governo del vescovo a quello dei cittadini'. In *Storia di Milano*, vol. 3, 3–236. Milan, 1954.

Barni, Gian Luigi. 'Milano verso l'egemonia'. In *Storia di Milano*, vol. 3, 238–393. Milan, 1954.

Bartoloni, Franco. 'Per la storia del Senato Romano nei secoli XII e XIII'. *BISIME* 60 (1946), 1–108.

Basile Weatherill, Martina. 'Una famiglia "longobarda" tra primo e secondo millennio: i "da Intimiano"'. In *Ariberto da Intimiano*, edited by E. Bianchi et al., 311–33. Milan, 2007.

Becker, Claudia. *Il comune di Chiavenna nel XII e nel XIII secolo*, translated by Gian Primo Falappi. Chiavenna, 2002.

Behrmann, Thomas. 'L'atto giuridico e il suo pubblico'. In *Legislazione e prassi istituzionale nell'Europa medievale*, edited by Gabriella Rossetti, 175–208. Naples, 2001.

Behrmann, Thomas. 'Von der Sentenz zur Akte'. In *Kommunales Schriftgut in Oberitalien*, edited by Hagen Keller and Thomas Behrmann, 71–90. Munich, 1995.

Bellomo, Manlio. *Ricerche sui rapporti patrimoniali tra coniugi*. Milan, 1961.

Benson, Robert Louis. 'Political *renovatio*'. In *Renaissance and Renewal in the Twelfth Century*, edited by idem et al., 339–86. Cambridge, MA, 1982.

Berti, Graziella, and Tongiorgi, Liana. *I bacini ceramici medievali delle chiese di Pisa*. Rome, 1981.

Besozzi, Leonida. 'Hobedientia de Abiasca et de Clari'. *Bollettino storico della Svizzera italiana* 96 (1984), 103–32.

Biscaro, Gerolamo. 'Gli avvocati dell'arcivescovo di Milano nei secoli XI e XII'. *Archivio storico lombardo*, 4th series, 5 (1906), 5–29.

Biscaro, Gerolamo. 'I maggiori dei Visconti, signori di Milano'. *Archivio storico lombardo*, 4th series, 16 (1911), 5–76.

Bisson, Thomas N. *The Crisis of the Twelfth Century.* Princeton, 2009.

Blasco Ferrer, Eduardo. 'Consuntivo delle riflessioni sul cosiddetto privilegio logudorese'. *BSP* 70 (2001), 9–41.

Blomquist, Thomas W., and Osheim, Duane J. 'The First Consuls at Lucca: 10 July 1119'. *Actum Luce* 7 (1978), 31–38.

Bocchi, Francesca. 'Sul titolo di "consul" in età alto medievale'. *Zbornik radova Vizantološkog Instituta* 18 (1978), 51–66.

Bognetti, Gian Piero. *Studi sulle origini del comune rurale.* Milan, 1978.

Bordone, Renato. '"Civitas nobilis et antiqua"'. In *Piemonte medievale*, 29–61. Turin, 1985.

Bordone, Renato. *La società cittadina del Regno d'Italia.* Turin, 1987.

Bordone, Renato. 'Le origini del comune di Genova'. *ASLSP* 42.1 (2002), 237–59.

Bordone, Renato. 'Le origini del comune in Lombardia'. In Giancarlo Andenna et al., *Comuni e signorie nell'Italia settentrionale: la Lombardia*, 317–26. UTET *Storia d'Italia*, vol. 6. Turin, 1998.

Bordone, Renato. 'Tema cittadino e "ritorno alla terra" nella storiografia comunale recente'. *Quaderni storici* 52 (1983), 255–77.

Borino, Giovanni Battista. 'Cencio del prefetto Stefano'. In *Studi gregoriani*, vol. 4, edited by idem, 373–440. Rome, 1952.

Bosisio, Alfredo. 'Il comune'. In *Storia di Brescia*, vol. 1, edited by Giovanni Treccani degli Alfieri, 561–710. Brescia, 1961.

Bosisio, Alfredo. *Origini del comune di Milano.* Milan, 1933.

Bottazzi, Marialuisa. 'Tra papato e impero'. *Studi medievali* 47 (2006), 305–50.

Bougard, François. *La justice dans le royaume d'Italie de la fin du VIIIe siècle au début du XIe siècle.* Rome, 1995.

Brezzi, Paolo. *Roma e l'impero medioevale (774–1252).* Bologna, 1947.

Bruce, Travis. 'The Politics of Violence and Trade: Denia and Pisa in the Eleventh Century'. *Journal of Medieval History* 32 (2006), 127–42.

Bruni, Stefano, Abela, Elisabetta, and Berti, Graziella. *Ricerche di archeologia medievale a Pisa*, vol. 1. Florence, 2000.

Bulla, Gian Paolo. 'Famiglie dirigenti nella Piacenza del XII secolo alla luce delle pergamene di S. Antonino'. *Nuova rivista storica* 79 (1995), 505–86.

Busch, Jörg W. *Die Mailänder Geschichtsschreibung zwischen Arnulf und Galvaneus Flamma.* Munich, 1997.

Cammarosano, Paolo. *Studi di storia medievale. Economia, territorio, società.* Trieste, 2009.

Cammarosano, Paolo. *Tradizione documentaria e storia cittadina*. Siena, 1988.

Cantini, Federico. 'Ritmi e forme della grande espansione economica dei secoli XI–XIII nei contesti ceramici della Toscana settentrionale'. *Archeologia medievale* 37 (2010), 113–27.

Capitani, Ovidio. 'Da *Landolfo* Seniore a *Landolfo* Iuniore'. In *Atti del 110 Congresso internazionale di studi sull'alto medioevo*, 589–622. Spoleto, 1989.

Capitani, Ovidio. 'Storiografia e riforma della chiesa in Italia'. *Settimane di studio* 17 (1969), 557–629.

Carocci, Sandro. *Baroni di Roma*. Rome, 1993.

Carocci, Sandro, and Vendittelli, Marco. *L'origine della Campagna Romana*. Rome, 2004.

Caso, Anna. *I Crivelli*. Città di Castello, 1994.

Cassandro, Giovanni. 'Un bilancio storiografico'. In *Forme di potere e struttura sociale in Italia nel Medioevo*, edited by Gabriella Rossetti, 153–73. Bologna, 1977.

Castagnetti, Andrea. 'Da Verona a Ravenna per Vicenza, Padova, Trento e Ferrara'. In *La vassalità maggiore*, 345–491.

Castagnetti, Andrea. 'Feudalità e società comunale'. In *Medioevo Mezzogiorno Mediterraneo*, edited by Gabriella Rossetti and Giovanni Vitolo, vol. 1, 205–39. Naples, 2000.

Castagnetti, Andrea. 'Feudalità e società comunale II'. Available online at http://www.rm.unina.it/biblioteca/scaffale/c.htm#Andrea Castagnetti.

Castagnetti, Andrea. 'Il primo comune'. In *Storia di Venezia*, vol. 2, 81–130. Rome, 1995.

Castagnetti, Andrea. 'Introduzione'. In *La vassalità maggiore*, 7–23.

Castagnetti, Andrea. 'L'età precomunale e la prima età comunale (1024–1213)'. In *Il Veneto nel medioevo*, 1–162. Verona, 1991.

Castagnetti, Andrea. *Società e politica a Ferrara dall'età postcarolingia alla signoria estense (Sec. X–XIII)*. Bologna, 1985.

Cattaneo, Carlo. 'La città: considerata come principio ideale delle istorie italiane [1858]'. In idem, *Scritti storici e geografici*, edited by Gaetano Salvemini and Ernesto Sestan, vol. 1, 383–437. Florence, 1957.

Ceccarelli Lemut, Maria Luisa. 'Bernardo Maragone "provisor" e cronista di Pisa nel XII secolo'. In *Legislazione e prassi istituzionale a Pisa (secoli XI–XIII)*, edited by Gabriella Rossetti, 181–99. Naples, 2001.

Ceccarelli Lemut, Maria Luisa. 'Enrico da Pisa (Henricus plebanus)'. *DBI* 42 (1993), 751–52.

Ceccarelli Lemut, Maria Luisa. 'I consoli e i magistrati del Comune di Pisa dalla comparsa del consolato (1080/1085) al 1189'. *BSP*, forthcoming.

Ceccarelli Lemut, Maria Luisa. *Medioevo pisano*. Pisa, 2005.

Ceccarelli Lemut, Maria Luisa. 'Pisan Consular Families in the Communal Age'. In *The 'Other Tuscany'*, edited by Thomas W. Blomquist and Maureen F. Mazzaoui, 123–52. Kalamazoo, 1994.

Ceccarelli Lemut, Maria Luisa. 'Terre pubbliche e giurisdizione signorile nel *comitatus* di Pisa (secoli XI–XIII)'. In *La signoria rurale nel medioevo italiano*, edited by Amleto Spicciani and Cinzio Violante, 87–137. Pisa, 1998.

Ceccarelli Lemut, Maria Luisa, and Garzella, Gabriella. 'Optimus antistes'. *BSP* 70 (2001), 79–103.

Celli, Roberto. 'Il ruolo del parlamento nel periodo formativo dei Comuni'. In *Poteri assemblee autonomie (il lungo camino verso la sovranità popolare)*, 17–40. Udine, 1989.

Chiappa Mauri, Luisa. 'A Milano nel 1164'. *Archivio storico lombardo* 118 (1992), 9–36.

Chiodi, Giovanni. 'Roma e il diritto romano'. *Settimane di studio* 49 (2002), 1141–1254.

Ciccone, Gaetano. 'Famiglie di titolo comitale nel territorio di Livorno e Porto Pisano'. *BSP* 57 (1988), 117–56.

Classen, Peter. *Burgundio von Pisa*. Heidelberg, 1974.

Classen, Peter. *Studium und Gesellschaft im Mittelalter*. Stuttgart, 1983.

Coleman, Edward. 'Bishop and Commune in Twelfth-century Cremona'. In *Churchmen and Urban Government in Late Medieval Italy, c. 1200– c. 1450*, edited by Frances Andrews and Maria Agata Pincelli, 25–41. Cambridge, 2013.

Coleman, Edward. 'Representative Assemblies in Communal Italy'. In *Political Assemblies in the Earlier Middle Ages*, edited by Paul S. Barnwell and Marco Mostert, 193–210. Turnhout, 2003.

Coleman, Edward. 'The Italian Communes'. *Journal of Medieval History* 25 (1999), 373–97.

Collavini, Simone. 'Sviluppo signorile e nuove strategie onomastiche'. In *Studi di storia offerti a Michele Luzzati*, edited by Silvio P. P. Scalfati and Alessandra Veronese, 73–85. Pisa, 2009.

Constable, Olivia Remie. *Trade and Traders in Muslim Spain*. Cambridge, 1994.

Conte, Emanuele. *Servi medievali*. Rome, 1996.

Corsi, Maria Luisa. 'Note sulla famiglia da Baggio (secoli IX–XIII)'. In *Contributi dell'Istituto di storia medioevale*, vol. 1, 166–204. Milan, 1968.

Cortese, Ennio. *Il diritto nella storia medievale*, vol. 2. Rome, 1995.

Cortese, Maria Elena. 'Aristocrazia signorile e città nell'Italia centro-settentrionale (XI–XII sec.)'. In *I comuni di Jean-Claude Maire Vigueur*, edited by Maria Teresa Caciorgna, Sandro Carocci, and Andrea Zorzi, 69–94. Rome, 2014.

Cortese, Maria Elena. *Signori, castelli, città*. Florence, 2007.

Cowdrey, H. E. John. *Pope Gregory VII, 1073–1085*. Oxford, 1998.

Cowdrey, H. E. John. 'The Mahdiya Campaign of 1087'. *English Historical Review* 92 (1977), 1–29.

Cowdrey, H. E. John. 'The Papacy, the Patarenes and the Church of Milan'. *Transactions of the Royal Historical Society* 5th series, 18 (1968), 25–48.

Cremaschi, Giovanni. *Stefanardo da Vimercate*. Milan, 1950.

Cristiani, Emilio. *Nobiltà e popolo nel comune di Pisa*. Naples, 1962.

D'Acunto, Nicolangelo. 'Il prefetto Cencio di Giovanni Tignoso nelle fonti del suo secolo'. *BISIME* 95 (1989), 1–44.

D'Amia, Amerigo. *Diritto e sentenze di Pisa*. Milan, 1962.

Dartmann, Christoph. *Politische Interaktion in der italienischen Stadtkommune (11.–14. Jahrhundert)*. Ostfildern, 2012.

De Angelis, Gianmarco. '"Omnes simul aut quot plures habere potero"'. *Reti medievali rivista* 12 (2011), 151–94.

De Angelis, Gianmarco. *Poteri cittadini e intellettuali di potere*. Milan, 2009.

Degrandi, Andrea. 'Vassalli cittadini e vassalli rurali nel Vercellese del XII secolo'. *Bollettino storico-bibliografico subalpino* 91 (1993), 5–45.

Delfino, Maria Antonietta. 'Per la storia della classe dirigente del Comune di Pisa: i da Ripafratta'. Tesi di laurea, Università di Pisa, relatore Cinzio Violante, 1971–72.

Delumeau, Jean Pierre. *Arezzo. Espace et sociétés, 715–1230*. Rome, 1996.

Delumeau, Jean Pierre. 'Des Lombards de Carpineto aux Bostoli'. In *I ceti dirigenti dell'età comunale nei secoli XII e XIII*, 67–99. Pisa, 1982.

Di Renzo Villata, Maria Gigliola. 'La formazione dei "Libri Feudorum"'. *Settimane di studio* 47 (2000), 651–721.

Dilcher, Gerhard. *Die Entstehung der lombardischen Stadtkommune*. Aalen, 1967.

Dilcher, Gerhard. 'I comuni italiani come movimento sociale e forma giuridica'. In *L'evoluzione delle città italiane nell'XI secolo*, edited by Renato

Bordone and Jörg Jarnut, 71–98. Bologna, 1988.

Doran, John. 'The Legacy of Schism'. PhD thesis, Royal Holloway, University of London, 2008.

Faini, Enrico. *Firenze nell'età romanica (1000–1211)*. Florence, 2010; the appendices to the book are available online at http://eprints.unifi.it /archive/00001977/01/11-Faini.pdf.

Faini, Enrico. 'Le tradizioni normative delle città toscane'. *Archivio storico italiano* 171 (2013), 419–81.

Farina, Isabella. 'Per la storia della classe dirigente del Comune di Pisa: i Sismondi'. Tesi di laurea, Università di Pisa, relatore Gabriella Rossetti, 1969–70.

Fasola, Livia. 'Una famiglia di sostenitori milanesi di Federico I'. *QF* 52 (1972), 116–218.

Fasoli, Gina. *Dalla 'civitas' al comune nell'Italia settentrionale*. Bologna, 1969.

Fedele, Pietro. 'Il leopardo e l'agnello di casa Frangipane'. *ASRSP* 28 (1905), 207–17.

Fedele, Pietro. 'L'êra del Senato'. *ASRSP* 35 (1912), 583–610.

Fedele, Pietro. 'Le famiglie di Anacleto II e Gelasio II'. *ASRSP* 27 (1904), 399–440.

Ferrara, Roberto. 'La scuola per la città'. *ASLSP* 29.2 (1989), 595–647.

Filangieri, Luca. 'Famiglie e gruppi dirigenti a Genova (secoli XII–metà XIII)'. Dottorato di ricerca, Università degli studi di Firenze, 2010.

Fiore, Alessio. 'Dal diploma al patto'. In press.

Fiore, Alessio. *Signori e sudditi*. Spoleto, 2010.

Fisher, Craig B. 'The Pisan Clergy and an Awakening of Historical Interest in a Medieval Commune'. *Studies in Medieval and Renaissance History* 3 (1966), 143–219.

Fissore, Gian Giacomo. *Autonomia notarile e organizzazione cancelleresca nel comune di Asti*. Spoleto, 1977.

Fissore, Gian Giacomo. 'Origini e formazione del documento comunale a Milano'. In *Atti del 110 Congresso internazionale di studi sull'alto medioevo*, 551–88. Spoleto, 1989.

Fissore, Gian Giacomo. 'Problemi della documentazione vescovile astigiana per i secoli X–XII'. *Bollettino storico-bibliografico subalpino* 71 (1973), 417–510.

Framing Clement III, (Anti)pope, 1080–1100, edited by Umberto Longo and Lila Yawn. In *Reti medievali rivista* 13.1 (2012), http://rivista.retimedievali.it.

Franceschi, Franco, and Taddei, Ilaria. *Le città italiane nel Medioevo, XII–XIV secolo*. Bologna, 2012.

Franchini, Vittorio. 'Il titolo di *consul* in Ravenna a traverso l'alto medio evo'. *Bullettino della società filologica romana* II (1908), 33–44.

Fried, Johannes. *Die Entstehung des Juristenstandes im 12. Jahrhundert*. Cologne, 1974.

Frugoni, Arsenio. *Arnaldo da Brescia nelle fonti del secolo XII*. Rome, 1954.

Frugoni, Arsenio. 'Sulla "Renovatio Senatus" del 1143 e l'"Ordo equestris"'. *BISIME* 62 (1950), 159–74.

Fugazza, Emanuela. *Diritto, istituzioni e giustizia in un comune dell'Italia padana*. Padua, 2009.

Fugazza, Emanuela. '"In palatio episcopi, in pleno conscilio campana sonante congregato . . .". *Bollettino storico piacentino* 103 (2008), 3–34.

Garzella, Gabriella. 'Cascina'. In *Cascina*, vol. 2, by Marinella Pasquinucci, Gabriella Garzella, and Maria Luisa Ceccarelli Lemut, 69–108. Pisa, 1986.

Garzella, Gabriella. 'Marignani, Azzi, Alabarba'. In Rossetti et al., *Pisa nei secoli XI e XII*, 65–124.

Garzella, Gabriella. *Pisa com'era*. Naples, 1990.

Giardina, Camillo. *Storia del diritto*, vol 1. Palermo, 1963.

Giulini, Giorgio. *Memorie della città, e della campagna di Milano, ne' secoli bassi*, vols. 4 and 5. Milan, 1760–65.

Goez, Elke. *Beatrix von Canossa und Tuszien*. Sigmaringen, 1995.

Goldberg, Jessica. *Trade and Institutions in the Medieval Mediterranean*. Cambridge, 2012.

Grillo, Paolo. 'A Milano nel 1130'. *BISIME* 109 (2007), 219–35.

Grillo, Paolo. 'Aristocrazia urbana, aristocrazia rurale e origini del comune nell'Italia nord-occidentale'. *Storica* 19 (2001), 75–96.

Grillo, Paolo. 'Cavalieri, cittadini e comune consolare'. In *I comuni di Jean-Claude Maire Vigueur*, edited by Maria Teresa Caciorgna, Sandro Carocci, and Andrea Zorzi, 157–76. Rome, 2014.

Grillo, Paolo. 'Il comune di Vercelli nel secolo XII'. In *Vercelli nel secolo XII*, 161–88.

Grillo, Paolo. 'La frattura inesistente'. *Archivio storico italiano* 167 (2009), 673–700.

Grillo, Paolo. *Milano in età comunale (1183–1276)*. Spoleto, 2001.

Grillo, Paolo. 'Una fonte per lo studio dei comuni rurali lombardi all'inizio del secolo XII'. In *La costruzione del dominio cittadino sulle campagne,* edited by Roberta Mucciarelli, Gabriella Piccinni, and Giuliano Pinto, 59–76. Siena, 2009.

Grundman, John P. *The Popolo at Perugia, 1139–1309.* Perugia, 1992.

Guzzardi, M. B. 'Erizi'. In Rossetti et al., *Pisa nei secoli XI e XII,* 127–68.

Hall, Martin, and Phillips, Jonathan. *Caffaro, Genoa and the Twelfth-century Crusades.* Aldershot, 2013.

Halphen, Louis. *Études sur l'administration de Rome au moyen âge.* Paris, 1907.

Hamilton, Louis I. 'Memory, Symbol, and Arson'. *Speculum* 78 (2003), 378–99.

Hay, David J. *The Military Leadership of Matilda of Canossa, 1046–1115.* Manchester, 2008.

Herklotz, Ingo. *Gli eredi di Costantino.* Rome, 2000.

Hiestand, Rudolf. 'Iudex sacri Lateranensis palatii'. *Deutsches Archiv* 43 (1987), 62–80.

Hubert, Étienne. *Espace urbain et habitat à Rome du Xe siècle à la fin du XIIIe siècle.* Roma, 1990.

Hubert, Étienne. 'Rome au XIVe siècle'. *Médiévales* 40 (2001), 43–52.

Iapoce, Benedetta. 'La famiglia Federici tra l'XI ed il XV secolo'. Tesi di laurea, Università di Pisa, relatore Maria Luisa Ceccarelli Lemut, 1993–94.

Inguscio, Agostino. 'Reassessing Civil Conflicts in Genoa, 1160–1220'. DPhil thesis, Oxford University, 2012.

Jones, Philip. 'Economia e società nell'Italia medievale. La leggenda della borghesia'. In *Storia d'Italia. Annali,* vol. I, 187–372. Turin, 1978.

Jones, Philip. *The Italian City-State.* Oxford, 1997.

Keller, Hagen. 'Die Entstehung der italienischen Stadtkommunen als Problem der Sozialgeschichte'. *Frühmittelalterliche Studien* 10 (1976), 169–211. (Now in idem, *Il laboratorio politico,* 45–101.)

Keller, Hagen. 'Die soziale und politische Verfassung Mailands in den Anfängen des kommunalen Lebens'. *Historische Zeitschrift* 211 (1970), 34–64.

Keller, Hagen. 'Die Stadtkommunen als politische Organismen in den Herrschaftsordnungen des 11.–13. Jahrhunderts'. In *Pensiero e sperimentazioni istituzionali nella 'Societa Christiana' (1046–1250),* edited by Giancarlo Andenna, 673–703. Milan, 2007.

Keller, Hagen. 'Einwohnergemeinde und Kommune'. *Historische Zeitschrift* 224 (1977), 561–79.

Keller, Hagen. 'Gli inizi del comune in Lombardia'. In *L'evoluzione delle città italiane nell'XI secolo*, edited by Renato Bordone and Jörg Jarnut, 45–70. Bologna, 1998.

Keller, Hagen. *Il laboratorio politico del Comune medievale*. Naples, 2014.

Keller, Hagen. 'La decisione a maggioranza e il problema della tutela della minoranza nell'unione dei comuni periferici di Chiavenna e Piuro (1151–1155)'. *Clavenna* 39 (2000), 9–56. (Now in idem, *Il laboratorio politico*, 263–309.)

Keller, Hagen. 'Mailand im 11. Jahrhundert'. In *Die frühgeschichte der europäische Stadt im 11. Jahrhundert*, edited by Jörg Jarnut and Peter Johanek, 81–104. Cologne, 1998. (Now in idem, *Il laboratorio politico*, 229–62.)

Keller, Hagen. 'Pataria und Stadtverfassung, Stadtgemeinde und Reform'. *Vorträge und Forschungen* 17 (1973), 321–50.

Keller, Hagen. *Signori e vassalli nell'Italia delle città (secoli IX–XII)*, translated by Andrea Piazza. Turin, 1995.

Kershaw, Ian. 'Working Towards the Führer'. *Contemporary European History* 2 (1993), 103–18.

Kinney, Dale. 'S. Maria in Trastevere from Its Founding to 1215'. PhD thesis, New York University, 1975.

Krautheimer, Richard. *Rome. Profile of a City, 312–1308*. Princeton, 1980.

La pianura di Pisa e i rilievi contermini, edited by Renzo Mazzanti. Rome, 1994.

La vassalità maggiore del Regno Italico, edited by Andrea Castagnetti. Rome, 2001.

Lane, Frederic Chapin. 'At the Roots of Republicanism'. *American Historical Review* 71 (1966), 403–20.

Lane, Steven G. 'The Territorial Expansion of a Political Community: Pavia, 1100–1300'. PhD thesis, The University of Chicago, 1995.

Lansing, Carol. *The Florentine Magnates*. Princeton, 1991.

Laspeyres, Ernst Adolph. *Über die Entstehung und älteste Bearbeitung der Libri feudorum*. Berlin, 1830.

Laudage, Johannes. 'Rom und das Papsttum im frühen 12. Jahrhundert'. In *Europa an der Wende vom 11. zum 12. Jahrhundert*, edited by Klaus Herbers, 23–53. Stuttgart, 2001.

Lenzi, Mauro. *La terra e il potere*. Rome, 2000.

Lucioni, Alfredo. *Anselmo IV da Bovisio arcivescovo di Milano (1097–1101)*. Milan, 2011.

Luglié, Giuseppa Immacolata. 'I da Caprona'. In Rossetti et al., *Pisa nei secoli XI e XII*, 171–221.

Lütke Westhues, Peter. 'Beobachtungen zum Charakter und zur Datierung der ältesten Statuten der Kommune Pistoia aus dem 12. Jahrhundert'. *QF* 77 (1977), 51–83.

Mainoni, Patrizia. 'A proposito della "rivoluzione fiscale" nell'Italia settentrionale del XII secolo'. *Studi storici* 44 (2003), 5–42.

Mainoni, Patrizia. 'Sperimentazioni fiscali e amministrative nell'Italia settentrionale'. In *Pensiero e sperimentazioni istituzionali nella 'Societa Christiana' (1046–1250)*, edited by Giancarlo Andenna, 705–59. Milan, 2007.

Maire Vigueur, Jean-Claude. *Cavaliers et citoyens*. Paris, 2003.

Maire Vigueur, Jean-Claude. 'Comuni e signorie in Umbria, Marche e Lazio'. In *Storia d'Italia*, edited by Giuseppe Galasso, vol. 7.2, 323–606. Turin, 1987.

Maire Vigueur, Jean-Claude. *L'autre Rome*. Paris, 2010.

Maire Vigueur, Jean-Claude, and Faini, Enrico. *Il sistema politico dei comuni italiani (secoli XII–XIV)*. Milan, 2010.

Martini, Luciana. 'Per la storia della classe dirigente del Comune di Pisa: la "domus Gualandorum"'. Tesi di laurea, Università di Pisa, relatore Gabriella Rossetti, 1975–76.

Matzke, Michael. *Daibert von Pisa*. Sigmaringen, 1998.

Mayer, Ernst. *Italienische Verfassungsgeschichte von der Gothenzeit bis zur Zunftherrschaft*, 2 vols. Leipzig, 1909.

Mazzi, Angelo. *Studi bergomensi*. Bergamo, 1888.

Menant, François. 'Bergamo comunale'. In *Storia economica e sociale di Bergamo. Il comune e la signoria*, 15–181. Bergamo, 1999.

Menant, François. *Campagnes lombardes au moyen âge*. Rome, 1993.

Menant, François. *L'Italie des communes (1100–1350)*. Paris, 2005.

Menant, François. 'La prima età comunale'. In *Storia di Cremona. Dall'alto medioevo all'età comunale*, edited by Giancarlo Andenna, 198–281. Cremona, 2004.

Menant, François. 'Une forme de distinction inattendue'. In *Écritures de l'espace social*, edited by Didier Boisseuil et al., 437–56. Paris, 2010.

Meneghini, Roberto, and Santangeli Valenzani, Riccardo. *Roma nell'altomedioevo*. Rome, 2004.

Miccoli, Giovanni. *Chiesa gregoriana*. Rome, 1999.

Milani, Giuliano. *I comuni italiani*. Bari, 2005.

Milani, Giuliano. *L'esclusione dal comune*. Rome, 2003.

Milani, Giuliano. 'Lo sviluppo della giurisdizione nei comuni italiani del secolo XII'. In *Praxis der Gerichtsbarkeit in europäischen Städten des Spätmittelalters*, edited by Franz-Josef Arlinghaus et al., 21–45. Frankfurt, 2006.

Mohr, Melissa. *Holy Sh*t*. Oxford, 2013.

Molho, Anthony. 'The Italian Renaissance, Made in the USA'. In *Imagined Histories: American Historians Interpret the Past*, edited by Anthony Molho and Gordon Wood, 263–94. Princeton, 1998.

Montelli, Emanuela. 'Impiego dei mattoni nella casa dei Crescenzi in Roma'. In *Actas del sexto Congreso nacional de historia de la construcción, Valencia, 21–24 octubre 2009*, edited by S. Huerta et al., 909–18. Madrid, 2009.

Montelli, Emanuela. *Tecniche costruttive murarie medievali*. Rome, 2011.

Moore, Robert I. 'Family, Community and Cult on the Eve of the Gregorian Reform'. *Transactions of the Royal Historical Society* 5th series, 30 (1980), 49–69.

Moscati, Laura. *Alle origini del comune romano*. Rome, 1980.

Moscati, Laura. 'Benedetto "Carushomo" *summus senator* a Roma'. In *Miscellanea in onore di Ruggero Moscati*, 73–87. Naples, 1985.

Moscati, Laura. '"Una cum sexaginta senatoribus"'. *Clio* 20 (1984), 531–45.

Muir, Edward. 'The Italian Renaissance in America'. *American Historical Review* 100 (1995), 1095–1118.

Niermeyer, Jan Frederik. *Mediae latinitatis lexicon minus*. Leiden, 1976.

Occhipinti, Elisa. 'I *capitanei* a Milano'. In *La vassalità maggiore*, 25–34.

Occhipinti, Elisa. 'I Visconti di Milano nel secolo XII'. In *Formazione e strutture dei ceti dominanti nel medioevo*, edited by Amleto Spicciani, vol. 3, 123–35. Rome, 2003.

Occhipinti, Elisa. *L'Italia dei comuni*. Rome, 2000.

Oldfield, Paul. *City and Community in Norman Italy*. Cambridge, 2009.

Olivieri, Agostino. 'Serie dei consoli del comune di Genova'. *ASLSP* 1.3 (1860), 157–626.

Opll, Ferdinand. *Stadt und Reich im 12. Jahrhundert (1125–1190)*. Vienna, 1986.

Osheim, Duane J. *An Italian Lordship*. Berkeley, 1977.

Overmann, Alfred. *La contessa Matilde di Canossa*, translated by Guerrino Beda. Rome, 1980.

Padoa Schioppa, Antonio. 'Aspetti della giustizia milanese dal X al XII secolo'. In *Atti del 11o Congresso internazionale di studi sull'alto medioevo*, 459–549. Spoleto, 1989.

Padoa Schioppa, Antonio. 'Il ruolo della cultura giuridica in alcuni atti giudiziari italiani dei secoli XI e XII'. *Nuova rivista storica* 64 (1980), 265–89.

Palumbo, Pier Fausto. *Lo schisma del MCXXX*. Rome, 1942.

Panero, Francesco. 'Istituzioni e società a Vercelli dalle origini del comune alla costituzione dello Studio (1228)'. In *L'università di Vercelli nel medioevo*, 77–165. Vercelli, 1994.

Pavoni, Romeo. 'Dal Comitato di Genova al Comune'. In *La storia dei Genovesi*, vol. 5, 151–75. Genoa, 1985.

Pensabene, Patrizio. 'La Casa dei Crescenzi e il reimpiego nelle case del XII e XIII secolo a Roma'. In *Arnolfo di Cambio e la sua epoca*, edited by Vittorio Franchetti Pardo, 65–76. Rome, 2006.

Peri, Illuminato.'Ordinamento del comune consolare'. *Atti della Accademia di scienze, lettere e arti di Palermo*, parte 2, *Lettere*, 4th series, vol. 2 (1950–51), 65–198.

Pescaglini Monti, Rosanna. *Toscana medievale*. Pisa, 2012.

Petersohn, Jürgen. 'Der Brief der Römer an König Lothar III. vom Jahre 1130'. *Deutsches Archiv* 50 (1994), 461–507.

Petersohn, Jürgen. *Kaisertum und Rom in spätsalischer und staufischer Zeit*. Hannover, 2010.

Petralia, Giuseppe.'La percezione della "nuova città"'. In *Il moderno nel medioevo*, edited by Amedeo de Vincentiis, 135–51. Rome, 2010.

Petralia, Giuseppe. 'Le "navi" e i "cavalli"'. *Quaderni storici* 103 (2000), 201–22.

Petti Balbi, Giovanna.'Caffaro'. *DBI* 16 (1973), 256–60.

Petti Balbi, Giovanna. *Caffaro e la cronachistica genovese*. Genoa, 1982.

Petti Balbi, Giovanna. *Governare la città*. Florence, 2007.

Pini, Antonio Ivan. 'Il comune di Ravenna fra episcopio e aristocrazia cittadina'. In *Storia di Ravenna*, vol. 3, edited by Augusto Vasina, 201–57. Venice, 1993.

Placanica, Antonio. 'L'opera storiografica di Caffaro'. *Studi medievali* 36 (1995), 1–62.

Poloni, Alma. *Trasformazioni della società e mutamenti delle forme politiche in un Comune italiano*. Pisa, 2004.

Poly, Jean-Pierre. *La Provence et la société féodale, 879–1166*. Paris, 1976.

Pratesi, M. C.'I Visconti'. In Rossetti et al., *Pisa nei secoli XI e XII*, 3–61.

Provero, Luigi. *Dai marchesi del Vasto ai primi marchesi di Saluzzo*. Turin, 1992.

Puglia, Andrea. 'Fuori della città'. In *"Un filo rosso"*, edited by Gabriella Garzella and Enrica Salvatori, 171–94. Pisa, 2007.

Puglia, Andrea. 'L'origine delle famiglie pisane Sismondi e Casalberti'. *BSP* 66 (1997), 83–104.

Puglia, Andrea. 'Reazioni alla dominazione canossiana e costruzione della memoria dell'autonomia cittadina'. *BSP* 77 (2008), 33–47.

Putnam, Robert D., with Leonardi, Robert, and Nanetti, Raffaella Y. *Making Democracy Work*. Princeton, 1993.

Racine, Pierre. *Plaisance du Xème à la fin du XIIIème siècle*. Paris, 1979.

Radding, Charles M. *The Origins of Medieval Jurisprudence*. New Haven, 1988.

Rao, Riccardo. *Comunia*. Milan, 2008.

Redi, Fabio. *Pisa com'era*. Naples, 1991.

Rege Cambrin, Laura. 'La famiglia dei Casalei dalle origini alla metà del XIII secolo'. Tesi di laurea, Università di Pisa, relatore Maria Luisa Ceccarelli Lemut, 1988–89.

Renzi Rizzo, Catia. '*Pisarum et Pisanorum descriptiones* in una fonte araba della metà del XII secolo'. *BSP* 72 (2003), 1–29.

Reynolds, Susan. *Fiefs and Vassals*. Oxford, 1994.

Rippe, Gérard. *Padoue et son contado (Xe–XIIIe siècle)*. Rome, 2003.

Ronzani, Mauro. *Chiesa e "Civitas" di Pisa nella seconda metà del secolo XI*. Pisa, 1996.

Ronzani, Mauro. 'Dall'*edificatio ecclesiae* all'*Opera di S. Maria*'. In *Opera*, edited by Margaret Haines and Lucio Riccetti, 1–70. Florence, 1996.

Ronzani, Mauro. 'L'affermazione dei Comuni cittadini fra Impero e papato'. In *Poteri centrali e autonomie nella Toscana medievale e moderna*, edited by Giuliano Pinto and Lorenzo Tanzini, 1–57. Florence, 2012.

Ronzani, Mauro. 'La "casa di Gontulino"'. *BSP* 74 (2005), 503–22.

Ronzani, Mauro. '"La nuova Roma"'. In *Momenti di storia medioevale pisana*, edited by Ottavio Banti and Cinzio Violante, 61–77. Pisa, 1991.

Ronzani, Mauro. 'Le prime testimonianze dell'attività dei consoli pisani in quattro documenti del 1109 relativi ai rapporti fra l'autogoverno cittadino e i discendenti dei conti dell'età ottoniana'. In *Quel mar che la terra inghirlanda*, edited by Franco Cardini and Maria Luisa Ceccarelli Lemut, 679–705. Pisa, 2007.

Ronzani, Mauro. 'Le tre famiglie dei "Visconti" nella Pisa dei secoli XI–XIII'. In "Un filo rosso", edited by Gabriella Garzella and Enrica Salvatori, 45–70. Pisa, 2007.

Ronzani, Mauro. 'Nobiltà, chiesa, memoria famigliare e cittadina a Pisa fra XI e XV secolo'. In Società, istituzioni, spiritualità, 739–66. Spoleto, 1994.

Rossetti, Gabriella. 'Ceti dirigenti e classe politica'. In Rossetti et al., Pisa nei secoli XI e XII, xxv–xli.

Rossetti, Gabriella. 'Costituzione cittadina e tutela del contado, una vocazione originaria a Pisa tra XI e XII secolo'. In Legislazione e prassi istituzionale a Pisa (secoli XI–XIII), edited by Gabriella Rossetti, 105–61. Naples, 2001.

Rossetti, Gabriella. 'I caratteri del politico nella prima età comunale'. BSP 70 (2001), 53–63.

Rossetti, Gabriella. 'Il comune cittadino: un tema inattuale?' In L'evoluzione delle città italiane nell'XI secolo, edited by Renato Bordone and Jörg Jarnut, 25–43. Bologna, 1988.

Rossetti, Gabriella. 'Il lodo del vescovo Daiberto sull'altezza delle torri'. In Pisa e la Toscana occidentale nel Medioevo, vol. 2, 25–47. Pisa, 1991.

Rossetti, Gabriella. 'Le istituzioni comunali a Milano nel XII secolo'. In Atti del 110 Congresso internazionale di studi sull'alto medioevo, 83–112. Spoleto, 1989.

Rossetti, Gabriella. Percorsi di Chiesa nella società medioevale. Pisa, 2008.

Rossetti, Gabriella. 'Pisa e l'impero tra XI e XII secolo'. In Nobiltà e chiese nel medioevo, edited by Cinzio Violante, 159–82. Pisa, 1993.

Rossetti, Gabriella. 'Società e istituzioni nei secoli IX e X: Pisa, Volterra, Populonia'. In Atti del 50 Congresso internazionale di studi sull'alto medioevo, 209–338. Spoleto, 1973.

Rossetti, Gabriella, et al. Pisa nei secoli XI e XII: formazione e caratteri di una classe di governo. Pisa, 1979.

Rossini, Rosa. 'Note alla "Historia Mediolanensis" di Landolfo iuniore'. In Contributi dell'Istituto di storia medioevale, vol. 1, 411–80. Milan, 1968.

Rota, Antonio. 'La costituzione originaria del comune di Roma'. BISIME 64 (1953), 19–131.

Rovai, Barbara. 'La famiglia de Curte tra l'XI ed il XIV secolo'. Tesi di laurea, Università di Pisa, relatore Maria Luisa Ceccarelli Lemut, 1993–94.

Salvatori, Enrica. Boni amici e vicini. Pisa, 2002.

Salvatori, Enrica. 'I presunti "capitanei delle porte" di Milano e la vocazione cittadina di un ceto'. In *La vassalità maggiore*, 35–94.

Salvatori, Enrica. 'Il corsaro pisano Trapelicino'. *BSP* 76 (2007), 31–56.

Salvatori, Enrica. 'Lo spazio economico di Pisa nel Mediterraneo: dall'XI alla metà del XII secolo'. BISIME 115 (2013), 119–52.

Salvatori, Enrica. 'Spazi mercantili e commerciali a Milano nel medioevo'. In *Spazio urbano e organizzazione economica nell'Europa medievale*, edited by Alberto Grohmann, 243–66. Perugia, 1994.

Savigni, Raffaele. *Episcopato e società cittadina a Lucca da Anselmo II (+1086) a Roberto (+1225)*. Lucca, 1996.

Scalia, Giuseppe. 'Il carme pisano sull'impresa contro i Saraceni del 1087'. In *Studi di filologia romanza. Scritti in onore di Silvio Pellegrini*, 1–63. Padua, 1971.

Scalia, Giuseppe. '"Romanitas" pisana tra XI e XII secolo'. *Studi medievali* 13 (1972), 791–843.

Scalia, Giuseppe. 'Tre iscrizioni e una facciata'. *Studi medievali* 23 (1982), 817–59.

Scavi MM3, edited by Donatella Caporusso, vol. 1. Milan, 1991.

Schmitz-Esser, Romedio. '*In urbe, quae caput mundi est*. Die Entstehung der römische Kommune (1143–1155)'. *Innsbrucker historische Studien* 23–24 (2004), 1–42.

Schramm, Percy Ernst. *Kaiser, Rom und Renovatio*. Leipzig, 1929.

Schultz, Knut. "*Poiché tanto amano la libertà . . .* ", translated by Paola Massardo. Genoa, 1995.

Schumann, Reinhold. *Authority and the Commune. Parma, 833–1133*. Parma, 1973.

Schwarzmaier, Hansmartin. *Lucca und das Reich bis zum Ende des 11. Jahrhunderts*. Tübingen, 1972.

Schweppenstette, Frank. *Die Politik der Erinnerung*. Frankfurt, 2003.

Scott, Tom. 'A Historian of Germany Looks at the Italian City-State'. *Storica* 47 (2010), 7–59.

Sergi, Giuseppe. *Potere e territorio lungo la strada di Francia*. Naples, 1981.

Settia, Aldo A. *Comuni in guerra*. Bologna, 1993.

Settia, Aldo A. *Rapine, assedi, battaglie*. Bari, 2002.

Sinatti d'Amico, Franca. *La gerarchia delle fonti di diritto nelle città lombarde*, vol. 1. Florence, 1962.

Skinner, Quentin. *The Foundations of Modern Political Thought*, vol. 1. Cambridge, 1978.

Soldi Rondanini, Gigliola. 'Cagapesto (Cacapisti, Pesto), Gerardo'. *DBI* 16 (1973), 279–82.

Solmi, Arrigo. 'L'Amministrazione finanziaria del regno italico nell'alto medio evo'. *Bollettino della società pavese di storia patria* 31 (1931), 1–288.

Spinelli, Marina. 'Uso dello spazio e vita urbana a Milano tra XII e XIII secolo'. In *Paesaggi urbani dell'Italia padana nei secoli VIII–XIV,* 253–73. Bologna, 1988.

Storti Storchi, Claudia. *Intorno ai Costituti pisani della legge e dell'uso (secolo XII).* Naples, 1998.

Stroll, Mary. *Calixtus II (1119–1124).* Leiden, 2004.

Stroll, Mary. *The Jewish Pope.* Leiden, 1987.

Strothmann, Jürgen. *Kaiser und Senat.* Cologne, 1998.

Struve, Tilman. 'Heinrich IV. und die *fideles cives* der städtischen Kommunen Oberitaliens'. *Deutsches Archiv* 59 (1997), 497–553.

Sturmann, Carmela. 'La "domus" dei Dodi, Gaetani e Gusmari'. In Rossetti et al., *Pisa nei secoli XI e XII,* 225–336.

Tabacco, Giovanni. 'Interpretazioni e ricerche sull'aristocrazia comunale di Pisa'. *Studi medievali* 3 (1962), 707–27.

Tabacco, Giovanni. 'Le istituzioni di orientamento comunale nell'XI secolo'. In idem, *Sperimentazioni del potere nell'alto medioevo,* 339–67. Turin, 1993.

Tabacco, Giovanni. *The Struggle for Power in Medieval Italy,* translated by Rosalind Brown Jensen. Cambridge, 1989.

Tangheroni, Marco. 'La prima espansione di Pisa nel Mediterraneo: secoli X–XII'. In *Medioevo Mezzogiorno Mediterraneo,* edited by Gabriella Rossetti and Giovanni Vitolo, vol. 2, 3–23. Naples, 2000.

Thumser, Matthias. 'Die Frangipane'. *QF* 71 (1991), 106–163.

Thumser, Matthias. 'Die frühe römische Kommune und die staufischen Herrscher in der Briefsammlung Wibalds von Stablo'. *Deutsches Archiv* 57 (2001), 111–47.

Thumser, Matthias. *Rom und der römische Adel in der späten Stauferzeit.* Tübingen, 1995.

Ticciati, Laura. 'S. Casciano'. In *Progetti e dinamiche nella società comunale italiana,* edited by Renato Bordone and Giuseppe Sergi, 101–239. Naples, 1995.

Ticciati, Laura. 'Strategie familiari della progenie di Ildeberto Albizo—i Casapieri—nelle vicende e nella realtà pisana fino alla fine del XIII secolo'. In *Pisa e la Toscana occidentale nel Medioevo,* vol. 2, 49–150. Pisa, 1991.

Tiné, Renata. 'I discendenti del "senior" Stefano: i "Baldovinaschi" nella Pisa dei secoli XI–XIII'. Tesi di laurea, Università di Pisa, relatore Mauro Ronzani, 1996–97.

Toubert, Pierre. *Les structures du Latium médiéval.* Rome, 1973.

Toubert, Pierre. 'Scrinium et palatium'. In idem, *L'Europe dans sa première croissance*, 419–61. Paris, 2004.

Vallerani, Massimo. 'La riscrittura dei diritti nel secolo XII'. In *Zwischen Pragmatik und Performanz*, edited by Christoph Dartmann et al., 133–64. Turnhout, 2011.

Vallerani, Massimo. 'Tra astrazione e prassi'. In *Praxis der Gerichtsbarkeit in europäischen Städten des Spätmittelalters*, edited by Franz-Josef Arlinghaus et al., 135–53. Frankfurt, 2006.

Vasina, Augusto. 'Consoli e mondo comunale nelle città dell'area ravennate-esarcale'. In *Società, istituzioni, spiritualità*, 975–1022. Spoleto, 1994.

Vasina, Augusto. *Romagna medievale.* Ravenna, 1970.

Vendittelli, Marco. 'Romanorum consules'. In *La nobiltà romana nel medioevo*, edited by Sandro Carocci, 211–36. Rome, 2006.

Vercelli nel secolo XII. Vercelli, 2005.

Vespignani, Giorgio. *La Romània italiana dall'esarcato al Patrimonium.* Spoleto, 2001.

Violante, Cinzio. 'I "da Besate"'. In *Nobiltà e chiese*, edited by Cinzio Violante, 97–156. Pisa, 1993.

Violante, Cinzio. 'I laici nel movimento patarino'. In *I laici nella «societas christiana» dei secoli XI e XII*, 597–697. Milan, 1968.

Violante, Cinzio. *La Pataria milanese e la riforma ecclesiastica*, vol 1. Rome, 1955.

Violante, Cinzio. *La società milanese nell'età precomunale.* Bari, 1953.

Violante, Cinzio. 'Pievi e parrocchie nell'Italia centro-settentrionale durante i secoli XI e XII'. In *Le istituzioni ecclesiastiche della "societas christiana" dei secoli XI–XII. Diocesi, pievi e parrocchie*, 643–799. Milan, 1977.

Violante, Cinzio. 'Una famiglia feudale della 'Langobardia' nel secolo XI'. In *Studi filologici letterari e storici in memoria di Guido Favati*, vol. 2, 653–710. Padua, 1977.

Volpe, Gioacchino. *Medio evo italiano.* Florence, 1961.

Volpe, Gioacchino. *Studi sulle istituzioni comunali a Pisa*, 2nd edition. Florence, 1970.

von der Höh, Marc. *Erinnerungskultur und frühe Kommune*. Berlin, 2006.

Waley, Daniel, and Dean, Trevor. *The Italian City-Republics*, 4th edition. Harlow, 2010.

Wandruszka, Nikolai. *Die Oberschichten Bolognas und ihre Rolle während der Ausbildung der Kommune (12. und 13. Jahrhundert)*. Frankfurt, 1993.

Whitton, David. 'Papal Policy in Rome, 1012–112'. DPhil thesis, Oxford University, 1979.

Wickham, Chris. *Community and Clientele in Twelfth-century Tuscany*. Oxford, 1998.

Wickham, Chris. 'Consensus and Assemblies in the Romano-Germanic Kingdoms'. *Vorträge und Forschungen*, in press.

Wickham, Chris. *Courts and Conflict in Twelfth-century Tuscany*. Oxford, 2003.

Wickham, Chris. *Framing the Early Middle Ages*. Oxford, 2005.

Wickham, Chris. 'Getting Justice in Twelfth-century Rome'. In *Zwischen Pragmatik und Performanz*, edited by Christoph Dartmann et al., 103–31. Turnhout, 2011.

Wickham, Chris. 'Justice in the Kingdom of Italy in the Eleventh Century'. *Settimane di studio* 44 (1997), 179–255.

Wickham, Chris. 'La signoria rurale in Toscana'. In *Strutture e trasformazioni della signoria rurale nei secoli X–XIII*, edited by Gerhard Dilcher and Cinzio Violante, 343–409. Bologna, 1996.

Wickham, Chris. 'La struttura della proprietà fondiaria nell'agro romano, 900–1150'. *ASRSP* 132 (2009), 181–238.

Wickham, Chris. *Land and Power*. London, 1994.

Wickham, Chris. 'Property-ownership and Signorial Power in Twelfth-century Tuscany'. In *Property and Power in the Early Middle Ages*, edited by Wendy Davies and Paul Fouracre, 221–44. Cambridge, 1995.

Wickham, Chris. *Roma medievale*. Rome, 2013.

Wickham, Chris. 'The "Feudal Revolution" and the Origins of Italian City Communes'. *Transactions of the Royal Historical Society* 6th series, 24 (2014).

Wickham, Chris. 'The Financing of Roman City Politics, 1050–1150'. In *Europa e Italia*, edited by Paola Guglielmotti et al., 437–53. Florence, 2011.

Wolf, Heinz Jürgen. 'Il cosiddetto "Privilegio logudorese" (1080–1085)'. *BSP* 59 (1990), 7–47.

Zabbia, Marino. 'Tra modelli letterari e autopsia'. *BISIME* 106 (2004), 105–38.

Zerbi, Piero.'La Chiesa ambrosiana di fronte alla Chiesa Romana dal 1120 al 1135'. *Studi medievali* 4 (1963), 136–216.

Ziese, Jürgen. *Wibert von Ravenna. Der Gegenpapst Clemens III. (1084–1100)*. Stuttgart, 1982.

INDEX

aristocracy (*cont'd*)
178; commune building and,
2, 6, 9–14, 16, 18, 171–73,
176, 182, 185, 200, 203; hegemony and, 13, 55, 157, 182,
199–202; Milan and, 22–27,
30–32, 36–46, 50–57, 60–
65; military and, 2, 6, 11–12,
14, 22, 25–26, 36, 46, 53–55,
60, 81, 99, 146, 171–72, 176,
178; new aristocracy and,
122, 124–25, 139, 142, 147;
nobiles and, 18, 23, 78, 122,
139, 159; Pisa and, 68, 81,
83, 85, 90, 99, 109, 115–16;
Rome and, 9, 120–47, 150–
59; *valvassores* and, 2. *See also*
families
Arnaldo of Azzano, *iudex*,
172, 193
Arnaldo of Brescia, 152,
154–55
Arnate, 42
Arnolfo, historian of Milan, 21,
23
Arno river, 69, 74, 77, 79, 95–96
artisans: commercialism and,
8, 13, 52, 140, 142, 151–52,
154, 175, 193; commune
building and, 8, 13, 175, 193;
Cremona and, 175–76; Milan
and, 52; Padua and, 177–79;
Rome and, 140, 142, 151–52,
154
assemblies: *collectio* and, 23, 27;
commune building and, 11,
18, 172, 176, 181, 188–89,
195–200; *concio* and, 27,

29–33, 62–64, 85, 130, 174,
177, 200; *contio* and, 30–31,
90, 154–55; Landolfo and,
31; legitimacy and, 11; Milan
and, 27–28, 31, 62; Pisa and,
87; *placita* and, 11, 25, 28,
34, 39, 47, 62, 64, 75, 77, 97,
100–101, 106–7, 123–24,
163, 172, 196, 199; Rome
and, 141
Asti, 14, 161; Adelaide and, 168;
bishops and, 165–66, 169–
70, 189; castles and, 167;
cathedrals and, 167–68; *cives*
and, 168; commercialism and,
166–67; consuls of, 166–70;
documentation of, 166–69,
171; episcopal system and,
167; prominent families of,
185; S. Anastasio, 168; vassals and, 167–68
Avvocati family of Lucca, 19–20,
181
Avvocati family of Milan, 40

Babillonia, Leone de, 107
Baggio, Anselmo da. *See* Alex-
ander II
Baggio family, 24, 26
Balearic Islands: archbishops
and, 73; Muslims and, 67;
Pisa's wars with, 67–68, 70,
73, 86, 88, 92–93, 100, 104,
107–8, 142; pope and, 73
ballistas, 79
Banti, Ottavio, 10, 197
Baona family, 192
Barcelona, 88, 107